SLAYER

The Next Generation

D1601405

By the same author:

Slayer: An Expanded and Updated Unofficial and Unauthorised Guide to Buffy the Vampire Slayer

Hollywood Vampire: A Revised and Updated Unofficial and Unauthorised Guide to Angel

High Times: An Unofficial and Unauthorised Guide to Roswell

Inside Bartlet's White House: An Unofficial and Unauthorised Guide to The West Wing

By the same author with Paul Cornell and Martin Day:

The New Trek Programme Guide

X-Treme Possibilities

The Avengers Dossier

By the same author with Martin Day:

Shut It! A Fan's Guide to 70s Cops on the Box

SLAYER
The Next Generation

Keith Topping

First published in Great Britain in 2003 by
Virgin Books Ltd
Thames Wharf Studios
Rainville Road
London
W6 9HA

A catalogue record for this book is available from the British
Library.

ISBN 0 7535 0738 2

Typeset by TW Typesetting, Plymouth, Devon
Printed and bound in Great Britain by
Mackays of Chatham PLC

Contents

Full List of Episodes

Slayer: The Next Generation

is dedicated to

Tony and Jane Kenealy,

Clay Eichelberger,

and

Mike Like

Thick as Thieves

The author wishes to thank the following for their invaluable encouragement and contributions to this book: Ian Abrahams, David Alder, Michael Billinghurst, Rupert Booth and Trina Macgregor, Sean Brady, Jo Brooks, Matt Broughton, Wendy Comeau (thanks for all the scones), Neil Connor (for dealing with another PC-related crisis), Allison Costa, Michael Cule, Peter Darvill-Evans (whose ultimate *fault* this book is), Doug Dean, Alexandre Deschampes, Kathryn Fallon, Nicola Guess, Jeff Hart, David Howe, Dave and Lesley McIntee, Ian McIntire, Scott Marshall, Alan Miller, David Miller at *Shivers*, John Molyneux, the legendary Ian Mond, Ingrid Oliansky, Eva Palmerton, Sarah Parker, Alex Popple, Leslie Remencus, Jill Sherwin, Jim Smith, Tom Spilsbury at *TV Zone*, Paul Steib and Wendy Wiseman, Billy Stewart, Jim Swallow and Mandy Mills, Witold Tietze, Yochanan and Veda Urias, (the *real*) Maggie Walsh, Bill and Jacque Watson, Christopher Weimer, Kyle Whitehead, Thomas Whitney, the Fat Dragon Ladies, everyone at Gallifrey One (see you all in February) and CONvergence, especially Anna Bliss, Stephanie Lindorff, Windy Merrill and Jody Wurl.

Respect is duly given to the late Simon Raven, whose novel *Doctors Wear Scarlet* first got me interested in vampires. To David Bailey, Paul Condon, Paul Cornell and Caroline Symcox, Davy Darlington, Simon Guerrier, Jim Sangster and all of my pals on the *BuffyWatchers* and *Gallyfriends* mailing lists. *Keep the faith*. And to numerous website custodians who spared the time to answer my, no doubt annoying, emails. Details of many of these sites can be found in the chapter 'Buffy and the Internet'.

A *special* thank you to my Scooby Gang: my long-suffering editor Kirstie Addis, Martin Day (*my* Watcher), Diana Dougherty, Rob Francis (who *again* went for the doughnuts), Robert Franks, Shaun Lyon and Jason

Tucker (invaluable critique), Paul Simpson (who provided transcripts of his interviews with many of the cast and crew), Kathy Sullivan (without whom, as ever, there would be *no* book), Susannah Tiller (proofreading and significant contributions to the **Playing the Homophobia Card** section), Graeme Topping and the great Mark Wyman. All of whom, once again, loaned this ongoing project their boundless enthusiasm and talent for the duration. So, next year, same place, same time, OK?

This book was written, re-written, and generally mucked-about-with on location, in Newcastle upon Tyne, Van Nuys, North Hollywood, Minneapolis, London, Paris and various airports and hotels in between.

Hey ho, let's go . . .

What's the Sitch?

For those readers who have regularly purchased the steadily increasing bulk of *Slayer* over three previous editions, you'll notice a few subtle changes this time. It's smaller for one thing. But, as my mum always used to tell me, it's not size that's important . . .

Anyway . . .

Quite frankly, *Slayer* was turning into something akin to *Wisden*: a bloated repository of all knowledge, that could only be dipped into and not read cover-to-cover for pleasure. The third edition covered the first five years of *Buffy*'s history and, as one of my friends said when the book came out, 'could be subtitled *The WB Years*'. This seemed a perfect opportunity to draw a line under the past and start afresh with a new approach for subsequent editions. Hence, *Slayer: The Next Generation*.

So, this time I'm focusing on the most recent, sixth, season of *Buffy* – now at its new home in the US on the UPN network – and on the very changed Sunnydale that the last year has witnessed. A word about these changes: they haven't *all* been universally popular. Critical acclaim has never been far from *Buffy*'s doorstep: last year, the series gained Emmy and Golden Globe nominations and made the 10-best lists of critics from *Time*, *TV Guide* and *USA Today*. But fandom can be a far more difficult beast to please. TV fandoms are strange places for the uninitiated. They grow up around a particular show primarily because of the quality of the product – otherwise people wouldn't become fans in the first place. But, by their very nature, fandoms tend to become hypercritical seething pools of discontent if, in the consensus of the majority (or, often, a vocal *minority*), whatever it was that made the show good in the first place is lost or replaced. There's an element of that around *Buffy* at the moment which may surprise those readers without Internet access.

The term 'jumping the shark' in Internet-speak refers to a single defining moment when a TV series reaches its critical (if not, necessarily, commercial) peak and, from there, it's all downhill. In other words, it's the point at which some of a series' fans start to say 'it's not as good as it used to be, is it?' There's actually a website that celebrates such moments and invites nominations at *www.jumptheshark.com*. The '*Buffy*'s jumped-the-shark' doomsayers have been loudly out in force over the past few months. November 2001's musical episode, **107**, 'Once More, With Feeling' was, a portion of fandom has apparently decided, *the* moment. Which is, to me, not dissimilar to those *Harry Potter* fans who are less interested in serious literary debate and more interested in whether Scooby-Doo would belong to Gryffindor or Hufflepuff in bizarro-world.

The problem, in *Buffy*'s case, is one of a consistent quality which has set it apart from virtually everything else on TV. A case of hyperbole? Not a bit of it. *Buffy* has been for the last five years, quite simply, the best television programme in the world. OK, maybe *The West Wing* or *24* are up there with it, but *that's* the extraordinary level at which *Buffy* competes. Witty, inventive, scary, dangerous, clever, its use of teen-angst metaphor and media-referencing have been an absolute revelation to many cynical old hacks like myself. But this quality, it seems, eventually jades some viewers into expecting the unique every week. Now into its sixth year and after over one hundred episodes, one could be forgiven for thinking that it's OK for a series to coast along on its strengths and settle for the if-it-ain't-broke-don't-fix-it formula. To, in effect, go down the Rolling Stones route and spend a year replaying the greatest hits to stadium audiences. That's exactly what happened at *Star Trek: The Next Generation* around year six. It happened, too, on *The X-Files*. So, everybody had a bit fun and got self-referential and a touch indulgent, and the ratings stayed healthy. But in both cases the seven year itch was just around the corner.

Is this an analogous situation with *Buffy*, then? Well, one can argue on relative quality issues all night – that's down to individuals. But the one thing that *Buffy hasn't* done this year – and this is pretty much agreed by everyone – is to stand still and look backwards. Instead, there's been not so much a gradual evolution in characterisation but rather an 'asteroid hitting earth and destroying all life'-style leap in terms of focus and direction. It all started at the end of season five. What are you gonna do now, we asked? Kill our lead character, they replied. Oh, OK, what do you do for an encore?

TV fans, generally, are conservative people by nature and are resistant to change in their favourite shows. Ironically, in *Buffy*'s case, the series' highly literate and articulate fanbase seems to be a notable exception to this. Those who have been complaining are doing so, largely, because there hasn't been, they feel, *enough* development. These people are not idiots by any stretch of the imagination, they really care about their show and they want it to be great. So it's probably worth acknowledging that there *is* validity in some of those charges, particularly over the characterisation of core characters. In one of his regular Internet postings during summer 2001, Joss Whedon indicated that the key theme of *Buffy*'s sixth season would be, as he described it, 'oh, grow up.' But some fans, it seems, don't like the idea of Buffy, Xander and Willow growing up. They prefer them to be perpetual teenagers caught in a netherworld between the nightmares and nostalgia of childhood and the real-life, everyday horrors of the adult world and the boring stuff that *we* have to deal with: jobs, relationships, money problems. That's perfectly understandable – most people watch TV to escape the trivialities of life, not to celebrate them. I've always believed, however, that Whedon and his writers have the ability to deal (either through metaphor or straight drama) with these characters, whom we've watched develop over five years, at *any* age. And, more importantly, that the production team are taking the advice of *Hamlet*, on the purpose of drama, very literally. To hold a mirror up to nature. In other words, to show the audience what we *need* whether we want, or even *deserve*, it or not.

Another common complaint among the more vocal dissidents has been the series' apparent willingness to move away from the fantastical villains that it featured in the past and, instead, to make the main nemesis(es) of season six a *troika* of sexually repressed fanboys who live in their mom's basement and whose schemes involve freeze-rays and jet-packs while arguing about *Star Wars* trivia. The series, itself, even alluded to this discontinuity in **117**, 'Normal Again'. The idea of militant terrorist fans – Black Anoraks, if you will – may be a touch close to home for some (on occasion myself included, see **113**, 'Dead Things'). Self-parody aside, however (and the production team have gone out of their way to assure fans that the *troika* are not a dark mirror pointed in *their* direction but, rather, a caustic expression of Whedon and co themselves), some fans still regard the idea of Buffy fighting *normal* people – if you can consider Warren, Jonathan and Andrew to be normal – as abhorrent. Of course, the counter argument to that is after you've fought a *god* like Glory, where else are you going to go except to the opposite extreme?

So, it's been a rough year in the *Buffy*verse in many ways. We've had storylines about addiction, betrayal, loneliness, fear. We've seen people that we know and admire die, or leave, or suffer unbearable heartbreak. We've been to the brink of the apocalypse again and it's been darkness all the way. And we've found that, ultimately, love redeems. Which is, always has been, and will remain, *Buffy*'s mission statement and what sets it apart from its contemporaries. 'The best television show in the world?' *Rolling Stone* called it eighteen months ago. Who am I to argue?

It is, because in *Buffy*, love conquers everything.

Headings

Dreaming (As Blondie Once Said) is Free: Lots of TV series do cool dream sequences. *Buffy* does *magnificent*, surreal, scary, funny ones – as you'll find listed here.

Dudes and Babes: Who's hot and who's *not* among the beautiful people of Sunnydale. I'm grateful to a plethora of fans (of various sexualities) for gleefully adding suggestions and the odd secret fantasy to this section.

Authority Sucks!: Which aspect of square conformity is trying to bring 'the kids' under its thumb this week. A category for would-be anarchists everywhere.

Mom's Apple Pie: Aspects of traditional US family life either shown or subverted. We also keep an eye on Buffy's (often tempestuous) relationship with her younger sister, Dawn and how, in the absence of their deceased mother, Joyce, Buffy is rapidly turning into a parent. With all of the horrors *that* entails. Brian Lowry, writing in the *Los Angeles Times*, notes: 'Parents on most of WB's teen-orientated shows – *Dawson's Creek, Buffy, Felicity* and *Zoe, Duncan, Jack & Jane* – aren't just absent or inept; rather, in the few scenes they're given they are frequently clueless, bullying or dysfunctional, in need of a stern lecture from their kids regarding morality.'

Denial, Thy Name is Joyce: A category that details Joyce Summers's amazing propensity for self-delusion and how it's starting to rub off on other characters, especially her daughters. Kristine Sutherland, who plays Joyce, in a thoughtful, revealing interview with Paul Simpson, confessed: 'A parent of an adolescent has to walk a very fine line, and sometimes what's called for is a healthy dose of denial and looking the other way. [It's] an amazing powerful thing . . . I really believe in the power of denial.' We've all noticed.

It's a Designer Label!: Fashion statements, tips and victims are detailed here, along with the lengths of the skirts involved. *Buffy*'s costume designer Cynthia Bergstrom does, in fact, select clothes for the cast from LA fashion stores like Neiman Marcus, Fred Siegel Flair, Tommy Hilfiger, Macy's, Contempo Casuals and Traffic. However Sarah Michelle Gellar has, according to *Entertainment Weekly*, 'put the kibosh on turtlenecks and microminis, which is why Buffy's criminally short skirts vanished after season one.'

References: Pop-culture, Generation X and general homages to all things esoteric. In previous editions I've occasionally pointed out where characters 'misquote' from a text. It has been suggested, rightly, that more often than not such misquotations are deliberate allusions and that 'paraphrasing' might be a more accurate way to describe these.

Geek-Speak: A section that tries to catch all of Warren, Jonathan and Andrew's media referencing and general *sadness*.

Bitch!: Girls will be girls . . . All those moments that make the little boys twitch nervously.

Awesome!: The monsters that menace Sunnydale. The action sequences. The 'funny bits'. All of the things that make viewers say '*Cool!*'

Valley-Speak: From 'the netherworld known as the 818 area code' and for those who, *like*, don't understand what's, *you know*, being said. *Totally. Dude*. The series' unique teen-speak described by *Buffy*'s creater Joss Whedon as 'twisting the English language until it cries out in pain.'

Cigarettes and Alcohol: An occasional category dealing with teenage naughtiness of the nicotine-and-lager variety.

Logic, Let Me Introduce You to This Window: Goofs, plot holes and continuity errors.

I Just *Love* Your Accent: Examples of *Buffy*'s charmingly Californian view of the British.

Quote/Unquote: The dialogue worth rewinding the video for.

Other categories appear occasionally, including some new to this edition. Most should be fairly self-explanatory. **Critique** details what the press made of it all while

Comments from the production crew and cast have been added where appropriate. **Soundtrack** highlights the series' excellent use of music. You know the format by now.

Keith Topping
His Gaff
Merrie Albion
October 2002

It's a Joss-Thing

'I was there almost all the way through shooting. I eventually threw up my hands because I could not be around Donald Sutherland any longer. It didn't turn out to be the movie that I had written. They never do, but that was my first lesson. Not that the movie is without merit, but I just watched a lot of stupid wannabe-star behaviour . . .'

Joss Whedon on the film
Buffy the Vampire Slayer (1992)

Joe Whedon was born in New York on 23 June 1964, and was raised in uptown Manhattan where he grew up as a confirmed anglophile watching British PBS television series like *Masterpiece Theater* and *Monty Python's Flying Circus*. His interest in superhero comics, ghost stories and other bizarre tales of the unexplained was unusually intense, even for a child of this particular era. It seemed 'deeper, more consuming than in other children,' he later noted. 'While they were all outside playing, I was indoors, fascinated by a stack of comic books.'

Whedon attended the classy Riverdale High School in New York. It was the worst time of his life. He describes himself at this age as painfully shy and, to this day, doesn't admit to having a single happy memory of those awkward teenage years. 'I was one of those kids who no one pays attention to, so he makes a lot of noise and is wacky.' Though high school was akin to a horror movie for him, to make matters worse 'girls wouldn't so much as poke me with a stick.' So, as with many emotionally bruised and shy young people, rather than face these demons out in the open, he spent much of his time isolated at home reading comics and novels by science fiction authors like Frank Herbert and Larry Niven. On one occasion in an art class, Whedon drew a self-portrait in which his hand disappeared, because he thought that he was becoming invisible to people and that no one would ever love him. This was to become a key element in an idea he was already formulating about a movie set during the teenage years in which traditional horror motifs of vampires and demons are subservient to the *real* problems of growing up as an isolated outsider. 'Basically, school is about alienation and horror,' Joss notes. 'I was very unhappy in high school all the time.' Asked, by *DreamWatch*, how much like his subsequent character Xander Harris he, himself, was as a teenager, Whedon is willing to admit: 'Less-and-less as he gets laid more-and-more.' His education also included a, slightly happier, period at Winchester Public School in England. ('My mother was a teacher,' he adds. 'She was on sabbatical in England so I had to go *somewhere*.')

On his return to the US, Whedon studied film at Connecticut's Wesleyan University in 1987. College turned out to be a much more pleasurable experience than high school. '[It] rocked. I was still miserable for most of the time, but in a party way,' he adds wryly. After graduating, Whedon decided to follow in the family tradition and became the world's first third-generation television writer. His grandfather, John, was a pioneering TV writer in the 1950s and scripted episodes of *The Dick Van Dyke Show*, *The Donna Reed Show* and *Leave it to Beaver*. Joe's father, Tom, was also an award-winning auteur, producing *The Golden Girls* and writing for *The Dick Cavett Show*, *Alice* and *Benson*. Older brother, Zachery, is also a theatre playwright. Whedon's father urged him to try writing a TV script ('so I could make enough money to move out of the house,' he alleges). Broke and without any job prospects, he moved to Los Angeles and decided to change his name to Joss, meaning 'lucky' in Chinese.

After writing many speculative movie scripts in his late teens, and working in a video store by day to pay the rent, Joss finally landed a writing job on the popular sitcom *Roseanne*. (He would also subsequently produce the TV version of the hit movie *Parenthood*.) 'My life was completely about film,' he told *teen movieline*. '[I] learned about filmmaking by analysing two particular movies, *Johnny Guitar* and *The Naked Kiss*.' However with his encyclopedic fanboy knowledge of horror movies and comics, Whedon had always wanted to write for that market (one of his favourite films remains Stanley Kubrick's *The Shining*) and he freely acknowledges the influence of two stylistically fascinating modernist vampire movies – *The Lost Boys* and *Near Dark* (both 1987) – on the concept of *Buffy*. 'I watched a lot of horror movies as a child,' Whedon told *The Big Breakfast*. 'I saw all these blonde women going down alleys and getting killed and I felt really bad for them. I wanted one of them to kill a monster for a change. So I came up with *Buffy*.'

Whether *Buffy the Vampire Slayer* should be regarded as an example of Joss Whedon's incredible writing talent or as a triumph for his persuasive skills is (to this day) unclear, but the very fact that the concept ever made it beyond its initial one-line description more than suggests the latter. Joss's movie script for *Buffy*, written when he was just 21, suffered four years of rejection before finding a supporter in producer Howard Rosenman.

However, the eventual film, made in 1992, disappointed Whedon bitterly. But as a young writer at the very bottom of the Hollywood ladder he had little control over the finished product. Director Fran Kuzui increased the camp factor and downplayed the terror in the script. 'When you wink at the audience and say nothing matters, you can't have peril,' notes Joss. To him, that was the end of the project and, over the next four years Whedon became one of Hollywood's hottest movie screenwriters. He worked primarily as a script doctor – sometimes uncredited, though for rapidly increasing salaries – on movies like *Twister*, *Waterworld*, *Speed*, *Alien: Resurrection* and *Toy Story* – for which he was Oscar nominated. 'Most of the dialogue in *Speed* is mine, and a bunch of the characters,' Joss told Tasha Robinson. 'I have the only poster left with my name still on it. Getting arbitrated off the credits of *Speed* was *not* fun. In *Twister*, there are things that weren't the way I'd intended them, whereas *Speed* came out closer to what I'd been trying to do.' *Waterworld* was an even more frustrating experience for Joss. 'I refer to myself as the world's highest-paid stenographer,' he says. 'People ask me, "What's the worst job you ever had?" [I say] "I once was a writer in Hollywood . . ." Talk about taking the glow off [the movie industry].' *Waterworld*, he notes, was a good idea, 'but the script was the classic, "They write a generic script and don't care about the idea." When I was brought in, there was no water in the last 40 pages. It all took place on land, or on a ship. I was basically taking notes from Kevin Costner, who was very nice to work with, but he's not a writer. So I was there for seven weeks, and accomplished nothing. I wrote a few puns, and some scenes that I can't even sit through because they came out so bad. It was the same situation with *X-Men*.'

As he told *Entertainment Weekly* in 1997: 'I always look at my movie career as an abysmal failure,' and certainly most of his early original screenplays (including *Suspension*, which he described as '*Die Hard* on a bridge') were optioned but never produced. Then, out of the blue, in 1996 Joss was asked by Sandollar Productions to revive *Buffy* as a TV format. *Buffy*, and its highly charged Los Angeles spin-off *Angel*, have subsequently become two of *the* great TV success stories of the 90s and Whedon remains much in demand in Hollywood, writing *Titan A.E.*, *Atlantis: The Lost Empire* and contributing to *X-Men*. His next TV project will be an SF thriller called *Firefly* due to debut on Fox in the fall of 2002.

Producing a show like *Buffy*, one would assume that Joss is a great lover of gore, yet he isn't by any stretch of the imagination. 'I love horror movies. I also love science fiction and fantasy. I love any world that is different from the one I'm in right now. I think I mostly love the supernatural because I don't believe in it and, therefore, I love the escape of it.' Joss likes to listen to movie scores and praises the work of James Cameron, Shawnee Smith and Gene Colan. His horror genre influences include *Tomb of Dracula*, *Morbius* and numerous movies including the previously mentioned *The Lost Boys* and *Near Dark*, *Blade* and the remake of *The Blob*. He thinks that *The Night of the Comet* is hugely underrated and adored the stage version of Frank Langella's *Dracula*.

What makes Joss an outsider in a cut-throat industry is his drive and his passion to work. Near the end of *Buffy*'s fourth season in early 2000, he was rushed to hospital for an emergency appendectomy. After his operation, within 48 hours he was back at the studio writing the season finales for *Buffy* and *Angel*. Described by virtually everyone who has ever met him as down-to-earth and soft-spoken, with a wicked sense of humour, patience and thoughtfulness, Joss is married to Kai Cole, a textile and interior designer. They live with their four cats in Los Angeles. Still, at heart, a comics and TV fanboy like many of the people who watch his shows, Joss is alleged to have attended several conventions in 1998 and 1999 under the pseudonym of 'Mr Spratt', until he became instantly recognisable to fans. Something of a Renaissance man, Joss has also written an acclaimed comic mini-series (*Fray*) for Dark Horse, turned his hand to songwriting for the musical *Buffy* episode **107**, 'Once More, With Feeling' and is currently working on a proposed Rupert Giles *Buffy* spin-off co-production with the BBC and an animated *Buffy* series for Fox. He achieved a lifetime ambition in September 2002 with the release of the soundtrack to his *Buffy* musical on CD. 'Very occasionally,' Joss wrote in the sleeve notes, 'life doesn't Suck!' These are busy and exciting times for this most talented of TV auteurs and his young cast and crew as they continue to produce the two best shows on television.

'Previously on *Buffy the Vampire Slayer ...*'

The little Californian town of Sunnydale, 80 miles north of
Los Angeles, population 38,500 (give or take the odd
victim of blood-draining or sacrificial-disembowelling),
seems like the end of the world to sixteen-year-old
schoolgirl Buffy Ann Summers. When she moves there,
with her recently divorced mother, Joyce, Buffy is looking
for a fresh start after her expulsion from a previous school
(there was that nasty business of the gym burning down).
On her first day at Sunnydale High, she befriends two local
nerds, Xander Harris and Willow Rosenberg, which automatically excludes her from the cool set led by formidable
rich-girl Cordelia Chase. Buffy also meets the school's
English librarian Rupert Giles, her Watcher. Because, as
we soon discover, Buffy is actually The Slayer: a one-per-
generation clan of stake-wielding super-babes whose purpose it is to rid the world of vampires, demons and the
forces of darkness.

Buffy is initially reluctant to kick-start her slaying career
since that was what got her into so much trouble in the
past, but Giles persuades her that, though it's a dirty job,
someone's got to do it ('Welcome to the Hellmouth'). With
the help of her new friends, and a mysteriously dark and
handsome brooding-hunk of sexy-maleness, Angel, Buffy
is able to defeat the diabolical schemes of local vampire
king, The Master, and his disturbingly alluring acolyte,
Darla ('The Harvest'). Buffy soon discovers that her
vocation is not *just* about vampires, however, when she
finds herself dealing with the body-swop shenanigans of
former-cheerleader-turned-witch Catherine Madison and
her teenage daughter, Amy ('The Witch'), a substitute
teacher with a more than healthy desire for young boys
('Teacher's Pet') and a group of her fellow students who

become possessed by demonic hyenas ('The Pack'). Buffy
is shocked to discover that Angel is actually a vampire
himself – albeit one with a soul, the result of a gypsy curse
('Angel'). However, she is given little time to dwell on the
ramifications of this as Willow is kidnapped by an Internet
demon ('I Robot ... You Jane'), a sinister ventriloquist
dummy stalks Buffy for unknown reasons ('The Puppet
Show') and everybody at school has their worst nightmares
come true ('Nightmares'). When a lonely psychopathic
invisible girl, Marcie Ross, begins to take her revenge on
those who ignored her in the past, Cordelia becomes an
unwilling member of the Slayerettes ('Out of Mind, Out of
Sight') and yet another attempt at bringing forth the
apocalypse by The Master is thwarted in spectacular
fashion by Buffy who even survives her own drowning to
halt the end of the world ('Prophecy Girl').

After a summer spent with her father in LA, Buffy
returns to Sunnydale still struggling to cope with the
ramifications of her resurrection and her first subsequent
test at the hands of The Master's apprentice, The Anointed
One ('When She Was Bad'). The arrival of super-cool
British vampire couple Spike and Drusilla alters the
underworld balance of power within Sunnydale ('School
Hard') as do the sinister machinations of one of Giles's
former friends, the warlock Ethan Rayne ('Halloween',
'The Dark Age'). Buffy's past, in the shape of doomed
ex-boyfriend Billy Fordham, adds to her problems ('Lie to
Me'). She is further shocked to discover that another
Slayer, Kendra, was called at the moment of Buffy's death
('What's My Line?'). To make matters worse, Joyce enjoys
a brief flirtation with a sinister new boyfriend who turns
out to be a psychotic serial-killing robot ('Ted'). When
Spike and Drusilla summon The Judge, a powerful demon,
to bring forth the apocalypse, Buffy and Angel share a
night of passion ('Surprise'), during which a single moment
of happiness removes Angel's soul and reverts him to his
demonic persona, Angelus ('Innocence').

It's not just Buffy who's having problems in the area of
teen romance. Willow finds herself attracted to quiet,

studious guitarist, Oz, just as he discovers he has become a werewolf ('Phases') and, after splitting up with Cordelia whom he'd been dating, a spell that Xander has had Amy cast to make him attractive to Cordy has disastrous side effects ('Bewitched, Bothered and Bewildered'). Now thoroughly evil, Angelus's campaign of psychological terror against Buffy and her friends reaches a deranged climax when he murders Giles's girlfriend, the technopagan teacher, Jenny Calendar ('Passion'). Even possession by the ghosts of two doomed lovers from the 1950s haunting the school is unable to bring Buffy and Angel together ('I Only Have Eyes for You'). It's hardly surprising that, when the school swimming team are turned into aquatic monsters, few people bat an eyelid ('Go Fish'). The final part of Angelus's masterplan, to summon the demon Acathla and end the world is thwarted by, of all people, a jealous Spike, who forms an unlikely alliance with Buffy. But, in doing so, Buffy has to reveal her secret identity to her mother and, having been forced to send Angelus to Hell to save the world from Armageddon, and been kicked out of school by the officious Principal Snyder, Buffy runs away from Sunnydale ('Becoming').

In Los Angeles, she finds her vocation again, defeating a demon who prays on homeless teenagers ('Anne'). She returns home to find that her friends, the self-styled Scooby Gang, have arranged a homecoming party which is subsequently attacked by voodoo-zombies ('Dead Man's Party'). Yet another new Slayer (a replacement for Kendra, whom Drusilla killed), Faith, shows up at the same time as jive-talking vampire Mr Trick ('Faith, Hope and Trick'). And we finally meet Sunnydale's oft-mentioned Mayor, Richard Wilkins, who turns out to be a really nice guy – except that he wants to rule the world ('Homecoming'). Angel is returned from Hell, with his soul intact ('Beauty and the Beasts'), all of the adults in Sunnydale become teenagers ('Band Candy') and Joyce and Giles *do it* on the hood of a police car. Twice. Faith's newly arrived Watcher, Gwendolyn, misuses dark power and Faith becomes disillusioned with the purpose of her gifts ('Revelations').

Willow and Xander finally realise that they've been attracted to each other all of their lives, and share an intimate moment (having been kidnapped by Spike) just as Oz and Cordy attempt to rescue them ('Lover's Walk'). Cordy becomes *very* upset by this and wishes Sunnydale into another reality, but Giles puts things to rights by smashing the amulet of the vengeance-demon, Anyanka ('The Wish'). Angel, confused over the reasons for his return from Hell, is haunted by The First Evil, and saved from suicide by a supernaturally suspicious snowstorm ('Amends'). Joyce is possessed and encourages the town to become a modern-day Salem ('Gingerbread'). Giles is sacked by the Watcher's Council when a test for the Slayer goes horribly wrong ('Helpless'). Xander enjoys a night where he, literally, becomes a man – in all sorts of ways – while his friends are saving the world from yet another apocalypse ('The Zeppo') and a replacement Watcher, Wesley Wyndam-Pryce, turns up and irritates the hell out of everyone ('Bad Girls'). Faith is seduced by 'the Dark Side of the Force' and (secretly at first, but later openly) allies herself with the Mayor ('Consequences') having murdered a man and then tried to pin the blame on Buffy. Willow wins back Oz, and becomes more proficient at witchcraft – to such an extent that she is able to conjure up an other-dimensional lesbian-vampire version of herself ('Doppelgängland'). Giles, Buffy and Angel trick Faith into revealing the Mayor's full apocalyptic plans ('Enemies') while Buffy gains telepathic powers and discovers a would-be murderer on campus ('Earshot'). As the Mayor's scheme heads towards Graduation Day, we discover that Cordy's family have lost all of their money in a tax fraud ('Choices'). Buffy and Angel finally admit what everybody has been telling them all year – that they have no future as a couple, and Buffy saves the school from Hell Hounds ('The Prom'). The Mayor's ascension to demon form (a huge snake) occurs during the ceremony but, with the help of the rest of the pupils of Sunnydale High, Buffy defeats the demon. As they prepare for college, Angel leaves Sunnydale behind for a new life in Los Angeles ('Graduation Day'). There, Angel is joined by Cordelia and, subsequently, Wesley, to run a detective agency who help the hopeless.

Buffy finds college tough at first, with a sassy vampire ('The Freshman'), an annoying roommate ('Living Conditions'), a Halloween fear-demon ('Fear Itself') and Spike, searching for a vampire Holy Grail ('The Harsh Light of Day'), to contend with. Xander finds himself dating, a now-human, Anya. Oz leaves town after finding that he is unable to control his werewolf side ('Wild at Heart') and, distraught, Willow's magic gets out of control ('Something Blue'). At Thanksgiving, the Scoobies have to contend with a Native Indian vengeance spirit ('Pangs'). Buffy begins dating handsome teachers' assistant, Riley Finn, but he, like her, has a secret identity as a member of The Initiative, a military squad of demon-killers who implant Spike with a microchip in his head that stops him from killing humans. Buffy and Riley discover each other's secrets when they come face-to-face fighting The Gentlemen, fairy-tale monsters who steal the voices of everyone in Sunnydale ('Hush'). Willow meets shy lesbian witch Tara Maclay, and the two begin a relationship. Giles is briefly turned into a demon, the result of a spell by Ethan ('A New Man'). Faith, in a coma since the Graduation Day massacre, wakes up ('This Year's Girl') and magically swaps bodies with Buffy ('Who Are You?') causing all sorts of mayhem before Willow and Tara reverse the effects. Neurotic nerdish outsider Jonathan Levinson performs an incantation that turns him into the most popular man in the world ('Superstar'), the only person who is immune to the effects of this being Adam, a sinister Frankenstein-like creation of The Initiative's leader Maggie Walsh. Adam has big plans for Buffy ('Goodbye Iowa'). Both Oz ('New Moon Rising') and Angel ('The Yoko Factor') return to discover that their places in the affections of Willow and Buffy respectively have been superceded. As Spike, secretly working for Adam, sows the seeds of discontent and betrayal among the Scooby Gang, it seems that Buffy and her friends are drifting apart. But, in the nick of time they realise their mistakes and, together, summon the mythical power of the first Slayer to destroy Adam ('Primeval'), albeit with a few decidedly strange consequences which manifest themselves in their dreams ('Restless').

Legendary vampire Dracula comes to Sunnydale to meet the Slayer he has heard so much about, but this is nothing to the surprises in store for the Scooby Gang when Buffy's sister, Dawn, gets kidnapped by the incompetent vampire, Harmony ('Real Me'). Hang on . . . Buffy's *sister*? Where'd she come from? Before that question can be answered, Xander's personality is split into two bodies ('The Replacement'), Riley suffers from the remnants of Initiative experiments on him ('Out of My Mind') and Tara's terrible secret is revealed – that she's a perfectly normal girl and not the demon as she'd been led to believe ('Family'). However, the big news around Sunnydale is the arrival of arrogant, bitchy, full-of-herself pan-dimensional god, Glory, searching for The Key, a mythical energy weapon hidden, by monks, in the form of . . . Dawn. Buffy is entrusted with this knowledge, and told that she must protect the girl from Glory who will use The Key to cause terrible destruction ('No Place Like Home'). Buffy pays Spike for information and is given a series of lessons in the true nature of being a Slayer ('Fool for Love') while Joyce begins to suffer from headaches ('Shadow') and a brain tumour is diagnosed ('Listening to Fear'). Buffy and Riley's relationship becomes unravelled due to misunderstanding and pride ('Into the Woods') and he leaves Sunnydale for a government-sponsored mission in South America. Anya and Xander come closer together when a Troll ex-boyfriend of Anya's wreaks havoc ('Triangle'). The Watcher's Council check up on Giles, now running the Magic Box shop, but Buffy magnificently turns the tables on them and gets Giles reinstated to his old job. But she still has to put up with Spike's growing (and disturbing) obsession with her ('Crush'), Dawn discovering her true status ('Blood Ties') and, most distressing of all, Joyce's sudden untimely death ('The Body').

As Spike makes sex-starved robotics genius Warren create a Buffy-replica for him ('Invention'), Buffy and her friends try to stop both Glory and crazed religious cult, The Knights of Byzantium, from learning the identity of The Key ('Spiral'). Dawn is captured by Glory and Buffy becomes catatonic, Willow having to enter Buffy's psyche to pull her back from madness ('The Weight of the World'). Finally, Buffy realises that the only way she can stop Glory and save Dawn (and the world, for what seems like the hundredth time) is to sacrifice herself ('The Gift').

Body Rock: Unsurprisingly, **94**, 'The Body' is a firm favourite among many of the *Buffy* cast and crew: 'It was so sad,' Amber Benson told Rob Francis. 'Kristine [Sutherland] was fantastic, walking around the set in her death make-up. And Emma did that amazing scene. They must have done it twenty times ... Everybody on the set was crying.'

'It was quite an experiment,' Joss told Francis. 'I thought everyone would hate [it]. I thought they'd go glassy-eyed and wish it was over. It wasn't supposed to be cathartic. Or helpful. It was just supposed to show what it's like in that situation for the first few hours [after death]. There's almost an element of boredom to grief that I wanted to show. But lots of people got something from it and that really moved me.' Joss went on to admit that the directional style had been hugely influenced by the films of PT Anderson (*Magnolia, Boogie Nights*). 'It's embarrassing how much,' he noted.

Critique: 'The most innovative drama on any non-cable network,' wrote *Time* magazine's James Poniewozik. 'A hilarious allegorical story of independence, relationships and mortality, told through scary stories.' Poniewozik drew particular attention to the storyline surrounding the introduction of Dawn: 'We'd never seen her before but the cast acted like she'd been there all along ... What first seemed like a clumsy way of adding someone to the cast turned out to be ... a great spoof on how aging TV shows meddle with their casts.'

Changing Channels

It was one of the TV stories of the decade, though it had little to do with what was taking place in Sunnydale. Tension erupted early in 2001 when *Buffy*'s production company, Fox, asked the WB network on which *Buffy* – then in its fifth season – was broadcast to pay $2 million per episode, effectively doubling the cost of carrying the show. WB executives replied they would pay $1.6 million, but no more, claiming that would mean they'd lose money on the series. Although only the WB's third-highest rated series (behind *7th Heaven* and *Charmed*), *Buffy* was easily its biggest revenue generator, with 30-second advertising-spots during episodes believed to be worth $100,000 each to the network.

'If we end up somewhere other than the WB, we'll be exactly the same show. Fox have supported us on everything,' Joss Whedon told the press. 'I think the fans will find us.' Still, Whedon was hopeful that *Buffy* would remain on familiar ground. He wasn't the only one. 'I will stay on *Buffy* if, and only if, *Buffy* stays on the WB,' Sarah Michelle Gellar told *E! Online* in an unguarded moment of clarity at the Golden Globes. The remarks enraged Fox executives, considering that Gellar was securely under contract until 2003 regardless of where *Buffy* ran. If the star was announcing serious intentions to quit, the studio's bargaining position in any forthcoming renegotiation could be seriously undermined. What happened next shows how frantic Hollywood players can become when a major deal is on the line. According to the *Los Angeles Times*' Scott Collins, Fox executive Sandy Grushow rang Gellar's representative Debbie Klein – whom he'd known since they were classmates in fifth grade – and reminded her of her client's binding contract. Subsequently, a wholesale retraction from the contrite star appeared. 'I'm not going anywhere. I can't stress that enough,' Sarah said, adding that 'Fox has been very good to me. I intend to stay with *Buffy* no matter what.'

Next, comments attributed to WB chief executive, Jamie Kellner, made Joss Whedon furious. 'To dismiss his own product angers me. It doesn't breed love,' Joss told the *Daily News*. Kellner was said to have argued vigorously against paying any more money for *Buffy*, telling *Entertainment Weekly* that it wasn't even the network's top-rated series and belittling the series' many adult viewers by asserting that it appeals mainly to teens. 'We have tremendous respect for Joss, Sarah and everyone associated with *Buffy*,' said WB spokesman Brad Turrell, manfully trying to defuse the row. 'They have delivered a consistently excellent program for five seasons.' Within weeks of the move, Kellner was no longer at the WB, having become CEO of the Turner Broadcasting System, like the WB, a subsidiary of AOL/Time-Warner.

A late-February 2001 deadline passed and Fox were now free to consider bids from such parties as ABC and UPN. The latter was an interesting, if unexpected, player in the deal. Home to the *Star Trek* franchise, WWF Wrestling and . . . not a lot else, UPN made a bid in March. Nick Brendon broke the news in an interview with *zap2it.com*. 'Apparently money talks,' he noted. Finally, in April, Fox announced that *Buffy* would be relocating from season six. UPN agreed to a two-year, 44-episode deal, reportedly paying $2.3 million per episode (and, it later emerged, broadcasting at a loss). UPN CEO Dean Valentine said: 'We are incredibly pleased to have *Buffy*, not just because it's one of the best shows on air and represents a new era in UPN's direction, but because Joss Whedon is one of the finest writers and producers in television.' Advertising revenue played a huge part in the decision, noted Adam Ware, UPN's chief operating officer, crediting *Buffy* and *Roswell* (which UPN also bought after it was dropped by the WB), for attracting The Gap and Maybelline to UPN. Joss was asked by *E! Online* if he watched UPN. 'No,' he replied, 'but I don't watch the WB either, apart from my own shows. You'll find that people who make TV [seldom] have time to watch it. The only exception for me is *The West Wing*.'

Although the media had considered UPN a long shot, the network was said to be passionate about the series and 'invested in its long-term success'. Needless to say, the WB were *not* impressed. In a terse statement they suggested that Fox had made 'an inauspicious decision for the television industry by taking one of their programs off a nonaffiliated network and placing it on a network in which they have a vested interest' (Fox and UPN were allegedly discussing a merger).

There was little reason for anyone outside the two networks to care much about *Buffy* moving. The show's many fans had no difficulty finding it when it returned in September. In a way, what was more interesting was a broader issue: how the WB had succeeded with its strategy of becoming a TV network primarily for teenage girls, and how UPN – with their acquisition of *Buffy* and *Roswell* – seemed to be trying to capture the same demographic. With shows like *Buffy*, *Charmed*, *Angel*, *Popular*, *Gilmore Girls* and *Roswell*, the WB made itself a first stop for every advertiser selling clothes, cosmetics, CDs and cell phones. 'I think, the [right] strategy is doing shows with a lot of strong teen characters,' Jamie Kellner had noted, 'but teen characters that have family units.' The price UPN eventually paid for *Buffy* made no sense to Kellner. That's because it only made sense at all as part of a broader deal that effectively guaranteed UPN continued affiliation with stations in New York, LA and other large markets.

Now, little more than a year after *Buffy* moved, the watershed shifts in the industry many predicted have not happened. Studios are still selling shows to networks with which they share no corporate affiliation. UPN didn't go out of business due to *Buffy*'s price tag, and the WB didn't collapse without the show. What's more, the WB's charges that Fox sold *Buffy* to UPN because News Corp. (Fox's parent company) was planning to take a stake in UPN hasn't happened either. UPN remains a wholly owned subsidiary of Viacom – and few industry insiders expect that to change.

But there *have* been ramifications. Thanks to *Buffy* and their other new hit, *Enterprise*, UPN has finally started to shed its old image. The strong performance of both shows helped the network's overall 2001–02 ratings jump 15 per cent in total viewers, 13 per cent in adults 18–49 and 19 per cent in the 18–34 demographic. It topped the WB in all three categories. The WB, despite a strong May sweep that helped re-establish some momentum, had a somewhat disappointing year, though this wasn't due to declines on Tuesdays. The network smartly shifted *Gilmore Girls* into *Buffy*'s old slot and paired it with its hit-of-the-year, *Smallville*.

One of the key reasons UPN execs gave for buying *Buffy* was its ability to help the network create new programming. This hasn't happened either. If UPN can't launch a new hit on the strength of *Buffy* during the coming 2002–03 season, the deal's $2.3 million-per-episode will seem exorbitant. And while *Buffy* has helped UPN make dramatic gains in ad revenue, the show's per-episode price is still far higher than the amount of direct coin it pulls in. UPN president Leslie Moonves calls the *Buffy* pact 'a smaller version of Fox's first NFL deal. Fox lost a fortune on that, but as a result, became a major-league player.'

For the WB, losing *Buffy*, while painful psychologically, hasn't mattered much to the network's bottom line. 'They might have had slightly better ratings with *Buffy*, but they still had a decent year,' noted Josef Adalin. But, Fox/News Corp. seem to be the deal's biggest winners. Not only is *Buffy* a more profitable show, but – except for a feared WB boycott of Fox-made shows, which hasn't actually happened – the company felt hardly a pinch of negative reaction from other networks.

The next question, of course, is whether *Buffy* will continue after Fox's current deal with UPN expires. Sarah Michelle Gellar has been publicly noncommittal about returning for the 2003–04 season. Joss Whedon has been planning for such a possibility, and may be inclined to continue without Gellar (see 'Grrr! Arrgh!'). Leslie Moonves says he's hopeful the show will continue, but hasn't yet begun negotiations. 'It was a high price tag, but it increased the overall image for UPN,' he notes, and losing it would be like 'NBC losing *Friends*'. For now, there seems to be a feeling that last year's landmark deal ended up giving all sides something to be happy about – a surprise for many in a town obsessed with labelling victors and vanquished.

> *'Wherever I was, I was happy. At peace. I was warm.*
> *I was loved. I was finished. Complete.*
> *I don't understand about dimensions or theology . . .*
> *but I think I was in Heaven.'*
>
> – 'After Life'

Sixth Season (2001–2002)

Mutant Enemy Inc./Kuzui Enterprises/Sandollar Television/20th Century Fox
Created by Joss Whedon
Co-Producers: John F Perry, Marc David Alpert (101–15),
James A Contner (113, 118, 121)
Producers: Douglas Petrie (101–14), David Solomon, Gareth Davies,
Marc David Alpert (116–122)
Consulting Producer: David Greenwalt
Supervising Producers: Jane Espenson, Douglas Petrie (115–122)
Co-Executive Producer: David Fury
Executive Producers: Sandy Gallin, Gail Berman, Fran Rubel Kuzui,
Kaz Kuzui, Joss Whedon, Marti Noxon

Regular Cast:
Sarah Michelle Gellar (Buffy Summers)
Nicholas Brendon (Xander Harris)
Alyson Hannigan (Willow Rosenberg)
Anthony Stewart Head (Rupert Giles, 101, 104–8, 121–2)
Krístine Sutherland (Joyce Summers, 117)
Elizabeth Anne Allen (Amy Madison, 109–10, 112)
Dean Butler (Hank Summers, 117)
James Marsters (Spike)
Danny Strong (Jonathan Levinson, 104–5, 109, 111, 113, 117–22)
Emma Caulfield (Anya Jenkins, 101–16, 118–22)
Andy Umberger (D'Hoffryn, 116)
Marc Blucas (Riley Finn, 115)
Amber Benson (Tara Maclay, 101–10, 113–14, 116–20[1])
Michelle Trachtenberg (Dawn Summers)

---

[1] Uncredited in **120**, 'Villains'.

Adam Busch (Warren Meers, 104–5, 109, 111, 113, 117–20)
Amelinda Embry (Katrina Silber, 113, 120)
Tom Lenk (Andrew Wells, 104–5, 109, 111, 113, 117–22)
Jeff Kober (Rack, 110, 120–1)
Kirsten Nelson (Lorraine Ross, 112, 117)
Kali Rocha (Halfrek, 112, 114, 116, 118)
Marion Calvert (Gina, 112–13)
James C Leary (Clem, 105[2], 114, 116, 119–20)
Steven W Bailey (Cave Demon, 120–2)

101
Bargaining

US Transmission Date: 2 October 2001 [UPN]
UK Transmission Date: 10 January 2002 [Sky One]

Writer: Marti Noxon
Director: David Grossman
Cast: Franc Ross (Razor), Geoff Meed (Mag), Mike Grief (Klyed),
Paul Greenberg (Shempy Vamp), Bru Muller (Teacher),
Joy DeMichelle Moore (Ms Lefcourt), Robert D Vito (Cute Boy),
Harry Johnson (Parent #1), Kelly Lynn Warren (Parent #2),
Hila Levy (Pretty Girl), Richard Wharton (Homeowner)

Some months have passed since Buffy Summers, the
Vampire Slayer, sacrificed herself to save the world. The
Scooby Gang are using the Buffybot to maintain an
illusion and the population of Sunnydale – human and
demonic – remain unaware of the Slayer's death. Unfortunately, a cowardly vampire accidentally discovers the truth
and escapes to tell a gang of biker Hellion demons about
Sunnydale's best-kept secret. Meanwhile, as Giles makes
preparations to return to England, Willow, Tara, Anya
and Xander perform a powerful and dangerous spell at
Buffy's grave.

A Little Learning is a Dangerous Thing: Dawn's teacher
notes that the kids' model version of a utopian futuristic
society includes an extraordinary number of pizza par-
lours, but no schools.

---

[2] Credited as 'Loose Skinned Demon' in **105**, 'Life Serial'.

Denial, Thy Names Are Willow, Tara, Anya and Xander:
The resurrection ritual that the Scooby Gang intend to use
on Buffy's corpse is, according to Tara, against all the laws
of nature and practically impossible to do. But, with
Willow the driving force behind the idea, they are prepared
to try. Buffy didn't die a natural death, rather she was
killed by mystical energy. This means, Willow argues, that
her soul is most likely trapped in a Hell dimension just as
Angel once was (see **34**, 'Becoming' Part 2; **38**, 'Beauty and
the Beasts'). She offers no supporting evidence for this and,
as it turns out, she's wholly wrong (see **103**, 'After Life').

Denial, Thy Name is Spike: Poor Spike, he obviously still
bears the scars of an indescribable guilt because he failed
in his 'promise to a lady,' (see **100**, 'The Gift') to protect
Dawn which indirectly resulted in Buffy's death. He seems
to be dealing with it, however. His disdain for authority
briefly surfaces while he's talking to Dawn about school.
Then he realises that he's supposed to be a role model.
However, he seems to get very upset each time he's near to
the Buffybot which, he now realises, is no replacement for
the real thing.

The Conspiracy Starts at Home Time: Willow has managed
to get the Buffybot's head back on (see **100**, 'The Gift') and
it is currently impersonating Buffy to a reasonably satisfactory degree. Enough to fool Dawn's teacher, at least.
Willow has programmed the robot away from a penchant
for knock-knock jokes, though in trying to insert some new
puns, its speech patterns have taken on an abstract, dadaist
edge. Tara and Willow have, meanwhile, moved into the
Summers home with Dawn and are living in Joyce's old
room.

It's a Designer Label!: Tara's lovely red leather coat shares
top honours with the Buffybot's hot leather pants. Also
watch out for several T-shirts with number motifs on them,
worn by various Scoobies and clearly meant to mess with
the heads of viewers who believe they're a hidden reference
to something significant.

References: Conceptually, *From Dusk Till Dawn* and *The Uncanny X-Men* (Willow *is* Jean Grey in the opening scene. See **100**, 'The Gift'; **122**, 'Grave'), *Night of the Living Dead* ('Scenario: we raise Buffy from the grave. She tries to eat our brains'), *Nightmare on Elm Street* (Razor's Freddie Kruger-style finger weapons). Xander alludes to *The Fury* ('that way lies spooky carnival death'). Also, Dadaism (a nihilistic artistic movement of the early 20th century founded on principles of irrationality and irreverence towards accepted aesthetic criteria), Video Hut, the Discovery Channel. A *Rock the Vote* poster is briefly visible. Anya found the last known Urn of Osiris,[3] the artefact needed to resurrect Buffy, at the online auction site *e-bay* from a Desert Gnome in Cairo. He drove a hard bargain, but she got him to throw in a limited edition Backstreet Boys lunch box (she implies it's for Xander). Dawn's class are reading the American classic *Walden, or Life in the Woods* by Henry David Thoreau (1817–62). One of the vampires wears a Hanson T-shirt. The movie *Dude, Where's My Car* is on the billboard at the Sun Cinema. Keen eyed viewers may spot that it's still on later in the season almost two years after it last played in most US theatres. The movie is, apparently, a particular favourite with Marti Noxon.

Bitch!: Anya, on the Buffybot: 'I just think the concept of *chi* is a little tough for her to grasp. She's not the descendant of a long line of mystical warriors, she's the descendant of a toaster oven.'

Awesome!: Spike casually setting fire to the fat vampire who's throttling Giles. A lonely Dawn lying on the bed next to the robot version of her dead sister. The genuinely touching scene of Giles's departure from the airport, and his final words to his young friends: 'Just be careful.' The climax, Buffy's corpse coming to life.

---

[3] Osiris was the Egyptian god of the afterlife, brought back from the dead himself by his wife, Isis, following his murder by his brother Sutekh (or Set). A character based on Osiris appears in *Stargate SG-1*.

'You May Remember Me From Such Films and TV Series As . . .': Franc Ross was Tobias in *Amityville: Dollshouse*, and appeared in *A Whisper Kills*, *The West Wing*, *The 119*, *3rd Rock from the Sun* and *Sliders*. Geoff Meed was in *Brother*, *Passions*, *ER* and *Enterprise*. Bru Muller's movies include *Eating L.A.* and *Since You've Been Gone*. He also wrote and produced *Maxwell*. Paul Greenberg appeared in *The Godson*, *Ghost Mom* and *The Kids in the Hall*. Robert D Vito was in *Chicago Hope* and *Grownups*. Mike Grief appeared in *Big Brother Trouble*, *King's Pawn*, *Liar Liar*, *Malcolm in the Middle* and *Grosse Pointe*. Hila Levy played Samantha in *Lava Lounge*. Richard Wharton's CV includes *Will & Grace*, *Herman USA* and *The Fence*.

Don't Give Up The Day Job: Paint Foreman Lisa Gamel was a scenic artist on *Barb Wire*. Script Supervisor Suzanne McRobert's movies include *Geppetto*. Production Co-Ordinator Lisa Ripley Becker previously worked on *The X-Files*.

Valley-Speak: Xander: 'House o' chicks, relax. I'm a man. I have a tool.' And: 'Great googly-moogly.'
   Dawn: 'What's with the mega-witches?'

Cigarettes and Alcohol: Xander wanted to get Giles a can of Old English 800 as a parting gift. But the guy living in a box in front of the store wouldn't buy it for him. There's a lot of beer being drunk in the biker bar.

Sex and Drugs and Rock'n'Roll: Tara blows sobri root in a vampire's face. It's supposed to confuse him but, instead, it makes him peppy. Tara wonders, briefly, if the vampire might be taking prescription medication.
   Buffybot says she admires Spike's brain almost as much as his 'washboard abs'.

Logic, Let Me Introduce You to This Window: The Scoobies are trying to keep Buffy's death a secret from the world at large – one could suggest, therefore, that the gravestone is something of a give-away. Hidden or not, there's always the possibility that somebody who isn't supposed to will be walking through the Sunnydale woods and discover it. Why do only the Buffybot and Anya have stakes during the initial hunt (to be fair, Giles also has an axe, but nobody else seems to be tooled up)? And doesn't Anya's pointy stick seem rather blunt to be of much use? When Willow enters the Magic Box after getting the last ingredient for the spell, Tara says she's late, indicating that the Scoobies were expecting her earlier. But Willow subsequently tells Xander: 'I thought we weren't gonna meet till later?' There's no historical record of an Urn of Osiris which is, in any case, something of a contradiction since the ancient Egyptians mummified rather than cremated their dead. They did preserve vital organs in canopic jars although the vessel seen here doesn't look much like one of those (its neck is far too narrow to get something like a heart into). The sacrifice which accompanies the resurrection ritual appears to be similar to Greco-Roman necromantic rites rather than anything Egyptian. Giles's flight from Sunnydale airport is 'leaving for Los Angeles and continuing to London.' US airports *do* use this description for flights that will land at another airport to take on more passengers. But the idea of a transatlantic flight originating in Sunnydale with a stop-over in LA (just eighty miles away) is ludicrous. Given that, in most respects (location, geography, size etc.) Sunnydale is based on the Californian town of Santa Barbara, it's interesting to note that Santa Barbara airport is a municipal (dealing chiefly with commuter flights to gateway cities like Los Angeles, San Francisco and Denver) and not an international one. The Magic Box interior has been redesigned since last season. Why, when the Scoobies know that she frequently exhibits bizarre behaviour, is the Buffybot allowed to patrol the streets on her own? Who is with Dawn while all the other Scoobies are patrolling in the opening sequence? Willow wears a brown skirt in the scene where she asks Dawn to return her clogs. However, in the next scene, in the kitchen, she is wearing the same red shirt, but with a pair a jeans. Later, at

Xander's apartment, the skirt returns. Anya's hairstyle also changes between scenes. Twice. Anya, Tara and Xander are much closer together in some shots when they're in a circle with Willow than in others and, at one point, Anya and Tara swap positions.

I Just *Love* Your Accent: Spike wonders if Giles's life flashed before his eyes while he was being choked: 'Cuppa tea. Cuppa tea. Almost got shagged. Cuppa tea ...'

Motors: A whole gang of demon bikers on nasty great Harley Davidsons.

A Haven For the Bruthas: Hellions are road pirates. They raid towns, usually backwaters but, with the Slayer seemingly gone, they're thinking about making the Hellmouth their new home.

Cruelty to Animals: A poor innocent fawn cops it in the neck as part of Willow's resurrection ritual.

Quote/Unquote: Xander: 'Who made you the boss of the group?' Anya: 'You did ... You said "Let's vote", and it was unanimous ...' Tara: 'Then you made her this little plaque, that said *Boss of Us*. You put sparkles on it ...'

Notes: 'We need the world, and the underworld, to believe that Buffy is alive and well.' *Buffy*, as a series and a concept walks a thin line between doomed magnificence and cheeky observational comedy. Put simply, you never get quite what you expect. We know change is in the air, but the opening episode has one basic agenda: to reassure viewers, along with the population of Sunnydale (human *and* supernatural), that nothing has changed. New network, same show. But, of course, something *has*. Buffy's dead for a start. That's where we begin. For a long time, it's where we stay. So we get some lovely comedy sequences with the Buffybot and a bit of Bambi-murdering and snake-regurgitating to appeal to any passing WWF fans. It was to the relief of this author, therefore, that the production managed to do all this (including retelling the backstory for any first-time viewers) without too much repetition, hesitation or deviation. Best season opener since **13**, 'When She Was Bad'.

Giles intends to return to England. He's leaving the Magic Box in Anya's capable hands and intends to be a silent partner. He isn't, however, going anywhere near fast enough for an impatient Anya who wants it, like, *now*. Hank Summers has seemingly found out about the death of his wife (see **95**, 'Forever'), and has, at least, been in occasional telephone contact with Dawn (if not Buffy). Xander still hasn't told his friends about his and Anya's engagement (see **100**, 'The Gift'; **106**, 'All the Way'). Mr Davis and Ms Lefcourt are two of Dawn's teachers. When Anya was a demon (see **43**, 'The Wish') she once punished someone by making them check spreadsheets for eternity. Zombies don't eat brains, according to Anya, unless instructed to by their Zombie masters. When Anya is nervous she says money helps to calm her. Willow mentions Dawn's unsuccessful attempts to resurrect her mother in **95**, 'Forever'. Dawn notes that she is no longer The Key (see **83**, 'No Place Like Home') or, if she is, she doesn't open anything since the death of Glory. Xander owns a surfboard (one popular fan myth is that it's actually the one presented to Sarah Michelle Gellar for Outstanding Lifetime Achievement at the Teen Choice Awards in August 2001, but the July recording date of 'Bargaining' would seem to rule this out). As previously mentioned in **47**, 'The Zeppo', the alignment of stars and/or planets seems to be of vital significance to resurrection rituals (Tara mentions that 'Mercury is in retrograde').

Soundtrack: 'Permanence' by Static X can be heard in the demon biker bar.

Critique: 'Unlike *Law & Order*, you never know what's going to happen on *Buffy*,' notes Amy Elz. 'Will Buffy be attacked by her city's mayor who's now a giant snake? Will she be forced to kill her boyfriend to protect the world? Will she suddenly burst into song? Who knows! That is what makes it great.'

'Like *The X-Files* before it, *Buffy* deftly blends action and science fiction with astute writing and surprisingly impressive acting into a unique and fulfilling drama,' noted *Variety*'s Laura Fries. 'While other shows have utilised the sci-fi angle as a gimmick to revive characters, Whedon isn't one to compromise a story arc in order to please fans. Buffy may be back, but nothing is neat and tidy.'

Did You Know?: When Tara gives Giles the rubber finger monster as a parting gift, she wiggles it on her finger while saying, 'Grrr Arrrgh,' like the vampire in the Mutant Enemy logo at the end of each episode.

Ratings: The two hour *Buffy* season six premiere was a smash hit with viewers, scoring the second highest ratings in the show's history. UPN, were doubtless relieved that the massive cost of snatching the Slayer from the WB seemed to have paid off, as 7.7 million viewers tuned in. In typical mediaspeak, UPN announced that the episodes 'earned the network's best Tuesday ratings ever across all key demographics.' A delighted Joss Whedon told reporters that the figures had put 'a little more bounce in our step today, which is a good thing since we're shooting a musical episode.' He added, 'I don't usually look at ratings, [but] I'm pretty damn thrilled.'

Marti Noxon's Comments: Concerning Tara and Willow, Marti told *DreamWatch*: 'My mom is gay; she came out when I was thirteen. For the latter part of my childhood I was raised by two women so, definitely, some of the stuff that I have written about [Willow and Tara's] relationship has been informed by that. I'd say the only thing that really affected the storyline is something my mother told me; that being gay is really just about loving somebody. It's much less about the sex of that person.'

Joss Whedon's Comments: 'It's not a question of topping ourselves,' Joss told *TV Guide*. 'That's why in season four we did the finale as a dream show, because we'd *done* a giant battle the year before.' The move to UPN from the WB allows Joss a little more freedom, at least when it comes to the Willow/Tara relationship. 'I think UPN will probably be a simpler process, because [the first kiss] already happened. They basically said if something reads wrong, they'll let us know.'

102
Bargaining, Part 2

US Transmission Date: 2 October 2001
UK Transmission Date: 10 January 2002

Writer: David Fury
Director: David Grossman
Cast: Franc Ross (Razor), Geoff Meed (Mag), Mike Grief (Klyed)

Buffy's resurrection goes unnoticed as Razor's gang creates havoc in Sunnydale. Confused and disorientated, Buffy wanders through the carnage and eventually runs into the Scoobies, who realise that she had to dig her way out of her own grave. When the demons arrive for a final fight, Buffy's Slayer sensibilities kick in and she defeats them. Dawn eventually finds Buffy at Glory's tower where she, seemingly, wants to jump to her death again.

Denial, Thy Name is Willow: While nobody comes out of this story without having been through quite a bit of soul-searching, it's especially tough on Willow. Weakened by the tests that the Osiris spell put her through, Willow thinks she has blown her only chance of bringing Buffy back from, as she believes, Hell. When she and the others find Buffy alive, she is overjoyed if a little too anxious in making nervous excuses for Buffy's terrified, non-vocal response to them. Anya asks 'what's wrong with her?' Willow's snappy reply, 'nothing', is just a touch too quick for comfort.

References: There's a huge conceptual and visual debt to Edgar Allen Poe's *The Premature Burial* (specifically Roger Corman's 1962 movie adaptation). Also, *Peter Pan* ('how long have you known your girlfriend was Tinkerbell?'),

NORAD (the North American Air Defense based at Cheyenne Mountain in Colorado), Sam Peckinpah's *The Wild Bunch* (see **2**, 'The Harvest'; **24**, 'Bad Eggs'), electrical retailers Radio Shack and *Little Red Riding Hood* ('the better to cut you down to size, grandma'). Tara paraphrases Bob Dylan's 'If You Gotta Go, Go Now.'

Awesome!: A wild-eyed Buffy awaking in her coffin, realising she has been buried alive and, subsequently, bursting to the surface. Spike and Dawn on the motorbike. Anya, Willow and Tara's furious attack on Razor when he threatens Xander.

Valley-Speak: Mag: 'You got a bug up your crack, take it up with Razor. Until then, you do what he says and shut your hole. Before I rip you a new one.'
　　Xander: 'This is really starting to grate my cheese.'

Naming All the Stars: Xander tries to navigate by following the North Star. Only what he's following turns out to be either an aeroplane or a blimp.

Sex and Drugs and Rock'n'Roll: Razor tells the cornered Scooby Gang that his demons intend to enjoy themselves for a few hours. 'You might even live through it, except that certain of my boys got some anatomical incompatibilities that tend to tear up little girls.' And what about Xander? – Note that one of Razor's gang appears to be a girl-demon. One shudders to imagine what they have planned for Xander.

Logic, Let Me Introduce You to This Window: Spike complains about the lack of serious weaponry in the Summers' household. Didn't the big trunk he's looking in used to be full of them (and, as recently as **100**, 'The Gift' too)? When did the Scoobies get rid of them? Buffy's hair, post-exhumation, is remarkably clean for someone who has just dug through six feet of impacted dirt. The fact that it has also become darker since her death, however, *is* an accurate *post-mortem* effect (there's not much sunlight in a coffin). Dawn appears to follow Buffy into the alley from the same direction that Buffy herself came. So Dawn should have also run past, or been very close to, Willow, Tara, Anya and Xander. Dawn deduces that Buffy has returned from her grave on the strength of some very cryptic and irrational things that the, clearly on-its-last-legs, Buffybot tells her concerning 'the Other Buffy'. But, she's a smart kid so we can mark that one down as a combination of wishful thinking and a lucky guess. How could the Scoobies be so stupid as not to realise that the resurrection spell would have revived Buffy in her coffin? Given the levels of Willow and, to an extent Xander's, guilt and desperation to have their friend back that's perhaps understandable, but Tara at least should have realised.

Quote/Unquote: Xander: 'There's something you don't see very day. Unless you're us.'
    Razor: 'I'd better back off or you might pull a rabbit out of a hat.' Anya, to Willow and Tara: 'Don't do *that*.'
    Buffy: 'Is this Hell?'

Notes: 'We can handle a vampire or two, sure, but we've got a cavalcade of demons here.' The second half of the story takes a dismissive look at the new roads that the first episode offered and, in the midst of their construction, resurrects Buffy and throws her headfirst into an abject nightmare. Not the stuff about biker demons – that's *tame*, everyday Sunnydale stuff and she defeats them with barely a noncommittal dismissive grunt. No, the nightmare is that life is actually *worse* than death (see **103**, 'After Life'). This, then, is *Buffy* elegantly reaffirming its ultimate agenda. She's back and, despite some cosmetic changes, she's still beautiful.
    Xander bemoans his lack of male friends (something he also mentioned, specifically relating to Oz's departure, in **93**, 'I Was Made to Love You'). He does, however, get on well with a guy at work called Tito (see **104**, 'Flooded').

Critique: 'Overall *Buffy* has not been affected by the move to the UPN. It's the same smart, clever and thoroughly entertaining series it has always been,' noted *Cinescape*. 'The show is always reinventing itself, offing characters and bringing in new blood . . . If anything . . . the series is likely to finally break into the mainstream which has so far eluded the cult show . . . for the past five years. Buffy lives and let's hope for a long time to come.'

However, had the inevitable *Buffy*-backlash begun? Certainly, some mainstream US reviewers were distinctly lukewarm in their comments: 'I like the hero-quest mythology in her resurrection a lot more than I do Sarah Michelle Gellar's performance as the born-again Buffy,' wrote David Zuarwik in the *Baltimore Sun*. 'Tonight's two-hour premiere doesn't meet the normally high standards for the show, seeming oddly flat, unmoving and mostly unfunny.' 'Not special at all,' added Tim Goodman, while Alan Sepinwall in the *New Jersey Star Ledger*, felt the episode 'definitely falls into the "overwrought" category [and was] not pleasant to sit through.'

Did You Know?: The Willow Rosenberg – Bambi Murderer sequence in the first episode, was originally much longer and was edited prior to transmission. Needless to say the broadcast version suffered even further cuts in many overseas markets – notably Britain – along with the snake-regurgitating sequence and Buffy waking up in her coffin in Part 2. 'Some trims were made to the episode but these were kept to a minimum to make sure the scenes flowed and the essence and integrity of the storyline were maintained,' a Sky One spokeswoman told the *Media Guardian*. 'I believe the first episode was darker and sexier than is usual for *Buffy*,' she added. The spokeswoman noted that the rest of the series did not include such adult storylines and would not require cutting. It was somewhat surprising, therefore, to discover several cuts were also made to the following episode, **103**, 'After Life'. Fans were eventually given a chance to see the episodes uncut in the weekly late-night repeat on Sky One.

Cast and Crew Comments: Michelle Trachtenberg has been hinting that she may be involved in another *Buffy* spin-off show, or even take over as the Slayer when Sarah Michelle Gellar is ready to hang up her stake. In *TV Guide*, Michelle revealed that Joss had discussed two possible avenues: 'I've been asked if a spin-off or a continuation [of the show] would be of interest to me, and pretty much it is. I love my character. And the people I work with every day would be wonderful to work with for a while longer.' But then, Michelle was a fan of *Buffy* even before she joined the cast, due to her friendship with her former *All My Children* co-star Sarah Michelle Gellar. 'I began watching because of Sarah,' she told *BBC Online*. 'I always tried to think about ways for me to guest star on the show.' She even visited Sarah on the set some months before casting calls were made for the role of Dawn. 'I love finding little references in the script to past episodes because, as a fan, I know what they're talking about.'

'This isn't a show just for teenagers or just adults,' Sarah Michelle Gellar told the *Buzz*, 'it's for everyone.'

Joss Whedon's Comments: 'If Xander said "Dy-no-mite!" every time he killed a vampire, I'd tear my face off after about six episodes,' Joss told *Maxim* when asked why none of the *Buffy* characters had a catchphrase. Joss also touched on the real life consequences of increased promiscuity on the show. 'Vampires can't get diseases or make babies, so they're covered. We laid that in so Buffy could have sex with Angel without having to include the inevitable condom-shot.' Asked if he would ever watch an adult film à la the *Friends* spoof *Bouffet, the Vampire Layer*, Joss added 'there probably *is* a porno out there with that name, but I don't watch pornography. I just write it.'

103
After Life

US Transmission Date: 9 October 2001
UK Transmission Date: 17 January 2002

Writer: Jane Espenson
Director: David Solomon
Cast: Lisa Hoyle (Demon)

The repercussions of the resurrection spell has the Scoobies battling with a malevolent demon spirit created as a consequence of their actions. Buffy, meanwhile, realises that she was happier with the peace of the afterlife but cannot bring herself to tell her friends what they have done. She finds the only sympathetic ear available in Spike.

Dreaming (As Blondie Once Said) is Free: In one of the most revealing moments of the series, Spike tells Buffy that he saved her from having to die in Glory's apocalypse (see **100**, 'The Gift'). Not when it *counted*, of course. But every night after that in dreams. 'I'd see it all again, do something different. Faster or more clever. Dozens of times, lots of different ways.'

A Little Learning is a Dangerous Thing: Anya describes the demon that possesses various members of the Scooby Gang as 'a hitchhiker' saying that it's a standard way to travel between alternate dimensions. 'You mean some Hell-beastie rode back with Buffy and we're responsible?' asks Willow. It subsequently transpires that the reason for the manifestation is thaumogenesis, a by-product from the spell they cast to resurrect Buffy.

Dawn mentions five species of demons that are known to move transdimensionally: Skaggmore, Trellbane, Skitterers, Large and Small Bone-Eaters.

Mom's Apple Pie: By the end of the episode Buffy has assumed Joyce's former role within the Summers' household and has made Dawn's school lunch.

Denial, Thy Name is Buffy: Pointedly, Buffy not only refuses to discuss where she has returned from, but also spends the episode avoiding thanking her friends for their gift of life. Of course, it subsequently becomes clear that she's got a good reason to be so ungrateful.

The Conspiracy Starts at Home Time: Spike is outraged that, having worked with the Scoobies all summer, and saving all of their lives countless times, he was kept out of the loop regarding Buffy's resurrection. He believes the

reason for this was that Willow knew there was a chance
Buffy would come back 'wrong' and that Willow would be
forced to destroy the resulting abomination. 'She knew I
wouldn't let her. That's why she shut me out,' he says.
Although Xander is dismissive, blaming Spike's reaction
on his unrequited love for Buffy, he later questions Tara
about whether she or Willow knew there were likely to be
consequences from the resurrection spell.

Dig Your Own Hole: Spike immediately recognises the
injuries that Buffy's hands have suffered as being consistent
with someone smashing their way out of their coffin.

It's a Designer Label!: Lots of nice stuff here: Willow's
'tropical' pink nightshirt and fluffy red sleeveless top,
Anya's red pyjamas and Tara's tie-dyed shirt.

References: Xander's 'I've done a lot of fleeing through
these mean streets,' is probably an allusion to Martin
Scorsese's *Mean Streets* although that title, itself, was part
of a quotation from Raymond Chandler's *The Simple Art
of Murder*. Also, *Spider-Man* ('my senses are honed for
danger'), *Batman* ('holy *crap*!'), *Poltergeist, Scooby-Doo,
Where Are You!* ('makin' with the big-skeedaddle'), allusions to *I Know What You Did Last Summer* and *Super
Friends* (see **51**, 'Enemies').

Bitch!: The thaumogenesis demon attacks Willow and Tara
in the form of Buffy: 'Your hands smell of death. Filthy
little bitches, rattling the bones. Did you cut a throat? Did
you pat its head?' (a reference to Willow's slaughter of the
fawn in **101**, 'Bargaining' Part 1).
      Dawn tells Xander to drive fast. He protests he can't.
Dawn: 'I could drive faster and I can't drive!'

Awesome!: Spike's angry confrontation with Xander about
being kept ignorant concerning the spell. Buffy watching as
the faces of her friends on photographs become decayed,
skeletal corpses. The shocking moment when Anya is taken
over by the demon. Dawn's anguish that the others are
considering undoing the spell to send Buffy back.

Surprise!: The agonisingly sad final scene, and the revelation to Spike and the audience that, far from being stuck in Hell, Buffy was actually in Heaven (or something conceptually similar), and that being brought back to life is the *real* Hell to her.

Don't Give Up The Day Job: Production Designer Carey Meyer's CV includes *Mr Write*, *Payback*, *Every Breath* and *The Doors*. Lisa Hoyle's stunts can be seen in movies like *Austin Powers: The Spy Who Shagged Me*, *Go*, *Pearl Harbor* and *Charlie's Angels*.

Logic, Let Me Introduce You to This Window: Spike appears to have been waiting in the alley for some considerable time at the end of the episode as it's bright and sunny just a few metres away in both directions. Willow says she has contacted Giles in London to tell him about Buffy's resurrection. But Giles only caught the plane *that* afternoon (see **101**, 'Bargaining' Part 1). As it's now, seemingly, the early hours of the next morning, nowhere near enough time would have passed for him to have arrived in England (it's at least an eleven hour flight from Los Angeles to Heathrow).

What A Shame They Dropped . . .: from the shooting script, Anya: 'Why are you having us skulk around and meet in the backyard like conspiracy squirrels? Sitting on this arm is making my buttocks hurt.'

I Just *Love* Your Accent: Willow tells Tara that when she spoke to Giles on the phone he was glad to hear that Buffy was alive, 'but kinda weirded out. Lots of "dear Lord"s. I think I actually heard him cleaning his glasses.'

Motors: Spike is still riding the motorbike he acquired in the last episode.

Quote/Unquote: Spike: 'The thing about magic: there's always consequences.'

   Anya: 'Remember that bookstore? They became one of those books-and-coffee places and now they're just coffee. It's like evolution only without the *getting-better* part.'

Notes: 'Everything here is hard and bright and violent . . . This is Hell.' If there is one certainty in life, besides death and the rent man, it's that Jane Espenson's scripts can cheer up even a professional misanthrope. With a stylish humour that renders other great writers anaemic in comparison, there's no doubt about it, the girl's got real class. 'After Life' is among her best work and that's no surprise. That there's hardly a joke in it worthy of the name, however, is. This is *Buffy*'s first hesitant step towards establishing where it intended to go this season. A dark and troubled story, at times (particularly the ending) *achingly* sad, about how friendship can sometimes be blind (there are early hints that Willow is drifting too deeply into the belief that magic is a cure-all). Forget **94**, 'The Body', Forget **95**, 'Forever', 'After Life' is easily the least life-affirming, least celebratory episode of *Buffy* yet. And therein lies its true beauty.

Willow alludes to the passage of time being different in a Hell dimension to reality (see **35**, 'Anne'; **38**, 'Beauty and the Beasts'). Xander mentions Spike's doomed obsession with Buffy (see **92**, 'Crush'; **96**, 'Intervention'; **100**, 'The Gift').

Critique: Richard Matthews in the *Daily Telegraph* describes *Buffy* as: 'Superb. Great writing, great acting and a sense of invention that never patronises its audience, Joss Whedon remodelled the teen heroine as a kick-ass vampire hunter and resuscitated the horror genre. Actually, to dismiss it as horror is to do an injustice. Taking a leaf out of *Star Trek*'s book, *Buffy* uses its fantastical premise to explore emotional and psychological home truths. If you doubt its prescience, just click to the episode that prefigured the Columbine massacre and you'll see the light.'

Did You Know?: Before meeting fiancé Freddie Prinze Jr, Sarah Michelle Gellar made it a policy not to date actors according to the *teenhollywood.com* website. She made a pact with herself to avoid relationships within showbiz, but was forced to drop her philosophy when she met Prinze. 'With Freddie it's been difficult in the sense that I've never really had a public relationship,' notes Sarah. 'How much do you talk about it? If you say nothing, it makes them thirst for more. But you can't complain, "I have no privacy." When you take on this job, it's something you're aware of.'

You Sexy Thing: She may have once been voted the most gorgeous girl in the world, but don't tell Sarah Michelle Gellar she's sexy. Sarah would prefer to be famous for being clever. 'Being sexy is being confident,' she told *Infobeat* website. 'It's important to know you don't have silicone breasts falling out and a thigh-high skirt. Sometimes you meet people and they think, "Another cute little blonde actress." That's not who I am.'

Cast and Crew Comments: Is there a way in which *Buffy* could tackle something like the 11 September tragedy within its drama, James Marsters was asked by *Starburst*? 'They certainly tackled the whole Collumbine [sic] Massacre head-on,' he noted. 'Although it must be said that was more about accidental timing than [the writers] wanting to be topical.'

When he appeared on *Richard and Judy* in Britain, James was asked about his relationship with his fans: 'I enjoy meeting them,' he said. 'I think fans of *Buffy* tend to be pretty sophisticated. The writing on the show demands that you are hip to "get it". Irony is heavily used on the show, so, in general, the fans are pretty interesting to talk to. Actually, they're freaks and I'm a freak.' So Richard Madeley wondered if he got asked really detailed questions about what happens in the show. 'No,' replied James, deadpan. 'They usually just grab my bum!'

Jane Espenson's Comments: In several interviews, Jane has noted that she particularly enjoys writing for the character of Anya whom she regards as something of an alter ego for herself. Emma Caulfield's reaction to that? 'I'm very flattered,' she told *BBC Online*. 'I love Jane, I love her episodes and I have such a good time playing the character. I'm a lucky girl.'

In an online interview, Jane agreed that 'After Life' was a significant departure from her usual style: 'I don't remember how the assigning happened. I normally write comedy. I remember Joss saying, you don't have to do this one. I thought I'd give it a try and I had a wonderful time writing it. It's interesting finding other ways to be entertaining.' Jane often gets asked to name her favourite episode: 'I always say **40**, 'Band Candy',' she told Rob Francis. 'Because it was my first. However, I'm not sure if that's true anymore. I really like **73**, 'Superstar'.'

Joss Whedon's Comments: Has Joss really pulled back from the day-to-day running of *Buffy* and *Angel* as fan-rumours suggest? 'Certainly not enough to suit my wife,' he told *Cult Times*. 'The honest answer is yes-and-no. I keep to my own schedule now. I don't have to be here every second for the day-to-day shooting . . . but I still have a great love for this show that I can't cure myself of.'

104
Flooded

US Transmission Date: 16 October 2001
UK Transmission Date: 24 January 2002

Writers: Douglas Petrie, Jane Espenson
Director: Douglas Petrie
Cast: Todd Stashwick (M'Fashnik Demon),
Michael Merton (Mr Savitsky), John Jabaley (Tito),
Brian Kolb (Bank Guard)

Buffy finds herself having to contend with the financial and physical mundanities of running a household like burst pipes and home-improvement loans. She seeks the advice of a returned Giles, who also expresses his concern over Willow's action in bringing Buffy back from the grave at such risk to herself. To add to Buffy's problems, she has become the object of mischief for a *troika* of bored, nerdish would-be sorcerers.

Dreaming (As Blondie Once Said) is Free: Buffy tells Giles that she hasn't had trouble sleeping since her resurrection. Except for the dreams.

Authority Sucks!: An officious bank officer refuses to give Buffy a loan even after she saves his life from an enraged M'Fashnik demon.

Pretty Green: Money is definitely becoming an issue, Willow tells Buffy. Joyce had life insurance which should have left Buffy and Dawn covered, but hospital bills sucked up most of this. As the Loan Officer confirms, the only collateral Buffy has is her house, which has been losing equity over the years. For some reason, Sunnydale property values have never been competitive (that'll probably be something to do with the mortality rate?).

Mom's Apple Pie: Buffy makes a complete mess of preparing a temporary bed for Giles on the couch, apologising that her mother always did stuff like that so well. Joyce dealt with this sort of thing every day, Giles tells Buffy after the living room is trashed during her fight with the M'Fashnik. Joyce took one crisis at a time, without the aid of superpowers, and got through them all. So, Giles believes, can Buffy.

Denial, Thy Name is Willow: Buffy hasn't displayed a range of human emotions since she returned, Willow notes, which is why Willow is so pleased when Buffy briefly gets angry over money issues. The subtext of Willow's confusion (and, even, a pointed annoyance) that Buffy isn't more grateful to Willow for bringing her back from the dead (see also Willow's rather petty conversation with Tara in **103**, 'After Life') spills over into her confrontation with Giles. He clearly suspects that Buffy's return from wherever she was ('we still know nothing' he perceptively notes) has damaged her in some way. But this is arrogantly dismissed by Willow, who seems more concerned that Giles should be impressed by her magical prowess than with her friend's welfare. As Giles notes, 'you're a very stupid girl.'

The Conspiracy Starts at Home Time: The M'Fashnik comes from a long line of mercenary demons, known to perform acts of mayhem and slaughter for the highest bidder. The *troika* have hired it to create chaos while they rob the bank.

Work is a Four-Letter Word: Xander spends four hours trying to piece Buffy's smashed coffee table back together after the fight with the demon, before finally giving up.

It's a Designer Label!: Buffy's sexy grey top, Anya's cute summery dress with roses on it.

References: Genesis 7:15 ('we should start gathering up two of every animal'), *Teletubbies* ('Buffy go bye-bye'), Gloria Gaynor's 'I Will Survive' ('and so you're back . . .'). Anya, Dawn and Xander have a petty (though amusing) argument about Spider-Man's *modus operandi* ('Action is *his* reward'). Willow alludes to *The Blair Witch Project*.

Geek-Speak: A whiteboard lists the *troika*'s TO DO list. It's impressive stuff: CONTROL THE WEATHER, MINIATURIZE FORT KNOX, CONJURE FAKE I.D.S, SHRINK RAY, GIRLS, GIRLS, and THE GORILLA THING (dialogue suggests this means training gorillas to be their slaves). Jonathan also mentions a plan to create workable jet-packs (see **120**, 'Villains'), 'chicks, chicks, chicks,' and adds HYPNOTIZE BUFFY at the end (see **105**, 'Life Serial'). Also, *The Wizard of Oz* (Andrew training winged-monkeys to attack the school play, which seems to have been a version of *Romeo and Juliet* judging by Jonathan's comments), *The Simpsons* and the *Austin Powers* movies (the *troika*'s 'Super Villain' laugh being a hilarious cross between Dr Evil and Montgomery Burns), *Star Trek* ('let's back things up a parsec', Jonathan and Andrew voting using the Vulcan hand gesture) and *The Next Generation* ('make it so'), The Beatles ('for those long, lonely nights after a hard day's slaughter'), *Happy Days* ('Exactamundo') and *Star Wars* ('the force can sometimes have great power on the weak-minded'). Andrew is upset because Warren won't build him a robot replica of *Sleepy Hollow* actress Christina Ricci (however, see **119**, 'Seeing Red', concerning Andrew's sexuality).

With their ill-gotten gains from the bank robbery, Warren, Jonathan and Andrew have kitted out their lair with, among other things, a periscope from a Russian submarine, a flame-thrower, numerous action figures and a virtual-reality headset. Their decoration ideas seem to have been taken largely from various super-villain 'pads' in *Batman* and *The Avengers*. Cool.

Bitch!: Willow is relieved that Buffy is, at last showing some emotion. In an, unsuccessful, attempt to provoke another angry response from Buffy, Willow alleges that last semester, she slept with Riley. 'What the hell are you doing?' asks Buffy. 'Pissing you off,' replies Willow, to which Buffy responds: 'Yes. True. Why?' When Anya suggests that Buffy charge for slaying vampires Buffy replies: 'That's an idea . . . *you* might have.'

Awesome!: The pre-title sequence in the basement with the burst water pipe. Pure slapstick. Buffy's hilarious fight with the demon in the bank. Giles, Xander and Dawn's discussions on the pronunciation of 'M'Fashnik'. The flashback to the *troika*'s first meeting ('you guys wanna team up and take over Sunnydale?', 'OK!'). Giles's confrontation with Willow. After drowning the demon in the basement, Buffy's pissed-off look when Spike casually asks if she was aware the place is flooded.

Surprise!: The revelation that the evil masterminds behind the bank robbery are . . . wait for it, Warren, Jonathan and some other guy we've never seen before.

'You May Remember Me From Such Films and TV Series As . . .': Todd Stashwick appeared in *Angel*, *L.A.X.*, *Law & Order*, *Whacked*, *Dark Angel* and *Lucid Days in Hell*. The great Danny Strong, originally screen-tested for the role of Xander. He was Juke Box Boy in *Pleasantville* and appeared in *Saved By the Bell: The New Class*, *New Suit*, *Clueless* and *Spoof! An Insider's Guide to Short Film Success*. Adam Busch was Kyle in *Magic Rock* and

Manolo in *Léon*. He's also a member of the band Common Rotation. Tom Lenk appeared in *Boogie Nights* and *Popular*. John Jabaley was location manager on *L.A. Heat*, *Avalanche* and *The Chaos Factor*. Michael Merton appeared in *Felicity* and *General Hospital*. He's also a scriptwriter on animated series like *X-Men: Evolution* and *Buzz Lightyear of Star Command*.

Don't Give Up The Day Job: Director of Photography Raymond Stella's vastly impressive CV includes such movies as *What Women Want*, *Blade*, *Apollo 13*, *Braveheart*, *Schindler's List*, *Indiana Jones and the Last Crusade*, *Jurassic Park*, *The Thing*, *Escape from New York* and *Jaws of Satan*. Editor Lisa Lassek previously worked on *Killers* and *Just Add Love*.

Valley-Speak: Andrew: 'Hello, screen-wipe. New scene.'
   Warren, after Andrew's little speech about wormholes: 'Dude. Don't be a geek.'
   Willow: 'I *totally* kept it together.'

Cigarettes and Alcohol: Buffy is surprised that, in the Magic Box, Dawn is helping with the research. She asks if Dawn wants a pack of cigarettes too.

Logic, Let Me Introduce You to This Window: When Giles wears a short-sleeved shirt, his Eyghon tattoo is missing (previously seen in **20**, 'The Dark Age', **40**, 'Band Candy' and **70**, 'Goodbye Iowa'). Shouldn't Tara and Willow help Buffy out with the household finances since they live in the house too? Don't they pay rent or contribute to the food bill? Sponging *students*. As Buffy says, rather bitterly, when the phone rings: 'Who'd be calling? Everyone I know *lives* here.' Why does Warren just happen to have Buffy's name, address and phone number on a piece of paper in his back pocket to give to the demon on demand? There had been no forewarning prior to the M'Fashnik turning up that the Slayer would, in any way, be involved in their shenanigans. When the M'Fashnik smashes in the door of Buffy's house, Dawn and Giles are standing next to each other some distance away from it, yet Dawn is dramatically thrown to the floor in a flurry of splinters while Giles remains standing.

I Just *Love* Your Accent: In his few days back in England, Giles met with the Watcher's Council. He keeps a flat in Bath, saw a few old friends and almost made a new one which, he believes, is statistically impossible for a man of his age. He describes Buffy's childhood pillows as 'whimsical.'

Giles's Cranial Trauma: 'Now I know I'm back in America,' notes Rupert. 'I've been knocked unconscious,' referring to the numerous occasions in the past in which he ends up getting hit on the head with a blunt instrument (too many to list, but watch more than a couple of episodes and you'll find one).

Quote/Unquote: Giles: 'The magics you channelled are ... ferocious and primal ... You are lucky to be alive, you rank, arrogant amateur.' Willow: 'You're right ... I'm very powerful. And maybe it's not such a good idea for you to *piss me off*.'

Andrew: 'Aside from the moral issues, and the mess, we can get in trouble for murder.'

Notes: 'Way I see it, life is like an interstellar journey. Some go into hypersleep and travel at sub-light speeds, only to get where they're going after years of struggle, toil and hard work.' After three episodes of reformatting, at last, the *real Buffy*: 'Flooded', a razor-sharp tale of wishful thinking, drags the series back to the past. There are three elements of plot: Buffy's newly acquired financial worries, the return of Giles and its effect upon the group dynamic and the arrival of the season's first Big Bad, a *troika* of fanboy evildoers. Jonathan, Warren and Andrew are *fabulous*, a cunning mixture of the incompetence of Dr Evil and the sarcastic reference-dropping of *The Simpsons*' Comic Store Guy. Fans, who either didn't recognise a gentle bit of fun being poked in their direction, or who *did* and got the joke, quickly grew to *love* them. Doug Petrie and Jane Espenson neatly balance all of the elements necessary for a great *Buffy* episode though the final scene seems a bit perfunctory.

When Giles left he signed papers placing the Magic Box in Anya's complete control. Her first, hysterical, words to him on his return are: 'We are so glad to see you . . . *You can't have the store back.*' The *troika*'s headquarters are in the basement of Warren's mom's house (last seen, briefly, in **96**, 'Intervention'). Andrew is the younger brother of Tucker Wells, the insane ex-student who tried to release hellhounds on Buffy's prom night (see **54**, 'The Prom'). Jonathan remembers that he was at that event (he presented Buffy with her 'Class Protector' award) and Warren, seemingly, was too (he sneeringly alludes to the fact that he graduated while Andrew, possibly, didn't). 'I had nothing to do with the devildogs. I trained flying monkey-demons to attack the school play,' notes Andrew defensively. The others, actually, thought *that* was quite cool. Jonathan, like Andrew, is not keen on the idea of killing Buffy, reminding the others that she saved his life a whole bunch of times (specifically, **22**, 'What's My Line?' Part 2; **32**, 'Go Fish'; **52**, 'Earshot' and **73**, 'Superstar'). Plus, 'she's hot.' When Buffy sits on the porch with Spike and asks 'why are you always around when I'm miserable?' it's not only a reference to the climax of **103**, 'After Life', but also to a similar sequence in **85**, 'Fool for Love'.

Original UPN broadcasts of this episode included, during one of the advert breaks, a twenty second trailer for **107**, 'Once More, With Feeling' (at this stage still being publicly called 'Buffy: The Musical') which featured Alyson Hannigan in the recording studio adding her voice to the chorus of '(They Got) The Mustard (Out)'. Several similar behind-the-scenes trailers featured over the next few weeks in the lead-up to the episode's premiere.

The Comic: 'Reunion', a one-shot comic book authored by Jane Espenson, tells the story of what happened during Buffy and Angel's off-screen meeting between Los Angeles and Sunnydale after this episode (and *Angel*: 'Carpe Noctem'). Or, at least, what Xander, Anya and Dawn speculate may have happened during the rendezvous.

Critique: 'As *Buffy* gets ever darker, the comic relief offered by Emma Caulfield's irrepressible demon-turned-human Anya is more welcome than ever,' noted *TV Guide*. '[She] is blunt, literal, selfish and mercenary. Yet the vibrant Caulfield makes Anya tremendously likeable.' Concerning the *troika*, *sci_fi.ign.com*'s Susan Kuhn noted: 'I love that Espenson and Petrie give them all the little geeky flourishes (the Spockian gesture when voting, the snorty laugh) without plunging into over-the-top nerd stereotype. It's nice to see Jonathan getting some decent airtime post-'Superstar' – as long as these wannabe Lone Gunmen are handled with a light touch, they should provide plenty of giggles this season.'

Did You Know?: Nick Brendon nearly gave up acting before landing the role of Xander, according to the *Sydney Morning Herald*. Nick told Keith Austin that, having lost over twenty jobs before becoming an actor and during his early days in the profession, 'I was bored. I guess, I was destined to act.' Despite this, Brendon gave up his acting career once, after becoming sick of Hollywood. 'I was really stressed out and I wasn't having fun. The day I quit acting, a big weight lifted.' Fortunately, sometimes life deals out second chances, and within three months of changing his mind, Nick landed the part of Xander. He also spoke about the stresses of singing on 107, 'Once More, With Feeling.' 'I started having nightmares, like showing up at school without pants on.' So, if Nick was to gain a superpower in real life, what would it be? 'The ability to touch a book and know everything in it without spending days reading it,' he told Rob Francis. 'It's a knowledge-thing but, basically, I'm just a lazy bastard!'

Cast and Crew Comments: Amber Benson has revealed that you stand a better chance of a candlelit dinner for two with her if you work behind – rather than in front of – the camera. 'I tend to date the behind-the-scenes guys,' Amber told *Stuff* magazine. 'I've gone through an editor, a writer and a camera operator. I work so hard, I don't have much time to date.' Amber also admits she isn't one for Hollywood celebrity parties. 'If I ever go to one, I'm in the corner with a non-alcoholic drink. I don't feel comfortable. You know what the most fun is? When you're the only sober person there. You watch these people acting like total asses.'

A clever, articulate and talented young woman, Amber has already taken the first steps in establishing a career for herself outside of acting, by writing and directing her own movie, *Chance*, and scripting issues of the *Buffy* comic.

Jane Espenson's Comments: 'The co-writing experiences this year, were very different,' Jane told the online Succubus Club in an interview in May 2002. 'Doug and I tried something we hadn't tried before, I wrote a whole draft, he did his rewrite on it. Then I rewrote him and he rewrote me. It didn't really work, because both of us would throw out all the other person's stuff and write our own version. It was two views of Mount Fuji. Fury and I did it completely differently. I wrote a half and he wrote a half. That worked especially well for **105**, "Life Serial".'

'I feel there's a lot of Buffy that speaks to events that happen in real life that are traumatic or painful,' Jane told another online interview. 'They pulled **52**, 'Earshot,' because of Columbine. I was glad they'd delayed it because the episode felt weird in that context. But I was also glad they finally aired it, because I felt like it was exactly the thing that people needed to hear. You may feel all alone in your pain in high school like everyone is observing you, but in fact, nobody's paying any attention to you because everyone's in [their own] pain, and wrapped up in their own world. That was really important to say.'

Joss Whedon's Comments: 'I tend to plot the major story points, sometimes in conversation with the writers, [but] usually by myself. At the beginning of every year I figure out the basic steps when this is going to happen and who will write that script and when and where so-and-so dies,' Joss told Rob Francis. Does it worry him that, particularly on the Internet, fans take everything he says so seriously? 'Sometimes I do worry that I will say something like

"Sarah will die – we will kill off Buffy," and then fans will say "I heard a rumour." People, lighten up!'

105
Life Serial

US Transmission Date: 23 October 2001
UK Transmission Date: 31 January 2002

Writers: David Fury, Jane Espenson
Director: Nick Marck
Cast: Paul Gutrecht (Tony), Noel Albert Guglielmi (Vince),
Enrique Almeida (Marco), Jonathan Goldstein (Mike),
Winsome Brown (Woman Customer),
Christopher May (Male Customer), David J Miller (Rat-Faced Demon),
Andrew Cooper Wasser (Slime-Covered Demon),
Richard Beatty (Small Demon), Jennifer Shon (Rachel),
Jabari Hearn (Steve), Derrick McMillon (Ron), Clint Culp (Bartender),
Mark Ginther (Horned Demon), Alice Dinnean Vernon (Mummy Hand),
Marcia Ann Burrs (Professor Bellamy)[4]

As Buffy tries to acclimatise to her new life as a surrogate parent, return to college and attempt numerous part-time jobs to make some money, she again comes up against the *troika*. They plan to test the Slayer by casting spells which make her experience time distortions, magically appearing and disappearing demons and a time-loop. The Scooby Gang's less-than-sympathetic response means that Buffy turns to Spike. And alcohol.

Dudes and Babes: Anya suggests to Buffy that, when selling things to people she should 'do what I do: just picture yourself naked.' There is some *weird* stuff in that girl's head.

Authority Sucks!: Anya, mean-spiritedly, suggests that the shipping charges that Buffy neglected to include in her, extremely stressful, first sale as a retail clerk at the Magic Box, will be taken out of her salary. Buffy quits in protest.

---

[4] Uncredited.

Pretty Green: Buffy's financial woes continue, with her losing two jobs on the first day. But the gift of a, seemingly, large cheque from Giles will hold off the creditors for the moment.

A Little Learning is a Dangerous Thing: In sociology, Willow and her classmates are studying The Social Construction of Reality, with their professor, Mike. All of this goes right over Buffy's head and she considers 'maybe I should ease back in with some non-taxing classes, like introduction to pies, or advanced walking.' Tara is taking an Art Appreciation class. From the book she gives Buffy to look at, they appear to be concentrating on the Renaissance period.

Denial, Thy Name is Buffy: Buffy says that her meeting with Angel (see **104**, 'Flooded') was 'intense' but refuses to elaborate when (pointedly) questioned by the Scoobies.

Denial, Thy Name is Giles: He believes that the time anomalies Buffy suffers may be stress-related.

Denial, Thy Name is Xander: When the demons attack the construction site, Xander is horrified, telling Buffy: 'No, not here. Not at my job. That's *your* job!'

The Conspiracy Starts at Home Time: In their quest to become the 'crime lords of Sunnydale', the *troika* know that they must stay one step ahead of Buffy at all times. That's why they intend to throw her some magical tests, seeing which of them can shake her up the most and maybe find a weakness.

Work is a Four-Letter Word: Xander gets Buffy a labouring job on his building site. Since she isn't in a union Xander has to call in a few favours. Her strength is an advantage in overcoming the obvious sexism of the crew, but she's actually *too good* at it. As they get paid by the hour she's told to slow down. The foreman Tony seems, as Xander notes, pig-ignorant, rude, and a little hostile (with pretentions of sexual harassment). Ultimately Andrew's demons attack and put an end to Buffy's construction career. Xander himself is in charge of supervising the sheet rock hangers on the site.

Buffy, reluctantly, tries retail at the Magic Box, with hilarious consequences.

It's a Designer Label!: Some horrorshows here: Willow's orange shirt and Buffy's sparkly boob tube being major offenders. The *troika* wear some of the geekiest clothes seen thus far (especially Jonathan's hooped top). Buffy's shop-girl outfit is quite tasteful.

References: *Groundhog Day* (and numerous TV homages to it), Republican presidential candidate Bob Dole. Tara and Willow watch Nickelodeon's *Spongebob Squarepants*, apparently. Also, *Gidget* (see **3**, 'The Witch') and *Jeopardy*. Marco calls Buffy 'little Britney', the series' only reference so far to Ms Spears with whom it has been linked in the tabloids on so many occasions.

Geek-Speak: Warren and Jonathan find Andrew spray-painting a huge (conspicuous) mural of the Death Star on the side of their van. (When Jonathan points out that one of the Thermal exhaust ports is in the wrong place, Andrew proudly says he's using the Empire's revised designs from *Return of the Jedi*.) Andrew hopes that Buffy solves the time-loop faster than Data did on 'that episode of *TNG* where the Enterprise kept blowing up' ('Cause and Effect'). Warren adds: 'Or Mulder in that *X-Files* where the bank kept exploding' ('Monday'). 'Scully wants me so bad,' Andrew says, hopefully (but, see **Sex and Drugs and Rock'n'Roll**). The pair also allude to the Dead Parrot sketch from *Monty Python's Flying Circus* ('this mummy hand has ceased to be'). While observing Buffy's first hesitant steps in retail, Warren suggests the *troika* check the other channels for 'free cable porn'. When Andrew suggests they're like Doctor No, an argument ensues about who was the best James Bond. Warren admires Sean Connery, but Jonathan prefers the 'smooth' Roger Moore. Andrew liked Timothy Dalton. Warren's angry rant about the comedy aspects of *Moonraker* being 'inexcusable' (the pigeon doing a double-take, etc.), although representative of some of the louder, and more boring, voices in Bond fandom, is *way* off the mark. It's funny, and nowhere near as bad *A View to a Kill*.

Awesome!: The entire mummy's hand/*Groundhog Day* third act. As funny as *Buffy* has ever got. Most of the *troika* scenes are also hysterical, with the three bickering over which Bond was best, and dropping sci-fi injokes all over the place.

'You May Remember Me From Such Films and TV Series As ...': James C Leary played Kevin in *Los Beltrán*. Richard Beatty appeared in *Thick as Thieves* and wrote *Blindside*. Clint Culp was in *Every Dog Has Its Day*. Jonathan Goldstein appeared in *The Auteur Theory* and *Stranger*. Paul Gutrecht wrote and directed *What We Have*, and appeared in *The Disappearing Girl Trick*, *Dragonfly* and *Ally McBeal*. Jennifer Shon was in *NYPD Blue* and *Boston Public*. Mark Ginther played Lord Zedd in *Mighty Morphin Power Rangers: The Movie*, appeared in *Angel*, *P.U.N.K.S* and *Con Air* and was stuntman on movies like *Hoffa*, *Joe Versus the Volcano* and *Hologram Man*. David Miller's films include *Exposé* and *Deep Down*. Derrick McMillon appeared in *D Minus*. Christopher May was in *The Sky Is Falling*, *Just Sex* and *The Keeper*. Andrew Wasser's CV includes *Tricks*, *Grounded for Life* and *Beverley Hills 90210*. Alice Dinnean Vernon was a voice artist on *Aliens in the Family* and appeared as Sherry Netherland in the long-running *Sesame Street*. Noel Guglielmi was in *The Fast and the Furious* and *24*. Marcia Ann Burrs appeared in *Frasier*, *Judging Amy* and *7th Heaven*.

Don't Give Up The Day Job: Nick Marck began as an assistant director on *Carny*, *10*, *Battlestar Galactica*, *The Postman Always Rings Twice* and *Rehearsal for Murder* before directing *The Wonder Years*, *The X-Files*, *Dawson's Creek* and *Malcolm in the Middle*.

Valley-Speak: Andrew: 'Wicked cool!'

Cigarettes and Alcohol: Giles is seen drinking a glass of wine as the Scoobies have dinner at the beginning. Totally cheesed-off with the *Groundhog Day*-style time loop, Buffy goes to Spike's crypt to cadge his whisky. He then takes her to a seedy demon bar. This is the third time we've seen Buffy drunk (see **17**, 'Reptile Boy' and **61**, 'Beer Bad'). There are numerous cases of Bacardi in the back room where Spike plays poker with the demons.

Sex and Drugs and Rock'n'Roll: *Double entendre* overload. Concerning fried chicken, Willow notes that she is 'a breast girl,' before turning to Tara and whispering: 'But, then, you knew that.' Anya tells Buffy about a Magic Box customer who wanted to purchase a sapphire 'ding-dong' (a phallus, presumably). Jonathan asks the *troika* to hold hands when he's performing a spell. 'With each other?' asks a horrified Andrew. 'You know what homophobia really means about you?' asks Warren. How very insightful (see **119**, 'Seeing Red'). And as for Jonathan telling the others to 'Stop touching my magic bone,' well . . .

Logic, Let Me Introduce You to This Window: While undeniably fun, the 'fast forward freakout' section is logically insane. From the perspective of those for whom time is travelling at normal speed – i.e. *everybody but Buffy* – she must seem as though she's standing in some kind of a trance. 'Zoned out' as Tara puts it. Doesn't anyone think to call an ambulance, sit her down, or do something other than just ignore her including, at one point, somebody knocking her to the ground and not even stopping to ask if she's all right. This is especially true of Tara who, twice, simply walks off and leaves Buffy staring into space. During the fight with the three monsters at the construction site, Buffy (or rather, Sarah Michelle Gellar's stunt-double) dangles from a horizontal bar and does some gymnastic-style kicking. One of her kicks clearly misses its intended demon-target but he still falls down as though hit. How did Jonathan and co. get a mini-camera into the eye-socket of a skull that's in the private area of the Magic Box. No one except the Scooby Gang is allowed in there, as we've previously seen demonstrated (notably, **84**, 'Family'). Jonathan suggests that *The Living Daylights* (1986), the fifteenth James Bond film, was written for Roger Moore. Not, strictly speaking, true. Richard Maibaum and Michael Wilson's script was certainly started during post-production on *A View to a Kill* (1985), Moore's last movie in the role, but it wasn't even completed to first draft stage by the time Moore left and Dalton had been cast. Indeed, while most of the writing was going on, the actor they were trying to get to play Bond was Pierce Brosnan, then starring in *Remington Steele*. Ordinarily this point would be far too anoraky to include but, hell, this is the *troika* we're talking about.

Cruelty to Animals: At the bar, Spike gets involved in a card game with various demons, including Clem, for which the stake is kittens. 'They're delicious,' notes the Green Skinned demon.

Quote/Unquote: Giles: 'Think of the store as a library; it'll help you to concentrate on service . . .' Buffy: 'Yes. And then I'm going to marry Bob Dole and raise penguins in Guam.'

Notes: 'Someone's doing stuff to me. Messing up my life. Except that it was kind of pre-messed already.' If there was ever any doubt in the minds of fans that they, themselves, were being satirised by the *troika* (see **104**, 'Flooded') then this episode hits them over the head with the realisation. Hard. The dramatic components of this are, at best, questionable. The comedy potential, however, isn't wasted. You *will* laugh at much of this episode and, if you don't, then you're probably dead. *Groundhog Day*-style plot-devices and merriment aside, 'Life Serial' also contains a clever piece of social comment concerning the drabness of working life after the freedom of the teenage years. Buffy tries, unsuccessfully to fit her unique lifestyle in with the awful realities of earning a weekly wage. She tackles labyrinthine bureaucracy, sexism and the falseness of customer service with-a-smile. A smashing episode, then, which deals with big issues, but finds time for fabulous comedy and only really disappoints in the rather stale final act. Otherwise, lots to laugh at and lots to think about. The series in microcosm.

Buffy mentions that she left college when Joyce became sick (see **97**, 'Tough Love').

Soundtrack: 'Kidnapper Song' by the Masticators and 'Boom Swagger Boom' by Murder City Devils.

Critique: Marcus Ferrell, at *ZENtertainment.com* was 'glad [to see] more humor this week; too much darkness can get you down. Although the antics of the dorks were illogical, they were humorous, and an inventive way of testing someone's skills. No doubt this will be met with much weeping and gnashing of teeth.'

Did You Know?: How much of the geek stuff did Adam Busch need to learn? 'I had to do a lot of research to find out about *Dungeons and Dragons*,' he told Matt Springer. 'The first scene we shot together – me, Danny and Tom – was when we sat around the table playing *Dungeons and Dragons* . . . none of us knew how to play.'

Comedy is the New Horror: David Fury began his career as a New York stage actor, and a stand-up comedian, as well as working as a voice artist on numerous films (most famously providing several of the voices on *Raiders of the Lost Ark*). He graduated onto writing sitcom scripts. 'Joss was open to comedy writers rather than people who worked in one hour dramas,' he notes. Jane Espenson's story is a similar one. Having graduated from college in Northern California as a self-confessed '*Star Trek*-obsessed nerd,' she 'got into the Disney Writers Fellowship. I worked on a number of sitcoms like *Dinosaurs* [and] a bunch of shows you never heard of,' she told Rob Francis. 'Then I decided I wanted to make the switch to drama and ended up on *Buffy*.' 'When I got this job the show was already established,' Jane told an Internet interview. 'I didn't come to it intending to make any sort of social comment. I knew that it was a metaphor and that I would be talking about what it feels like to be a teenager. But I didn't quite understand that it would end up being so much about what it means to be human. It's not just about the experiences of being fifteen any more, if it ever was.'

Cast and Crew Comments: 'You can expect that Dawn will be getting a little more rebellious,' Michelle Trachtenberg told *Sci-Fi Wire*. 'Obviously, she has shown signs of being a kleptomaniac,' she added. 'I know that storyline will reach a certain pinnacle – that Buffy and Dawn will have to deal with [it].'

On the set, the mature 16-year-old still gets treated like a kid by her elder castmates. 'They're all very nice, but I'm not in on the dirty jokes,' she told *TV Guide*. 'No one cusses around me, either.'

Jane Espenson's Comments: '[There were] four different storylines, each in a separate act,' Jane told the Succubus Club. 'I wrote the last two, Mummy Hand in the Magic Shop and the Kitten Poker with Spike. That was a fun one, I like writing the comedies.'

Joss Whedon's Comments: Joss always had faith that *Buffy* would find a niche. 'When I say I'm not surprised that the show has gotten to 100 episodes, I sound like an ego with legs,' he told the *Los Angeles Times*. 'But *Buffy* makes sense to me, and I believed it would make sense to other people.'

106
All the Way

US Transmission Date: 30 October 2001
UK Transmission Date: 7 February 2002

Writer: Steven S DeKnight
Director: David Solomon
Cast: John O'Leary (Mr Kaltenbach), Kavan Reece (Justin),
Amber Tamblyn (Janice), Dave Power (Zack),
Charles Duckworth (Glenn), Dawn Worrall (Christy),
Emily Kay (Maria), Adam Gordon (Carl), Sabrina Speer (Girl),

Chad Erickson (Guy), Dominic Rambaran (Paramedic #1),
Anthony Sago (Paramedic #2), Lorin Becker (Witch Woman),
Lily Jackson (Witchypoo), Steven Anthony Lawrence (Chunky Kid)[5]

After Xander and Anya finally announce their engagement
to their friends, Dawn lies to Buffy and spends Halloween
night up to mischief with her friend Janice and two boys.
She develops a crush on one, Justin, and receives her first
kiss. However, the boys reveal themselves to be vampires.
Meanwhile, after Willow and Tara have a fight about
Willow's abuse of magic, Willow casts a spell on Tara to
make her forget.

Dudes and Babes: Xander lovingly looks at Anya and
Dawn dancing and tells Buffy, 'I'm gonna marry that girl.'
Buffy is *horrified*: 'What?! She's fifteen and my sister . . .
oh.'

Tara and Willow have their first significant argument
over Willow's casual abuse of magic (see **104**, 'Flooded').
Why use magic, Tara asks, when you can do something
naturally? But this seems too hard a concept for Willow to
get her head around. Willow assumes, wrongly, that Tara
and Giles have been talking about her behind her back and
says some hurtful things (Tara: 'What do you want me to
do, just sit back and keep my mouth shut?' Willow: 'That'd
be a good start'). Then she regrets it. At the episode's end,
with Tara still upset at her, Willow does something even
more questionable, and uses a spell to make Tara forget
they have been fighting (see **107**, 'Once More, With
Feeling' and **108**, 'Tabula Rasa' for the repercussions).

Authority Sucks!: After Dawn's first fumbling steps in
teenage romance, Buffy leaves it to Giles to hand out the
necessary chastisement. He is clearly not happy with Buffy
avoiding her quasi-parental responsibility (see **107**, 'Once
More, With Feeling').

A Little Learning is a Dangerous Thing: Dawn tells
Justin that witches don't, generally, look like traditional

---

depictions with broomsticks and warts. When Justin asks if she has any witch friends she blurts out that she's read about them in books.

Denial, Thy Name is Giles: Buffy discovers the reason Giles is always cleaning his glasses is so that he doesn't have to see what the Scooby Gang are doing.

Theft is a Five-Letter Word: Dawn admits to Justin that she has been stealing for some time, finally explaining her taking Anya's earrings in **96**, 'Intervention', and noting that she hasn't paid for lipstick 'since forever' (see **114**, 'Older, and Far Away'). She steals an amulet that she finds lying in the Magic Box which can be seen again, briefly, in her stash box in **107**, 'Once More, With Feeling'.

It's a Designer Label!: The Halloween costumes are fun, especially Anya's. Check out, in particular, Tara's lovely peach top and the skin-tight silver pants worn by the Bronze waitresses.

Dodgy Subject Matter: Mr Kaltenbach designed toy robots in the late 50s and got enormous pleasure from the joy they gave to children. However, there are dark hints of a terrible secret in his past when he talks about 'one little mistake and they took it all away'. This is, potentially, the series' first oblique reference to child sexual abuse (although **30**, 'Killed By Death' does so through metaphor).

References: The title is a Sammy Cahn/Jimmy Van Heusen song most famously recorded by Frank Sinatra. The lady customer at the Magic Box is dressed as Witchypoo, a character from Sid and Marty Kofft's classic 1970s children's serial *H.R. Pufnstuf*. Zach's 'Pumpkins, very dangerous, you go first,' is an allusion to *Indiana Jones and the Raiders of the Lost Ark*. Xander paraphrases *Henry V* ('once more into the breach.' See **100**, 'The Gift'). During the Magic Box sale Xander is dressed (unimpressively) as a pirate. Giles refers to him as Ahab, the captain in *Moby Dick*. Anya wears a Farrah Fawcett-Majors costume ('a special kind of angel called a Charlie. We don't have wings, we just skate around with perfect hair fighting crime'). Willow and Tara see a couple in the Bronze dancing suggestively dressed as Luke Skywalker and Princess Leia: 'Do they *know* they're brother and sister?' Willow asks. Mr Kaltenbach hums 'Pop Goes the Weasel'. Also *Fantasia* (specifically the Mickey Mouse 'Sorcerers Apprentice' sequence), *Toy Story* (Zack uses Buzz Lightyear's catch-phrase 'To infinity and beyond'), *JFK* ('just one little mistake'), *A Shot in the Dark* ('Summers' residence'), *Crimes and Misdemeanors*, Xander alludes to Stevie Smith's poem 'Not Waving, But Drowning' (see **65**, 'Something Blue'), *WWF Smackdown*, *Superman*, escapologist Harry Houdini (1874–1926) and Bobby Boris Pickett and the Crypt-Kickers' kitsch classic 'The Monster Mash'.

Bitch!: Buffy, on Spike: 'He was so much easier to talk to when he wanted me dead.'

Anya notes that June weddings traditionally have the biggest calls for vengeance.

Look at the expression on Willow's face when Xander announces his engagement. A mixture of bewilderment and hurt. Ooo, no subtext there, I don't think (see **21**, 'What's My Line?' Part 1; **39**, 'Homecoming'; **116**, 'Hell's Bells'; **122**, 'Grave').

Awesome!: Stick Giles in a silly costume and you're always guaranteed a good laugh. Plus, Anya doing the *Dance of Capitalist Superiority*. There's *always* something to be said for that. Also, Giles's fight with the two girl vampires. Best bit of the episode is Buffy asking all the assembled vampires if anybody came to the woods simply to make out, and two rather embarrassed people raise their hands.

'You May Remember Me From Such Films and TV Series As . . .': John O'Leary's impressive CV includes *All the President's Men*, *Demon Seed*, *Airplane!*, *The Haunted* and *Guardian Angel*. Kavan Reece appeared in *That '70s Show*. Amber Tamblyn played Katie in *Ring* and was in *Rebellious* and *General Hospital*. Dave Power appeared in *Band of Brothers*, *JAG* and *U–571*. Lorin Becker played Jenny in

Mid-Century. Emily Kay was Melissa in *Undressed* and appeared in *Grace Under Fire.* Adam Gordon was in *Kissing Miranda* and *The X-Files.* Steven Lawrence played Beans in *Even Stevens* and appeared in *Lord of the Road* and *Sabrina, the Teenage Witch.* Anthony Sago was in *Night Man.* Chad Erickson was a Camera Intern on *High Fidelity* and a Grip on *Placebo Effect.*

Don't Give Up The Day Job: Editor Marilyn McMahon Adams previously worked on *Dark Skies, Streets of Fire* and *Shattered Vows.*

The Drugs Don't Work: Spike likes to stir burba weed into the blood he drinks. This makes it all hot and spicy, apparently.

Valley-Speak: Janice: 'The Mominator thinks I'm staying at yours. Can't believe they fell for that one. Like, own a TV.'
    Dawn, on Justin: 'He's OK.' Janice: 'OK? Or, like, "Oh my god, I think I'm gonna pee my pants"?'
    Zack: 'Don't make me go *kung-fu* on you, man!'
    Willow: 'Me at fifteen? Hello, spaz. Hard to believe such a hot mama-yama came from humble, geek-infested roots?'

Cigarettes and Alcohol: Plenty of booze at the engagement party and, later, at the Bronze.

Classic *Double Entendre:* Xander intends to teach Anya a new game called Shiver Me Timbers. 'I'm not really much for the timber,' notes Tara.

Logic, Let Me Introduce You to This Window: Dawn doesn't react when Justin kisses her – surely it should be obvious that he's a corpse? Buffy tells Xander that she was 'out of commission' for three months. However, in **103**, 'After Life', Buffy asks Spike how long she was gone, and he replies 147 days which is almost five months. How, even with Slayer-strength, can slamming a car door on somebody's head decapitate them? Is Dawn ready to give herself to Justin and become a vampire just before Giles shows up? And, if she is, what changes her mind between this scene and the one a few minutes later when she and Justin are alone and she admits to liking him, before staking him? Is it because he says she's special because she's the Slayer's sister?

I Just *Love* Your Accent: Spike uses the British slang phrase 'nick', meaning to steal. When Xander and Anya announce their engagement, Giles notes: 'Where I come from, this sort of thing requires much in the way of libation.' Except we don't normally call getting plastered *that*. 'God save the Queen,' toasts Xander. The Pistols' version, hopefully.

Quote/Unquote: Buffy (outraged): 'Were you *parking*? With a vamp?' Dawn: 'I didn't know he was dead.' Justin: 'Living dead.' Dawn: 'Shut up.'
　　Carl: 'What's your malfunction, man?' Spike: 'It's Halloween, you nit! We take the night off. Those are the rules.' Carl: 'Me and mine don't follow no stinking rules. We're rebels.' Spike: 'No, *I'm* a rebel. You're an *idiot*.'

Notes: 'So what do you think? Lunchables? Or should we go all the way and turn 'em?' *Buffy* Halloween episodes traditionally tend towards the lighter end of the dramatic scale. This year's effort, once some hilarious establishing scenes in the Magic Box are done-and-dusted, goes for a more serious approach. Dawn takes centre stage for once, in a story about teen-romance. Of course, this being Sunnydale, you know automatically that the apparently nice high school boy she's kissing in the woods isn't all he seems. And the *obviousness* of that subplot's execution (and resolution), is why 'All the Way' is the least-apt title imaginable. It is a shame that the episode doesn't really work, because DeKnight's script has several sparkling moments and a deal of tasty *double entendre*. Sadly, though, the dramatic weight is carried, almost entirely, by the continuing story arc of Willow's abuse of magic and of Tara's growing concern. 'All the Way' is an episode that, while it's important in the overall theme of season – growing up – nevertheless sees the series, for one week at least, running on the spot.

When Anya sends Buffy to the Magic Box basement for supplies, Buffy notes: 'Don't blame me if we have this conversation over and over,' a reference to **105**, 'Life Serial'. Buffy talks to Giles about previous Halloween calamities: 'Costumes that take over your personality,' (**18**, 'Halloween') and 'wee Irish fear-demon-y thingies' (**60**, 'Fear Itself'). Dawn wanted to get a tattoo while Buffy was dead, but Willow says they wouldn't let her. The book Willow holds while angrily berating the Halloween witch over the perpetuation of stereotypes is called *Everyday Witchcraft*.

Soundtrack: 'Even If (It Is Love)' by Lift , 'How Do You Make Me Feel?' by Opus 1 Music Library, Colin Monster's 'Body of Binky', 'Living Life' by Box of Music, Strange Radio's 'Make Me a Star', Nikka Costa's 'Everybody Got Their Something' (which Willow, Xander and Anya are dancing to before Giles turns off the radio), 'Around My Smile' by Hope Sandoval and the Warm Inventions and Fonda's 'The Sun Keeps Shining on Me'. Man of the Year perform 'Just As Nice' at the Bronze.

Critique: 'Vampires, in *Buffy*, mutate horribly when they are about to suck blood,' noted Zoe Williams in the *Guardian*. 'They are aping the bodily aspects of puberty . . . [and] the vampiric lifestyle in *Buffy* is characterised by alienation, loneliness, guilt and self-loathing. Modern *Buffy* critics, therefore, find strong [elements] of Jean-Paul Sartre in the undead . . . Given its associations with the rite of passage into adulthood, vampire congress has long been taken as a metaphor for sex. It pretty much still is.'

Did You Know?: Oz fans hoping for the return of the popular werewolf guitarist were disappointed to learn that a planned appearance by Seth Green in this episode was scuppered at the very last minute. *E! Online* reported that while Seth was initially slated to appear in 'All the Way', he had to pull out due to scheduling conflicts.

Cast and Crew Comments: Spike's craving for nicotine may be second only to his thirst for blood, but in reality James

Marsters has given up cigarettes. As he told Kate O'Hare, 'for the last year [I've been] on the patch.' James now resorts to the same trick as *The X-Files*' Cigarette Smoking Man, William B Davis. 'Horrible herbal cigarettes. We smoke [fictional brand] Morley's. We're the only two characters on TV that do.' But, Spike will continue to puff away – after all, what's he got to lose? 'Spike doesn't care about his health. He's dead.'

Head On: When Tony Head appeared on *The Johnny Vaughan Show* in February 2002, he admitted that when he was in the musical *Chess* in London, he was pestered by a stalker: 'Stupidly, when we first got our flat in Battersea, I put my name in the telephone directory. [The Stalker] was on the phone and basically you'd say "Oh for God's sake, Carol, go away" and you'd put the phone down. Half an hour later you'd pick it up and she'd still be there.'

Joss Whedon's Comments: Asked about his writing process on the *BtVS Posting Board*, Joss noted '[it's] about two things: structure and emotion. I'm incredibly strict about working out a tight structure, every piece fitting, so there are not too many surprises in a first draft. But it all stems from emotion. What do we need to feel? What do [the characters] need to feel? With **78**, "Restless", I had to throw structure out the window. It was a poem. Though I knew what it meant and what the dramatic flow was, I literally had to sit there (or lie there – I got my appendix out during that script) and wait for the next thing. It was very liberating for me.'

107
Once More, With Feeling

US Transmission Date: 7 November 2001
UK Transmission Date: 14 February 2002

Writer: Joss Whedon
Director: Joss Whedon
Original Songs, Music and Lyrics: Joss Whedon

Songs Produced and Arranged: Jesse Tobias, Christophe Beck
Choreographer: Adam Shankman
Cast: Hinton Battle (Sweet), David Fury (Mustard Man),
Marti Noxon (Parking Ticket Woman),
Daniel Weaver (Handsome Young Man), Scot Zeller (Henchman),
Zachary Woodlee (Demon/Henchman), Timothy Anderson (Henchman),
Alex Estronei (Henchman), Matt Sims (College Guy #1),
Hunter Cochrane (College Guy #2)

For some mysterious reason, everyone in Sunnydale is compelled to reveal their innermost feelings through song and dance. While searching for the demon behind this disturbing situation, Buffy finally tells the gang the truth about where she was after she died, leaving Willow, in particular, devastated. Meanwhile, Tara discovers Willow's spell to make her forget their argument, and both Giles and Spike come to decisions concerning their future relationships with Buffy.

Dudes and Babes: When a couple of boys check out Tara as she and Willow are walking through the park, and Willow lovingly draws Tara's attention to it, Tara is amused: 'I'm cured. I want the boys!' Willow, jokingly, asks if she has to fight to keep Tara: 'Cos I'm not large with the butch.'

A Little Learning is a Dangerous Thing: Dawn notes that her maths homework seemed much more interesting at school when they were singing about it.

Denial, Thy Name is Everyone: The entire episode concerns those secrets that everyone is trying so to hard to keep, and failing miserably: Buffy's knowledge of having been torn out of Heaven and of subsequently finding life tough to deal with; Xander and Anya's fears about their impending marriage and their suitability for each other; Giles's belief that his presence in Sunnydale, and his attempts to play the father, is stopping Buffy from achieving all that she can and giving her an easy option each time a crisis looms; Spike's depth of feeling for Buffy and annoyance that she can't seem to make up her mind whether she wants to kill him or kiss him; and, Tara and Willow's fractured relationship through the seductive power of magic on Willow. Only Dawn manages to keep *her* secret (rampant kleptomania, see **96**, 'Intervention'; **106**, 'All the Way') intact. For the moment at least (see **114**, 'Older, and Far Away').

The Conspiracy Starts at Home Time: Believing that the charm Dawn, ahem, 'found' in the Magic Box is her own, Sweet tells her 'I come from the imagination/And I'm here strictly by your invocation.' He intends to take her to his underworld domain as his queen ('you and me wouldn't be very regal,' Dawn sings, horrified, 'I'm fifteen, so this queen-thing's illegal!'). It subsequently turns out that it was Xander who accidentally summoned Sweet by wishing for 'dances and songs. I just wanted to make sure we'd get a happy ending.' Sweet, though tempted, ultimately lets Xander off with the underworld queen-thing.

It's a Designer Label!: Buffy's leather jacket and stylish-but-affordable boots; Tara's gorgeous medieval-style turquoise top with padded sleeves and gypsy dress; Anya's black butterfly dress and red underwear; Xander's silk dressing gown; Willow's big furry coat and Dawn's light-blue sweater.

References: The title is a quotation from Joan Armatrading's 'Love and Affection' (see **57**, 'The Freshman'). The trio of street-sweepers that Giles, Xander and Anya walk past appear to be performing the dance of the Chimney Sweeps from *Mary Poppins*. Spike's 'get your kumbaya-yas out,' is an allusion to both the African hymn 'Kumbaya' and the Rolling Stones' 1970 LP 'Get Your Ya-Ya's Out'. Buffy paraphrases Shakespeare's *As You Like It* ('Life's a show and we all play our part') and I Timothy 6:12 ('fight the fight'). Spike refers to '76 Trombones' from *The Music Man*. Also, visual reference to the title-sequences of the James Bond movies (specifically *The Spy Who Loved Me*), Tim Burton's *Batman* (Sweet's 'Joker'-style suit and attitude) and Michael Powell and Emeric Pressburger's ballet masterpiece *The Red Shoes* (Dawn's dance with Sweet's minions), *Pinnochio* ('some day he'll be a real boy'), *Snow White and the Seven Dwarfs* ('Whistle while you work'), *The Karate Kid*, The Isley Brothers' 'Twist and Shout', *That's Entertainment*, *The Avengers* ('we're needed'), *The Addams Family* ('show time!'), *Superman* ('Merciful Zeus!'), award-winning journalist David Brinkley, Peruvian mambo singer Yma Sumac and *The Lord of the Dance*. Sweet claims to have bought the Emperor Nero (AD37–68) his first fiddle (presumably, the one he allegedly played while Rome burned). Xander's 'Respect the cruller, and tame the doughnut' is a probable reference to a Tom Cruise line in *Magnolia* concerning male and female genitalia. 'Going Through the Motions' paraphrases Duke Ellington's 'It Don't Mean a Thing (if it Ain't Got that Swing)'.

Bitch!: Buffy: 'So, Dawn's in trouble. It must be Tuesday.' Spike, on Buffy: 'I'm free if that bitch dies.'

Awesome!: The brilliantly silly opening graveyard/'Going Through the Motions' sequence. Anya's hysterical rock-opera Bunnies rant. The initial discovery that it's not just the Scoobies who have the urge to share their feelings through song ('They got/the mustard/*OUT*!!!'). Tara's love song for Willow by the lake, and particularly the bit where the two girls sitting nearby suddenly get up and start dancing. Xander and Anya's amusing 'retro-pastiche' production number. James Marsters giving it the works in 'Rest in Peace'. The moment of horror on the faces of the Scoobies when Buffy tells them it wasn't Hell they brought her back from, but rather Heaven. Spike saving Buffy from a fiery end with some harsh truths about the concept of living. The showstopping 'Where Do We Go From Here?'

Surprise!: Buffy and Spike's big kiss at the end.

'You May Remember Me From Such Films and TV Series As . . .': Broadway veteran Hinton Battle played Cat in the US version of *Red Dwarf* and Scarecrow in *The Wiz* and appeared in *Quantum Leap* and *These Old Broads*. Timothy Anderson's movies include *Boys and Girls*. Daniel Weaver played Vanilla Ice in *Austin Powers: International Man of Mystery*. Zachary Woodlee was in *Rock Star* and *Not Another Teen Movie*. Scot Zeller appeared in *America's Sweethearts*, *Charmed* and *Gilmore Girls*.

Do any of you really need to know who David Fury and Marti Noxon are? Fury played the pizza guy in *Chance* and the Goat Slayer in *Angel*: 'Reprise', while Noxon sang the 'Cordy' theme song on *Angel*: 'Birthday'. Satisfied?

Don't Give Up The Day Job: Jesse Tobias was guitarist with Red Hot Chili Peppers, Alanis Morrisette and, latterly, Splendid. Adam Shankman was choreographer on *The Flintstones*, *Boogie Nights*, *Scream 2*, *She's All That*, *Inspector Gadget* and *The Wedding Planner* (which he also directed). This episode also saw the welcome return to *Buffy* of its Emmy winning former-composer Christophe Beck whose effortlessly evocative music also graces *Stealing Harvard*, *Big Fat Liar*, *Wolf Girl*, *Bring It On*, *Bone Daddy*, *Life During Wartime*, *Mr October* and *Slap Her, She's French*.

Valley-Speak: Handsome Young Man: 'How can I repay . . .?' Buffy: 'Whatever.'

Cigarettes and Alcohol: Spike has a bottle of red wine that he intends to share with Buffy but which he instead throws against the wall of his crypt when his song gets emotional.

Sex and Drugs and Rock'n'Roll: Tara and Willow get all giggly at the Magic Box and, on a very obvious pretext, return home to go to bed. This is, surprisingly, much to Xander's disgust – he describes it as 'get-a-roominess' and then becomes embarrassed when he realises Dawn is sitting beside him. Dawn, herself, thinks Tara and Willow's attraction is romantic. Xander and Buffy chorus simultaneously that it's not. Subtext question: Borderline homophobia? Or a wish to get more research done into the causes of the singing and dancing? The author leaves it to the reader to decide. Anya says she's seen some previous examples of underworld child-bride deals, and they never end well. Except, maybe, once.

Logic, Let Me Introduce You to This Window: When Buffy enters the Magic Box she says 'good morning.' Subsequently, Dawn arrives from school. This, presumably, means the Scoobies were researching all day. Didn't Xander have to go to work and Tara and Willow to college? How did Sweet get in the Bronze when it's closed? Maybe he's a breaking-and-entering demon as well as a singing-and-dancing one? Immediately after Tara leaves Dawn alone at the house, Sweet's puppet-faced minions kidnap Dawn. But how did *they* get into, and out of, the house without Tara seeing them? During the dance number featuring Tara, Anya and Buffy, Emma Caulfield ends up about half a step behind in the movements. You can actually see Amber Benson glance off-camera as she notices this and, as she and Emma back out of focus, a grin appears on Amber's face. The entire Xander summoned Sweet plot-twist seems very illogical. Xander gives absolutely no indication prior to the end that he knows why any of this is happening despite his desperation to end it (surely he would have tried to hint at what he may have inadvertently set in motion to his friends, even if he didn't want to implicate himself?) A funeral is seemingly taking place *at night* while Spike does his big production number. Well, this is Sunnydale, I guess nothing should surprise us. Wouldn't it be interesting to know what Jonathan, Warren and Andrew were singing about while all of this is going on? Bet it'd be something to do with *Star Trek*.

I Just *Love* Your Accent: Spike tells Giles not to be a 'stupid git.'

Quote/Unquote: Giles: 'That would explain the huge backing orchestra I couldn't see and the synchronised dancing from the room service chaps.' And: 'I was able to examine the body while the police were taking witness arias.'

Anya, on bunnies: 'They're not just cute like everybody supposes/They got them hoppy legs and twitchy little noses . . .'

Buffy: 'I'm just worried this whole session's going to turn into some training montage from an eighties movie.'

Notes: 'All those secrets you've been concealing/Say you're happy now, once more, *with feeling*/Now I've gotta run, see you all in Hell!' If **66**, 'Hush' was a variant on media guru Marshall McLuhan's mantra that when people stop talking, they *start* to communicate, then 'Once More, With Feeling' takes theoretical McLuhanism to an entirely new level. But even this description doesn't really do the episode justice. When Joss Whedon first envisioned a musical episode of *Buffy*, some fans were loudly horrified. We needn't have worried. From its *Bewitched*-style title-sequences and knowing musical-comedy opening scenes, to the closing, big-chorus-kiss-and-curtains, this is fifty minutes of quite extraordinary television that displays more wit and imagination and has more things to say about relationships than most series can manage in their entire run. A story about hidden secrets, unspoken truths, stifled laughter behind half-closed doors and of the lengths to which people can go to avoid hearing what they don't want to hear, 'Once More, With Feeling' may well be the best *Buffy* episode yet. It's certainly the strangest. For the most part Whedon adheres to standard musical clichés while cleverly using his actors to their strengths. Tony Head, Amber Benson and James Marsters – all fine singers – carry off their well-staged set-pieces with considerable aplomb. Sarah Michelle Gellar (a novice, apparently) does a fine job with her three songs, while the amusing Emma Caulfied/Nick Brendon duet 'I'll Never Tell' is the episode's comedy highlight. Expect something different and you'll get what you want. Expect to be cringingly embarrassed by tone-deaf actors strutting their non-funky stuff, and you may be very pleasantly surprised.

At the end of 'Something to Sing About', Dawn tells Buffy 'The hardest thing in this world is to live in it,' repeating what Buffy told her in **100**, 'The Gift'. There are numerous continuity references within the songs: Willow's theory that 'some kid is dreaming and we're all stuck inside his wacky Broadway nightmare,' is a musical summation of **10**, 'Nightmares'. Tara's song is literal as she *is* still under Willow's amnesia spell (**106**, 'All the Way'). Anya notes that Xander's 'Penis got diseases from the Chumash tribe' (**64**, 'Pangs'). 'It's do or die' sing the Scoobies. 'Hey, I died twice,' replies Buffy casually (**12**, 'Prophecy Girl'; **100**, 'The Gift'). Giles is staying at a hotel having, presumably, got tired of sleeping on Buffy's couch. He mentions having brought his guitar with him to Sunnydale (see **74**, 'Where the Wild Things Are'). In addition to bunnies, Anya also seems to have a fear of midgets. Anya and Xander are reading *Tomorrow's Bride* magazine. Xander has a couple of the lava lamps in his apartment, along with the dartboard from his old basement seen in **65**, 'Something Blue'. The headline of *Sunnydale Press* (see **17**, 'Reptile Boy'; **33**, 'Becoming' Part 1; **48**, 'Bad Girls'; **55**, 'Graduation Day' Part 1; **66**, 'Hush'; **73**, 'Superstar'; **92**, 'Crush') is: MAYHEM CAUSED – MONSTERS CERTAINLY NOT INVOLVED OFFICIALS SAY.

The premiere broadcast of this episode ran approximately eight minutes longer than normal. Subsequent repeats in the US were edited to standard – circa 42 minute – length. Most initial overseas broadcasts, however, were the 50 minute version and that's the one that was released on video in the UK in 2002. In Marti Noxon's parking ticket song, the last (almost inaudible) line is: 'I'm not wearing underwear.' This is the first episode to feature a different title sequence and theme music, and the first to have an on-screen title. The Mutant Enemy logo monster *sings* 'Grrr Arrrgh' at the episode's end.

Soundtrack: The songs featured are: 'Overture/Going Through the Motions', 'I've Got a Theory', '(They Got) The Mustard (Out)', 'Under Your Spell', 'I'll Never Tell', 'The Parking Ticket', 'Rest in Peace', 'Dawn's Lament', 'What You Feel', 'Standing', 'Walk Through the Fire', 'Something to Sing About', 'What You Feel (reprise)' and 'Where Do We Go From Here?' The soundtrack has recently been released on CD, together with selections from Chris Beck's music on **78**, 'Restless', **66**, 'Hush' and **100**, 'The Gift'.

Critique: Predictably, this high-profile episode gained *Buffy* huge press coverage. Not since **94**, 'The Body (and, before that, **66**, 'Hush') had we seen such a range of magazines and newspapers lining up to heap praise on Joss's shoulders. 'Magnificently inspired,' wrote long-time champion of the show, Matt Roush in the influential *TV Guide*. 'A wildly ambitious, entertaining and unexpectedly moving experiment in form by the show's gifted creator Joss Whedon . . . At moments I could have sworn I'd died and gone to TV heaven.'

'Skepticism among even fans of the show is understandable,' noted Scott Pierce. '[but] this episode is a triumph . . . It's funny, shocking and heartfelt. It mocks itself without becoming a parody . . . This is the sort of risk-taking TV that the Emmys ought to reward but won't. Whedon was absolutely right when he says "There are people who never take genre shows seriously. It's a prejudice that I'll never understand. Because anything to do with fantasy turns them off, and anything humorous must not be meaningful."'

'Perhaps Whedon's best trait is that he's one of the most consistent writers in Hollywood, the equal of Aaron Sorkin or David E Kelley without question and one of the few whose work almost never takes a misstep,' wrote Tim Goodman who added that 'Once More, With Feeling' was not just an episode, 'it's a TV event . . . Forget audience-pleasing chestnuts. The impressive aspect is that these myriad song styles all contain original material that moves the narrative along while jump-starting the season. It's hard to overstate how thrilling this episode is instantly recalling the sophistication of Dennis Potter.'

'Not as good as **66**, "Hush" from two years ago, but better than many of this season's downer episodes (TV to slit your wrist by),' noted the *Post Gazette*. 'Whedon's talent as a clever lyricist almost equals his work as a dramatist. The songs advance the show's serialized plot while further defining the characters. He's clearly a musical theater buff, paying homage to the various styles within the genre.'

Time magazine declared the episode one of the ten TV highlights of 2001: 'You could apply the title of this audacious musical episode to the whole season of *Buffy*, which survived an acrimonious move from the WB to return smarter, funnier and dramatically richer than ever. Who'd have thought creator Joss Whedon (who taught himself piano to write the episode's surprisingly tuneful score, as well as the nimble lyrics) studied his Sondheim along with his sarcophagi?'

'A hugely clever premise that immediately excuses the essential absurd conceit of musicals – why is everybody suddenly breaking into song and dance?' added the *Washington Post*. 'A plot mechanism that makes perfect sense in a *Buffy* universe, where demons' spells continually undermine logic and the laws of nature. Whedon created an organic episode that not only referenced events in prior episodes and advanced existing plot points but also foreshadowed major developments.'

The Punk and the Godfather: James Marsters warned *TV Guide* not to expect a Celine Dion power ballad from Spike. 'We were in London on the dance floor, and Joss Whedon actually stopped dancing, going, "I'm in the middle of your song,"' relates the actor, who covers Tom Waits and Bruce Springsteen in his own one man stage show. 'Just today he said, "The last stanza needs more balls." He wants it to be really rock and roll.'

The fact that Spike is in love with Buffy can seemingly, motivate a heroism within the vampire. 'Or, if spurned,' James observes, 'it could drive to him to great acts of villainy. I don't know if Buffy will ever reciprocate Spike's feelings. I really think Spike is kind-of beneath her. He's evil – he just happens to be in love with a good person.'

Did You Know?: Sarah Michelle Gellar intended to have someone else sing her songs which she would merely lip-synch. When she realised how emotional they were, however, she didn't want anyone else singing them. In a television interview with Richard Blackwood, Sarah states that she *did* mime the songs, but presumably she means that she mimed while on set, having already recorded the soundtrack. Alyson Hannigan, on the other hand, was so lacking in confidence concerning her voice that she specifically requested to have no song of her own and very few singing lines.

Cast and Crew Comments: 'I'm not a singer and I hated every moment of it,' Sarah Michelle Gellar confirmed. 'It took something like nineteen hours of singing and seventeen hours of dancing in-between shooting four other episodes.' She wasn't the only one feeling apprehensive. 'Some of [the cast] were terrified,' says Joss, 'but they embraced it amazingly. They had to work after hours, doing singing lessons, dance rehearsals, training.' 'I'm more nervous about singing than dancing,' noted Michelle Trachtenberg, 'but I [took] some lessons and [in the end] it was fun.' By contrast, Anthony Stewart Head couldn't have been happier. But then he *was* in the middle of recording his debut album, *Music for Elevators*, at the time. 'Every season I would ask, Are we going to do the musical episode?' he said. 'Joss would say he wasn't ready.'

'The episode is not for everybody but I think it's a thing of brilliance,' noted Joss's collaborator Chris Beck. 'I consider it an honor to have been involved.' 'It's the most fun I've ever had,' Joss told the *BtVS Posting Board*. A self-confessed fan of Stephen Sondheim, Joss spent all summer writing the episode. '[He] came up with lyrics, melodies, the underlying chords/harmony, as well as general stylistic direction for each of sixteen numbers,' continued Beck. 'The songs started out as four-track recordings Joss made himself. I co-arranged and co-produced the songs with Jesse Tobias of Splendid. Joss was very much involved at every stage and often surprised me with the detail and specificity of his ideas, considering his lack of formal training and comparatively light musical experience.'

Marti Noxon's Comments: Marti insists the musical episode doesn't represent Joss's follow-up gimmick to Buffy's resurrection. 'It's definitely a privilege of our baroque period, but Joss has been wanting to do a musical since we started,' she told the *Seattle Times*. 'The question was

more of when would be the right time, and when he would
have the time.'

Joss Whedon's Comments: 'Yes, the musical is going to be
longer, maybe by about six minutes. So set your VCRs
accordingly, particularly since Tuesday night is the *only
time* the show will be broadcast in its entirety,' Joss told the
BtVS Posting Board. 'It will run again but cuts will be made.
Has anyone seen the bills posted in LA? I designed (with
much help from the masterful Jeph Loeb) a classic old style
musical poster and the brilliant Adam Hughes (he does
covers for *Wonder Woman* comics) painted it. It's something to see. After all this effort, I sure hope you don't all
hate the thundering crap out of the show. That'd be *oops*!'

108
Tabula Rasa

US Transmission Date: 13 November 2001
UK Transmission Date: 21 February 2002

Writer: Rebecca Rand Kirshner
Director: David Grossman
Cast: Raymond O'Connor (Teeth), Geordie White (Vamp #1),
Stephen Triplett (Vamp #2), David Franco (Vamp #3)

Grief-stricken over her stupidity in resurrecting Buffy,
Willow tries a spell to make Buffy forget that she was in
Heaven. As one might expect, given her recent track record
with magic, the spell goes awry and the Scooby Gang all
awake with amnesia, forgetting everything about their lives
including their relationships with each other, and the
existence of vampires.

Babes and Babes (Bring Your Own Subtext): Even with
amnesia it's blindly obvious to both Willow and Tara that
they're attracted to each other. It's interesting that Willow
uses the word selfish to describe herself (in relation to the
spell to resurrect Buffy). The last time she said something
similar was in **65**, 'Something Blue', an episode which also

concerned a spell of hers going disastrously wrong and having serious consequences not only for herself but also her friends.

A Little Honesty is a Dangerous Thing: With what could be her mantra after saying something remarkably tactless and inappropriate, if completely true, Anya sees Xander's horrified look and notes: 'I'm just saying what everyone's thinking,' (see **109**, 'Smashed').

Denial, Thy Name is Willow: Realising how selfish her actions were in bringing Buffy back (see **101**, 'Bargaining'), Willow suggests using yet more magic, a spell to make Buffy forget similar to the one used on Tara in **106**, 'All The Way'. Tara, needless to say, is outraged. Having discovered the violation of her own mind (a particularly insensitive thing for Willow to do considering Glory's 'brain-suck' on Tara in **97**, 'Tough Love'), Tara threatens to leave Willow if her abuse of magic continues. But Willow is blinded by her desire to 'help'. That may have been how it started, Tara argues, but now Willow is using spells to fix things she doesn't like, including Tara herself. Tara asks Willow to go a week without magic but, of course, she can't and after her spell goes disastrously wrong yet again, and her deception is discovered, Tara leaves her.

Real Gone Kid: Having finally admitted to himself in **107**, 'Once More, With Feeling' that his presence is holding Buffy back, Giles tells her that as long as he stays she will always turn to him if there's something that she feels unable to handle. And he'll step in because he can't bear to see her suffer (as in dealing with Dawn in **106**, 'All the Way'). He's taught Buffy all he can about being a Slayer, while her mother taught her everything she needs to know about life, Giles tells Buffy. But she is not going to stand on her own two feet until she is forced to. Therefore he's heading back to England and he plans to stay indefinitely.

Work is a Four-Letter Word: Teeth asks Buffy is she's ever given any thought to freelance work like debt collection.

It's a Designer Label!: Buffy's long white coat and matching polo neck, Willow's purple blouse. On the so-bad-it's-
hilarious side, there's Spike's tweed suit, dickie bow tie,
and deer stalker hat, worn as a disguise. Highly incon-
spicuous, mate.

References: How revealing that the name Buffy gives herself
when she loses her memory – Joan – is that of a legendary
teenage warrior and martyred saint. Hmm, messianic
complex anyone? Spike refers to the climax of the previous
episode (kissing Buffy) as being like *Gone With the Wind*.
The title of the episode is Latin for 'blank tablet'. Buffy
paraphrases *Macbeth* ('what we did is done'). Also, Allen
Funt the first host of *Candid Camera*, *Shazam!* ('holy
moly'), *Mary Poppins*. Unsure of his religious beliefs
Xander chants the traditional Christian prayer 'Now I lay
me down to sleep', the Jewish *Shema Yisrael*,[6] and the
Buddhist meditation mantra 'Om'. Spike quotes *The Book
of Common Prayer* ('dust to dust'). Giles sword-fighting
with the animated skeleton is a nod to Ray Harryhausen's
special effects on *Jason and the Argonauts*. Xander suddenly
laughs when he gets his memory back of seeing the comedy
King Ralph. Dawn sings the children's song 'The Ants Go
Marching One by One', one of many variants on the civil
war standard 'When Johnny Comes Marching Home'.

Awesome!: Spike's assumption that, because he and Giles are
both English, they're related ('There *is* a ruggedly handsome
resemblance,' says Anya). 'You *do* inspire a particular feeling
of familiarity and disappointment,' Giles adds helpfully.
Giles must be his father, Spike decides, and he adds how he
must hate Giles and his 'tarty stepmom' (Anya).

   Also, the Scoobies screaming when they open the door
to find two vampires waiting. And, subsequently, Xander
fainting. What a girl.

---

[6] The beginning of one of the most important Jewish prayers: *Shema
Yisrael, Adoshem Elokainu, Adoshem Echud*, which translates as: 'Hear,
O Israel, the Lord our God, the Lord is One,' and appears in
Deuteronomy 6:4.

'You May Remember Me From Such Films and TV Series As . . .': Raymond O'Connor appeared in *The Rock*, *Girls in Prison*, *Life Stinks* and *Babylon 5*. Stephen Triplett was in *Surveillance*. David Franco played Alan Morgan in *24* and appeared in *Holy Smoke* and *ER*.

Valley-Speak: Dawn: 'Fine, that's your purgative.' Buffy: 'Prerogative.' Dawn: 'Whatever, *Joan*.'
  Dawn: 'What kind of oogly-booglies?'

Sex and Drugs and Rock'n'Roll: At one point during the memory lapse, Willow tells Dawn 'I think I'm kind of gay,' repeating her thoughts about her vampire alter-ego in **50**, 'Doppelgängland'. Xander assumes that, because Willow is wearing a jacket with the name Harris sown into it, and that this is also his name that, maybe, he has *a brother* whom Willow is dating. Almost as revealing as Spike's secret wish to be Angel (see **Quote/Unquote**). Spike and Buffy move on from spell-induced snogging (**107**, 'Once More, With Feeling') to ending this episode doing some trauma-related making-out in the Bronze.

Slash-Fiction Fantasy Moment: Giles, to Spike: 'You're not too old to put across my knee, you know sonny.'

Logic, Let Me Introduce You to This Window: Why does Giles come to the conclusion that he was leaving Anya because he had a one-way ticket to England? Maybe Anya had another ticket herself. It's a bit of a leap (to, admittedly, a correct conclusion). When Xander breaks the crystal in the sewers, it's logical that Tara would guess what has happened, but how do Dawn and Xander seemingly know that it was Willow's spell that caused their amnesia? Willow certainly doesn't say anything. Giles's plane ticket on *Global Airlines* is going from Sunnydale to Los Angeles and then to London Heathrow (see **101**, 'Bargaining' Part 1, for the implausibility of this).

I Just *Love* Your Accent: One of Spike's finest moments as, during the amnesia, he sneers at Giles: 'He's got his crust all stiff and upper with that nancy-boy accent. You

Englishmen are always so ... Bloody hell. Sodding, blimey, shagging, knickers, bollocks, oh God. I'm English.' 'Welcome to the nancy-tribe,' notes Giles, dryly. Believing his name to be Randy, Spike asks: 'Why not just call me "Horny Giles"? Or "Desperate-for-a-Shag Giles"?'

'I never know what you're talking about,' Anya later tells Giles. 'Loo, shag, brolly, what the hell is all that?' Giles also uses 'balderdash' and 'chicanery' in everyday conversation.

Motors: Spike suggests the memory-challanged Scoobies take Giles's car to go to hospital, adding that he is sure Giles has some sort of mid-life crisis transport; something red and shiny and shaped like a penis. Ironically, Giles *did*, indeed, have just such a motor, introduced in **80**, 'Real Me'.

Cruelty to Animals: Spike owes Teeth forty kittens in gambling debts (see **105**, 'Life Serial'). Even with her amnesia, Anya's terror of rabbits continues and she, incompetently, manages to conjure up dozens of the poor creatures.

Quote/Unquote: A confused amnesiac Willow after Buffy has staked a vampire and watched it explode into dust: 'What did you just do?' Buffy: 'I don't know. But it was *cool*.'

Spike: 'I must be a noble vampire. A good guy. On a mission of redemption. I help the hopeless. I'm a vampire with a soul.' Buffy: 'A vampire with a soul? How *lame* is that?'

Notes: 'You did it the way you're doing everything. When things get rough, you don't even consider the options. You just do a spell. It's not what magic is for.' Not without some welcome belly-laughs (the entire second act with the bewildered amnesiac Scoobies in the Magic Box is particularly impressive), there's a bittersweet element to 'Tabula Rasa'. This *is* the end of an era in many ways, the departure of Tony Head being not least among them. The amnesia stuff leads to some genuinely hilarious conceits, though the least said about the downright silly subplot involving Spike, some kittens, and a Shark-headed extortion-demon who looks like a reject from *The Paul Merton Show*, the better. 'Tabula Rasa', to its credit, manages to work as both a characterisation exercise and a piece of action drama. With its emphasis on the contradictions of the Scooby Gang (just why *aren't* Willow and Xander a couple?), the episode has the chance to play subtle games and allow the audience, for once, to be several steps ahead of the characters. But the odd structure, and somewhat hurried and depressing nature of the final act end the episode on a downbeat note.

The suit Spike wears for most of the episode is reminiscent of the one he wore in Xander's dream in **78**, 'Restless'. During the same dream sequence, Giles said he thought of Spike as a son, and here Spike comes to that same conclusion. When asked by Buffy what he wants, Teeth replies a house in Bel Air with a generous-sized swimming pool. Don't we all?

Soundtrack: Michelle Branch performs a gorgeous version of 'Goodbye to You' in the Bronze at the episode's climax, intercut with various shots of Tara leaving Willow, Giles leaving on a jet plane, and Buffy and Spike getting interactive with their tongues. Her guitarist and musical director is Jesse Tobias (see **107**, 'Once More, With Feeling').

Critique: 'For five years, *Buffy* has been the least-watched great show on television, the most ridiculed by ignorati who think they're literati. Like its peers (*The West Wing*, *The Sopranos*, *ER*), Buffy is better than movies because its writer is the most important guy on the set,' noted Tim Appelo. 'A lack of sameness is why *Buffy* is confined to tiny networks and snubbed by Emmys. Television demands comforting rituals: the safely contained crises, the catchphrases, the familiar settings and static characters. *Buffy* is not afraid of exploring dark, unfamiliar places. This imperils her popularity.'

Did You Know?: Sarah Michelle Gellar doesn't have a high opinion of some of the *Buffy* merchandising currently filling the shelves. '[The Buffy action figure] looks more like Erik Estrada of *CHiPS* than me,' she told *BBC Online*. Besides which 'the audience of *Buffy* don't quite seem like doll-playing people if you know what I mean.'

You always know when a TV show has reached the merchandise hall of fame, however, when you can buy a pair of knickers with its name on them. Such an honour has recently been bestowed on *Buffy*. The black pants, emblazoned with a Slayer logo, are currently only available in small or medium sizes. Large and extra large versions are, apparently, on the way.

Head On: 'I've always had a wonderful time on the set, because they're all wonderful actors, and the casting is excellent,' Tony told Melissa Perenson. 'I always enjoy scenes I do with Sarah. We have a great deal of respect for each other, and they have a real resonance, which I think shows on screen. When I watch our scenes, you can always feel that there's a real strength there, a bond. And doing scenes with Alyson – fantastic. Nicky, James . . . they're all rare talents.'

Cast and Crew Comments: 'I've behaved like an unappreciative, almost disgruntled brat,' Emma Caulfield told the *Boston Globe*, describing her adversarial approach to the film and TV industry. 'I've peed on this business. So many people would kill to be in the position I'm in. I haven't deserved what I've gotten.' Emma's charmingly frank views are reminiscent of the character she plays. The 28-year-old actress had left acting after her stint as Brandon Walsh's girlfriend, Susan, in *Beverly Hills, 90210*. When she first guest-starred on *Buffy* in 1998, it was, she says, merely to 'make some quick cash and be on a show that I like'. Recently, while in Australia shooting a film, she had what she describes as 'an epiphany. I had this awakening there and I made peace with the fact that this business is not what I'm supposed to do. It's really a stepping stone for other projects,' she says. The owner of two cats, Caulfield wants to 'effect great change for the animals of the world'. On a similar theme, she told Rob Francis, 'for a while I've had the feeling that there's something I'm supposed to be doing but that I've somehow missed my calling. I think it has something to do with animal rights which I'm very passionate about.'

Marti Noxon's Comments: Talking to *BBC Online*, Marti stated that, if and when the Giles spin-off series *Ripper* is made, there may be crossovers to other parts of the Buffyverse. 'I think there would be some,' she told an online chat. 'It would primarily be a new cast, but, time and work permits and technicalities permitting, you'd see guests from the *Buffy* world.' Marti may even grace our shores herself. Asked if she would be working on *Ripper*, she noted: 'I'm actually eligible for dual citizenship. My father was born in Britain so my brother has worked in London and I know I can get a work permit. We get such a strong reaction from British fans, and we feel very gratified. We love you people too.'

109
Smashed

US Transmission Date: 20 November 2001
UK Transmission Date: 28 February 2002

Writer: Drew Z Greenberg
Director: Turi Meyer
Cast: Patrice Walters (Woman), John Patrick Clerkin (Man),
Jack Jozefson (Rusty), Rick Garcia (Reporter),
Kelly Smith (Innocent Girl), Jordan Belfi (Ryan), Adam Weiner (Simon),
Melanie Sirmons (Brie), Lauren Nissi (Girlfriend)

After breaking up with Tara, Willow successfully transforms Amy Madison back from her ratlike state and the two witches have a night of fun, drawing Willow further into her growing addiction. Meanwhile, Spike notices that his chip doesn't affect him when he hits Buffy, leading him to believe that she is no longer human.

Dudes and Babes: Amy believes she's been a rat for merely a matter of weeks; she still thinks that the Sunnydale High prom is coming up (see **54**, 'The Prom') and that there's a possibility Larry will take her. Willow, sadly, has to inform her that a) Larry's gay (see **27**, 'Phases'), b) Larry's *dead* (see **56**, 'Graduation Day' Part 2) and c) high school was over nearly three years ago, destroyed by 'a giant-snake-thing'. Amy later confides to Buffy that she's rather shocked that Willow is dating girls.

When Willow tells Amy that Xander is engaged, Amy wants to know what his fiancée is like. 'Thousand-year-old capitalist ex-demon with rabbit phobia,' notes Willow. 'That's *so* his type,' replies Amy who, herself, had a brief magic-influenced fling with Xander (see **28**, 'Bewitched, Bothered and Bewildered').

Divorce Sucks!: Dawn's reaction to the break-up of Willow and Tara is similar to that of a child caught in the middle of a separation triangle. Of course, she will have been through a similar experience before (at least, in the memories the monks created for her – see **83**, 'No Place Like Home') when Joyce and Hank divorced. Tara acts very like a mother towards her, taking her to a movie and for a milkshake but asking Dawn to promise she'll eat something green tonight.

A Little Learning is a Dangerous Thing: Buffy can't remember how the time difference between California and Britain works. For the uninitiated, Britain is eight hours ahead. So, when it's midnight in California, it's 8 a.m. in London.

Xander finds reference to what he believes may be the diamond eating frost-monster that they're looking for in a *Dungeons and Dragons* manual. Maybe that's where Warren and friends got the idea for the robbery in the first place?

Mom's Apple Pie: Buffy invites Amy to stay at the Summers' house until she gets her bearings. 'Everybody does,' she says, rather bitterly (see **103**, 'After Life', and her comments to Giles in **104**, 'Flooded').

Denial, Thy Name is Spike: As soon as he believes that his chip has stopped working, it's significant that Spike immediately tries to murder an innocent woman. For all of his protestations of having been changed by the experience, and by his love for Buffy, he is still, when all is said and done, a cold-blooded killer ('I know what I am. I'm evil').

Denial, Thy Name is Buffy: Responsible people are always so concerned with being good all the time, that when they finally get a taste of being bad they can't get enough of it argues Anya, concerning Willow. Buffy dismisses the suggestion that Willow can't handle her magic. Xander also believes that Willow has had a taste of something powerful; Anya adds that Tara was the only one holding her in check and now she's gone (see **110**, 'Wrecked').

Honesty, Thy Name is Anya: When Xander and Buffy seem reluctant to comment on Willow's use of magic while checking computer records, Anya is more forthright, saying that the others are 'la-la-la-ing' around the subject of Tara's leaving and scared to say anything to Willow. Then she stops and asks Xander if this – her lack of tact – is one of those things he was commenting on. One imagines *that's* a conversation they've had more than once (see, **66**, 'Hush' and Anya's comments concerning Giles's 'orgasm friend' and **108**, 'Tabula Rasa').

The Conspiracy Starts at Home Time: Buffy is about to admit to Willow her tryst with Spike over the previous two episodes but is distracted by Amy's return and the moment is lost (see **113**, 'Dead Things').

It's a Designer Label!: Willow's red T-shirt, Andrew's "I ♥ TOURING" T-shirt, Dawn's sparkly top, Buffy's leather skirt and, best of all, Spike's blue shirt and Amy's suede miniskirt and knee-length black leather boots. Tasty.

References: Buffy calls Spike 'Jessica Fletcher', the amateur-sleuth played by Angela Lansbury in *Murder, She Wrote*. Also, allusions to The Rolling Stones' 'Rocks Off', the bitter divorce of Tom Cruise and Nicole Kidman, *The Exorcist* ('head spinning?'), *Ellen* and *Star Trek: The Next Generation* ('you can play holodeck another time'). Dawn says of the movie that Tara took her to see: 'It was ironic when all those cute inner-city kids taught their coach a valuable lesson.' Suggestions on titles this plot could refer to include the Keanu Reeves vehicle *Hardball*, or the paranoid SF thriller *The Faculty*.

Geek-Speak: In the *Buffy* universe, seemingly, not only do all 703 episodes of the legendary British Science-Fiction TV series *Doctor Who* (1963–96) still exist,[7] but they are also all available on DVD. In Region 1, at least. The 80s comedy-SF show *Red Dwarf*, seemingly, isn't. Andrew descends from the ceiling of the museum à la Tom Cruise in *Mission Impossible*, or, for that matter, Frohike in the pilot episode of *The Lone Gunmen*. The reference to the Disney Hall of Presidents is a probable allusion to *Bill & Ted's Excellent Adventure*. The *troika* have a glitterball in their lair.

This episode sees the first hints of another layer to the *troika*: Andrew and Jonathan are in it for the kicks, the chicks, the money and a decent boost of self-esteem. And, mostly, because they get to play with such wonderful toys. But with Warren . . . there's clearly something darker (see **113**, 'Dead Things').

Bitch!: Spike: 'You're a tease, you know that, Slayer? Get a fellah's motor revving, let the tension marinate a-couple'o-days, then *bam*. Crown yourself the ice queen.' And, to Warren: 'Help me out here, Spock, I don't speak *loser*.'

Awesome!: Warren gets to use the blowtorch because his evil comrades are 'allergic to methane,' (Jonathan) and

---

[7] In reality over 100 of the 1960s monochrome *Doctor Who* episodes, from the William Hartnell and Patrick Troughton eras, are missing presumed wiped, from the BBC's shamefully incomplete archives. Occasionally film prints of an odd episode turn up in some obscure third-world dictatorship or in the hands of a private collector (the most recent find of such a gem was in 1999), but it's unlikely that we'll ever see television masterpieces like 'The Evil of the Daleks', 'Fury From the Deep' or 'The Web of Fear' in their entirety again.

'still afraid of *hot things*,' (Andrew). The freeze-ray. The moment of realisation for Spike when he hits Buffy and doesn't suffer from a headache. Dawn guilting Tara into staying. It's really sweet that Dawn knows the buttons to push and, even though she knows she's being manipulated, Tara stays anyway. Amy and Willow causing mayhem at the Bronze.

Surprise!: Amy, after Willow finally works out how to return her to human form (see **46**, 'Gingerbread'), screaming.

'You May Remember Me From Such Films and TV Series As . . .': The wonderful Elizabeth Anne Allen, like Julie Benz, auditioned for the role of Buffy and, though unsuccessful, was rewarded with the role of fan-favourite Amy. She was Shelly in *Silent Lies*, Carri in *Green Sails* and appeared in *Illegal Blue*. Patrice Walters appeared in *L.A. Confidential* and *The Practice*. Rick Garcia was in *Collateral Damage*, *24*, *The American President*, *The A-Team*, *CHiPs*, *The Fall Guy*, *Airwolf* and *The Incredible Hulk*. Jordan Belfi appeared in *Virgil* and *Remote* and was camera production assistant on *Wild Wild West*. Jack Jozefson's CV includes *Trade Day*, *Vic*, *Parker Lewis Can't Lose*, *Wild at Heart*, *NYPD Blue* and *Gas Pump Girls*. Adam Weiner played Alex in *Voyeur.Com*. Kelly Smith was in *Dead on Page Six* and *Naked Horror*.

Don't Give Up the Day Job: Drewz Greenberg has also written for the US version of *Queer as Folk* and acted in *The Rules of Etiquette*. Turi Meyer directed *Candyman: Day of the Dead* and *The Lot*.

Valley-Speak: Warren: 'Dude, that is so cool.'
  Jonathan: 'That's really neato, and stuff . . .'

Cigarettes and Alcohol: Amy and Willow go for a night of debauchery and mischief at the Bronze where they appear to be drinking Martinis.

Sex and Drugs and Rock'n'Roll: When she kissed him at the end of **108**, 'Tabula Rasa', Buffy tells Spike, she was 'thinking about Giles.' 'I always wondered about you two,' he replies angrily. When Spike tells Buffy that he's in love with her, she corrects him. 'You're in love with *pain*,' and an interesting little discussion about sadomasochism ensues. To put this brutally, Buffy's treatment of Spike for a long time has been less than satisfactory even if he is evil. He's, seemingly, a more than acceptable (even trusted) bodyguard for her sister, good enough to be used as an emotional crutch (dare one say soulmate?) on more than one occasion, but not to be treated as someone with feelings. 'You're a *thing*,' she tells him bitterly. Emotional trauma aside, it's not hard to see why all the Spike fans (they're mostly women, inevitably) often dislike Buffy so much. She's spent the last two seasons beating up someone who, effectively, can't fight back. Big girl. So, having acknowledged the unresolved sexual tension that's been building since the middle of season four (at least), they end the episode wrecking the abandoned house they find themselves in and then, ahem, *doing it*.

Logic, Let Me Introduce You to This Window: There's no station ID on the news report on KOUS (previously seen in **66**, 'Hush') as there are on all US TV broadcasts. The Boba Fett action figure is described as a 'limited edition mint-condition 1979 vintage', though *The Empire Strikes Back* wasn't released until May 1980.[8] It would be worth an awful lot more if it was still in its original packaging. When Warren takes the device to Spike's head, a reflection from Spike's skin can be briefly seen. And what exactly *is* the device and how does it enable Warren to 'take a look' at the chip without involving some surgery? From the results he gets all it seems to do is measure the strength of the signal being emitted which doesn't rule out several other types of malfunction. How come when Amy returns to human form, her hair is a different colour and a lot

---

[8] Some sources suggest the Fett action figure was, in fact, released in America in late 1979 to catch the Christmas market. Confirmation of this has proved impossible.

longer than it was in **45**, 'Gingerbread'? It's also ironic that she says how sorry she is about Joyce's death (see **94**, 'The Body'), since the last time Amy saw her, Joyce was part of a crazed mob of Sunnydale parents wanting to burn Amy at the stake. Where does Amy, who's taller than both Willow and Buffy, and thinner than Tara, get the various clothes that she wears and that all seem to fit her very well? In the Bronze, Amy and Willow play telepathic pool and nobody bats an eyelid. All right, it's nothing compared to the shenanigans they get up to later on and, as ever, this *is* Sunnydale we're talking about but surely somebody would have stopped and checked out their impressive display of mind control. The only crowd they seem to draw are two meatheads who want to dance with Amy. The question's been asked before, but it bears repeating: how do vampires have sex? It takes a deal of increased blood circulation for a man to get an erection. Plus it must be rather, you know, uncomfortable for Buffy (see **25**, 'Surprise'). Does Spike really strike anybody as the sort of person who'd be conversant with *Star Trek* terminology? Maybe it's not just *Passions* that does it for him (see **65**, 'Something Blue'; **90**, 'Checkpoint')? After all, he knew a bit about *The Empire Strikes Back* in **15**, 'School Hard'.

I Just *Love* Your Accent: The diamond that the *troika* stole was on loan from the British Museum. Spike orders Warren to look at his chip. 'Is that, like, British slang or something?' asks Warren.

Cruelty to Animals: Amy notes that, if rats could dance, they probably wouldn't gnaw so much.

Quote/Unquote: Buffy: 'How've you been?' Amy: 'Rat. You?' Buffy: 'Dead.'
    Willow: 'I keep expecting her to do ratty stuff. You know, licking her hands clean, shredding newspaper, leaving little pellets in the corner.' Buffy: 'Let's definitely not leave her alone in the house too long.'

Notes: 'The rules have changed ... Nothing wrong with me. Something wrong with *her*.' The funniest debut script since **40**, 'Band Candy', 'Smashed' is a statement of intent from a writer new to the series. Didn't *Buffy* used to be, like, all funny and stuff? Drew Greenberg seems to be asking. The return of Elizabeth Anne Allen is an obvious highlight as Amy takes Willow to the borders of the Dark Side for a night of witchy debauchery. Then, just when you think the episode can't possibly get any funnier, the *troika* turn up to steal a diamond using a 'freeze-ray'. Warren, Jonathan and Andrew continue to shine, even when Spike ignores their *Doctor Who* references (well, he's English, he would). 'Smashed' has all of this *and* some wonderful observational comedy surrounding Dawn and her relationship with Willow and Tara, though the episode's end of Buffy and Spike is signposted by two previous attempts to do, more-or-less, the same thing (see **107**, 'Once More, With Feeling' and **108**, 'Tabula Rasa'). Nevertheless, this represents the most witty and, musical episode aside, most inventive *Buffy* in some considerable time. A gem.

Amy mentions Principal Snyder getting eaten by the mayor (**56**, 'Graduation Day' Part 2). Her father is mentioned (see **3**, 'The Witch'; **110**, 'Wrecked'). She says she wishes there was a way to make him forget about the last three years. Willow says she can help her out but it might be an idea to sew her name in her clothes first (see **108**, 'Tabula Rasa'). When Buffy mentions all of the weird things that have been going on recently, Xander adds 'exploding lint' to her list, a reference to Buffy's description of the self-destructing surveillance device placed on her in **105**, 'Life Serial'. Anya notes that diamonds are excellent for cursing. Buffy always wanted a pony. The headline of the newpaper (presumably *Sunnydale Press*, see **107**, 'Once More, With Feeling') is: MUSEUM GUARD ATTACKED, FROZEN – BODY THAWED, REMAINS UNCONSCIOUS.

Soundtrack: Grunge rockers Virgil perform 'Vermillion Borders', 'Parachute' and 'Here' at the Bronze. When Amy and Willow do their prestidigitation, they are briefly replaced by girl-band Halo Friendlies doing a cracking version of 'Run Away'.

Critique: '"Why can't I feel," sang Buffy in a recent episode of the series on which teenagers go through hell – literally,' noted the *Boston Globe*. 'She'd already found eternal bliss in Heaven, but after a rude awakening of John Miltonian proportions, she lost paradise when her Scooby pals summoned her back to her so-called earthly life. Talk about teen angst; poor Buffy can't even enjoy the simple joys of resurrection.'

Did You Know?: Many fans would love to see *Buffy* in widescreen. But it seems this is unlikely to happen except on special occasions like **107**, 'Once More, With Feeling'. Joss Whedon prefers it that way: 'I like the idea that *Buffy* stays square,' he told *zap2it.com*. 'Most TVs are still square. Whereas *Angel*, [now filmed and broadcast in widescreen] I think of as a dark, melodramatic film, *Buffy* [is] a comforting TV show, even though it's the darkest, bleakest world. I want to keep it that way.'

The Love That Dares Not Speak its Name: So how will the Buffy/Spike relationship be resolved? 'There's going to be quite a bit of punching of noses, believe me,' hinted Marti Noxon. 'It's going to be a wild ride, that's for sure.'

Cast and Crew Comments: You have to excuse Sarah Michelle Gellar if she gets defensive about the show. After all, in many quarters, it has never gotten the respect it deserves. Which is why Gellar has no patience with people who can't see past the admittedly offbeat title and think the show is something far different from what it really is – people she describes, bluntly as 'stupid'. 'I don't mean to be rude,' she told *Deseret News*, 'but I think it's ignorance. This show is the most wonderful mix of brilliant, witty writing, phenomenal performances and evolving stories.'

Joss Whedon's Comments: 'The reason we stayed on the air in our first 13 [episodes] was because we had this incredibly strong Internet fanbase,' Joss told the *Chicago Tribune*.

'Thanks to those fans, *Buffy* is the highest profile cult show on television.' Joss promised in the same interview that he would never abandon *Buffy*'s cult roots in a bid for higher viewing figures. 'I'd rather have 100 people who *need* to see my show than 1,000 people who *like* to,' he said. 'I'll take the badge of *cult* and wear it very proudly. It means the show's affecting people on a different level.'

110
Wrecked

US Transmission Date: 27 November 2001
UK Transmission Date: 7 March 2002

Writer: Marti Noxon
Director: David Solomon
Cast: Fleming Brooks (Mandraz), Mageina Tovah (Jonesing Girl),
Michael Giordani (Jonesing Man), Colin Malone (Creepy Man),
Mark Oxman[9] (Espresso Pump Worker)

Buffy is ashamed of herself for having slept with Spike and determines to keep her liaison a secret from her friends. Meanwhile, keen for bigger thrills, Amy takes Willow to a warlock, Rack, whose powerful brand of spells quickly sees Willow hooked. While looking after Dawn, Willow decides she needs another fix. To escape a demon summoned by Willow's carelessness, she and Dawn steal a car, with disastrous consequences.

Dreaming (As Blondie Once Said) is Free: Willow's magic-induced hallucination featuring a red-skinned demon hiding in the grass is wicked stuff. It ends with that traditional horror movie motif: a woman in dire peril, and with Willow screaming her head off. That'll teach her to mess with the black arts.

A Little Learning is a Dangerous Thing: Xander realises that Willow's closeness to Amy is potentially dangerous.

---

[9] Uncredited.

He describes the coupling as Willow making herself a playmate who won't monitor her use of magic as Tara did. Seems he's learning a thing or two about honesty from his fiancée, though sadly, he doesn't say any of this to Willow herself.

Mom's Apple Pie: Having noted in **109**, 'Smashed', that Dawn's relationship with Tara is very much mother/ daughter, here we've got Willow presented as a classic incompetent father-figure. Always trying to do the right thing and usually making a complete and thoughtless hash of it. Where, exactly, that leaves Buffy in the equation is open to question, something neither Buffy nor Dawn themselves seem entirely sure about (see **111**, 'Gone').

Denial, Thy Name is Buffy: Buffy's back in the land of denial, trying to forget that she ever slept with Spike. After spending her time wavering between a sort-of acceptance of the situation ('it's not love') and angry rebuttals of him (see **109**, 'Smashed'), she makes the decision to try and cut him out of her life completely and ends the episode with her bed surrounded by garlic and clutching a cross. Too late, love. As he himself notes, 'I'm in your system now.' Yet still she treats him like scum even after he has tenderly taken care of her injured sister while she's too busy sorting out Willow. Poor deluded woman (see **111**, 'Gone').

The Conspiracy Starts at Home Time: Rack is a warlock/ pusher who deals, according to Spike, in dangerous black magic. His home/consulting rooms are downtown and 'cloaked'. They seem to exist in a different dimension altogether, and move around periodically to, as Amy suggests, keep Rack out of trouble. Spike notes that you have to be a witch or a vampire to be able to sense the building's presence. Rack is obviously mega-powerful (he was aware of Amy's life as a rat, see **45**, 'Gingerbread', noting that she was messing with spells that were out of her league and she should leave that sort of thing to the professionals).

It's a Designer Label!: For the forthcoming wedding, Anya can't decide whether to put her bridesmaids in cocktail dresses or the traditional burlap with blood larva (see **116**, 'Hell's Bells'). We get another look at Buffy's stylish-but-affordable boots (see **107**, 'Once More, With Feeling'). Amy's extremely tight black dress, Willow's studded denim jacket, Dawn's blue sweater and a whole episode full of cool leather coats (Buffy, Willow, Spike etc.). Check out also Anya's freshly dyed super-blonde hair.

References: Anya believes that home and garden guru Martha Stewart is a witch ('nobody could do that much decoupage without calling on the powers of darkness'). Also, actress Joan Crawford (Dawn's reference seems to be to the notorious biography movie about her as an overbearing and terrifyingly abusive mother, *Mommie Dearest*).

Bitch!: Notice how downright spiteful and condescending magicked-up Willow is towards Dawn.

Awesome!: Dawn slapping Willow across the face, and the later scene as Willow, addicted and in pain, literally hits rock bottom, and lies in the dirt at Buffy's feet weeping that she can't control herself. 'Get up,' says an angry Buffy, speaking for the entire audience. Also, the conversation between Buffy and Spike as they search for Rack's place is brilliant characterisation – Spike turning from a sleazy pervert obsessed with a girl who's out of his class into a totally out-of-the-closet romantic within three lines of dialogue. Epic. Best of all, Willow blissfully wallowing in the excesses of her magic-addled state, up on the ceiling and, like, *gone* (see **121**, 'Two to Go', *et al*).

'You May Remember Me From Such Films and TV Series As . . .': Jeff Kober played Bear in *The X-Files* episode 'Ice', was Dodger in *China Beach* and Booga in *Tank Girl* and appeared in *Enough*, *Coyote Moon* and *Enterprise*. Readers may recognise him best as 'Ray, the voice of Reef Radio' in those Bacardi adverts or as Zackary Kralik in **46**, 'Helpless'. Mageina Tovah was in *Y.M.I.* Michael Giordani appeared in *We Were Soldiers*. Colin Malone's CV includes *Art House, G vs E* and *Seinfeld*. Mark Oxman appeared in *The West Wing, Felicity* and *Catch Me If You Can*.

The Drugs Don't Work: Rack's price for feeding Willow's increasing addiction is to, as he describes it, 'take a little tour', which seems to involve him feeding from the powerful vibes that Willow gives off. It appears to be something of a quasi-erotic experience for both, ending with Willow smiling like she's just reached orgasm and Rack whispering that she 'tastes like strawberries' (see **121**, 'Two to Go'). Later, we see Amy spinning around, like a modern-day dervish, and clearly as high as a kite. Rack reclines on a sofa, holding in his hands what looks like a glass ball with a reflection of Amy trapped inside it. Rack looks up and there's Willow, literally on the ceiling, writhing in ecstasy. Hooked.

Valley-Speak: Dawn: 'A mother of all night-wedgies.' And: 'You're all sore and limpy.'
   Amy: 'It was awesome. This blowhard dude, first she made his mouth disappear?'
   Spike, to Buffy: 'You've had me by the short hairs. I love you. You know it. But I got my rocks back.'

Cigarettes and Alcohol: The 'smelly' guy in Rack's waiting room seems ready for a long wait as he puts his cigarettes and lighter on the table. Disgusted, Dawn leaves him to it.

Sex and Drugs and Rock'n'Roll: The opening shot. Rubble. Bits of splintered wood and plaster everywhere. The camera pans across to reveal a bare foot. Suddenly Buffy sits up, naked and holding her skirt to her chest. She looks around frowning, sensing that Spike's awake. Bruised and scratched, he looks up at her. 'When did the building fall down?' asks Buffy, confused. Yeah, I've had mornings like that too.
   Spike implies that he suspected the only thing better than killing a slayer would be having sex with one and that Buffy herself seems to be something of a vampire groupie.

Only one vampire ever got me hot, Buffy replies, but he's gone. Spike, on the other hand, is just convenient. Spike is clearly hurt by this and asks if she now intends to go back to treating him like dirt till the next time 'you get an itch you can't scratch?' 'I'm disgusted with myself,' notes Buffy. 'That's the power of your charms. Last night was the most perverse, degrading experience of my life.' Spike seems really pleased with this description.

Anya notes at the wedding she doesn't intend asking Xander to perform the groom's traditional rite of self-flagellation. Given that the couple have 'enjoyed spanking' (**69**, 'The I in Team') he'd probably have quite got off on that.

Logic, Let Me Introduce You to This Window: When Buffy wakes up next to Spike she immediately starts dressing. Before she leaves, Spike reveals he has her underwear. Surely she noticed that she didn't have them on while she was getting dressed? Rack must have been around Sunnydale for some time if Amy knows him, since she's been a rat for three years. How, therefore, have his and Buffy's (or, more importantly, Willow's) paths never crossed before? Amy says she'd better be getting home as her dad is expecting her. Since when? In the previous episode she was reluctant to contact Mr Madison and try to answer the inevitable questions about her absence. She may, of course, have telephoned him while she and Willow were out overnight (after they'd finished their amusing escapades at the Bronze). Bet that would have been a good conversation: 'Hi dad, No, I didn't run away from home, I've spent three years as a rat . . .' Willow says that the one thing she won't miss about magic is the time she kept stinky yak cheese in her bra. Wouldn't that have been a bit conspicuous in making her smell somewhat? Why, exactly, was Amy stealing sage (and other kitchen herbs) from Buffy's house? To give to Rack in exchange for another dose of his magic? Maybe, but, *sage*? Perhaps he's got some onions and wants to stuff a chicken?

I Just *Love* Your Accent: Spike uses the word bollocks for the fifth time in the series (**76**, 'The Yoko Factor'; **80**, 'Real Me'; **85**, 'Fool for Love'; **108**, 'Tabula Rasa').

Motors: When being chased by the demon, Willow and Dawn leap into a convenient car, which Willow commands to drive off. And crashes.

Quote/Unquote: Dawn: 'It was like a meat party in my mouth. OK, I'm just a kid, and even *I* know that came out wrong.'

Notes: 'She's as bad as I am. Worse. Bet she's at Rack's right now.' It's been some time since we've had a decent example of '*Buffy*-as-metaphor', which was, let's remember, once such an important part of the series' success. Doubly welcome, in an episode short on tension but high on blood-pumping, testosterone-soaked adrenaline, is a thoroughly harrowing and unpleasant study of the horrors of addiction. In the *Buffy* equivalent of *The Man With the Golden Arm*, Alyson Hannigan acts her little cotton socks off, reminding us all, if any reminder was needed, that Willow does, in fact, *rock*. 'Wrecked' is a strange, out-of-focus look at the dark path that Willow has travelled during the last year and a half. Echoing Faith's flirtation with The Dark Side in season three, Marti Noxon uses a clever mixture of Joyce Summers-style denial and pain to push Willow to the brink. That's all terrific stuff. Where 'Wrecked' is less successful is in its continuation of the Buffy/Spike riff that has, frankly, been mined to excess over the previous three episodes. How many more times do we need variations on the same basic episode end/beginning of 'they get-it-on', followed by 'she angrily regrets it'? The scenes work because Marsters and Gellar are, you know, *good*. But there's only so much repetition that a series can take before something radical is needed to shake it from its lethargy. The best bits of 'Wrecked' don't involve Buffy at all. That's a worry.

Xander catches Anya reading yet another bridal magazine (*Bride and Joy*). Some of the metaphors in the episode are really subtle (the burnt pancakes Tara was making for Dawn as a subconscious representation of her incendiary relationship with Willow, anyone?) Buffy accuses Spike of drawing out the search for Dawn, noting that he's done this sort of thing before (that's a bit unfair, the only previous occasion was in **92**, 'Crush'). Dawn suffers from a broken arm in the crash (see **111**, 'Gone').

Soundtrack: Laika's sexy 'Black Cat Bone' plays as Willow floats on the ceiling at Rack's place. The episode is also notable for Thomas Wanker's excellent, spooky, score.

Critique: 'More daring than ever, *Buffy* is glorious and revelatory in its willingness to face up to the messiness and potential danger of sex,' wrote Stephanie Zacharek. 'It may be the greatest postcoital line ever: "When did the house fall down?"'

Did You Know?: This episode is dedicated, onscreen, 'In Loving Memory of J.D. Peralta', a production assistant on *Buffy* who tragically died in November 2002 while 'Wrecked' was in production.

Cast and Crew Comments: 'People have stopped me in the street,' Tom Lenk told Lisa Kincaid. 'In fact I got stopped in a store [by] the night manager. [He said] "I have to know, are you on *Buffy*?" We had a twenty minute conversation. Fans always have something great to say.'

Marti Noxon's Comments: Marti revealed to *zap2it.com*, that the much-speculated scene in which Spike and Buffy finally have sex was the short version. It had to be cut after UPN executives complained the original was too explicit. As much as fifteen seconds were removed – an enormous amount in TV terms. Marti also commented on the decision to allow the tension between the characters to come to fruition. 'It's really a love-hate relationship in the strictest definition,' she said. 'It's still probably not the best choice for her [but she] kind of likes dark guys. The relationship is really about choosing someone who, in the long run, some of the safety of it is that you know it can't work.'

111
Gone

US Transmission Date: 8 January 2002
UK Transmission Date: 14 March 2002

Writer: David Fury
Director: David Fury
Cast: Daniel Hagen (Frank), Susan Ruttan (Doris Kroeger)

The *troika* build another new crime toy, an invisibility ray and, during their latest abortive stunt, accidentally hit Buffy with it. She takes advantage of her new situation by paying Spike a visit and playing devious games with some deserving cases. Jonathan, Warren and Andrew realise that the invisible objects are rapidly breaking down structurally and they kidnap Willow to force Buffy into the open.

Dudes and Babes: Spike finally stands up to Buffy regarding the whole shag-and-run situation. He feels that she's using him, and he's right.

There's a Ghost in My Crypt: Previously **31**, 'I Only Have Eyes For You' had confirmed that ghosts exist in the *Buffy* universe, and Spike is aware of this. Albeit, he seems to believe that spooks are tangible since this one is keen on grabbing his butt.

A Little Learning is a Dangerous Thing: Dawn's grades have fallen sharply in the last year, due in-part to her frequent lateness and absences from school. She has a special affection for a fertility statue of the god Kokopelli that originally belonged to her mother. Hopefully she's still naive enough not to know what it's for (see **3**, 'The Witch'). Spike seems to be enjoying watching a vampire movie in his crypt. Probably checking it out for inconsistencies.

Mom's Apple Pie: Willow is seemingly a dab-hand at cooking breakfast, making a tasty-looking ham omelette for Dawn which the latter refuses as she's still mad at Willow for, you know, stupidly endangering her life.

Denial, Thy Name is Xander: When Xander walks in on Invisible-Buffy and Spike having sex in Spike's crypt, the only way he could not know what's happening here would have been if he was nine *and* wasn't aware of Buffy's invisible status. Since Xander doesn't have either excuse one can only assume that he's having a Joyce Summers-style dose of deep denial.

Denial, Thy Name is Buffy: If Buffy is beginning to realise that her 'vacation from me' is a front for a deeper unhappiness, then a useful initial step mustn't end with her 'I don't want to die,' conversation with Willow. Taking responsibility for one's own actions instead of crying about and/or avoiding the consequences is an important one. Buffy harassing an annoying social worker insane is understandable, though she was simply doing her job and trying to ensure Dawn's welfare (which, as Doris points out, is something that Buffy should also be concerned with). Having sex with Spike only when she is, literally, not herself means that she doesn't have to, psychologically, deal with the consequences.

The Conspiracy Starts at Home Time: The diamond stolen from the museum (see **109**, 'Smashed') is called The Illuminata. There are rumours of it having quasi-mystical quantum properties. The *troika* need it to power their invisibility ray.

It's a Designer Label!: Buffy's tight red pants and puma T-shirt. There are lots of interesting T-shirt motifs on display including 'Bongo Bongo' (Andrew), 'Los Angeles USA' (Jonathan) and 'Skinny Skulls' (Willow).

References: *The Shining* ('all work and no play make Doris a dull girl'), *The X-Files* ('Xander and Anya are ... Muldering out what happened'), *Goldilocks*, *The Thing* ('for all we know she could be one of us'), *A Christmas Carol* ('I am the ghost of fashion victims past'), The Doors' 'The End' ('kill, kill, kill', see **19**, 'Lie to Me'), black actor Geoffrey Cambridge, Linda Creed and Thom Bell's blue-eyed soul classic 'Betcha By Golly Wow' (the most famous version is by The Stylistics) and *White Heat* ('so long, copper!'). When Buffy walks between parked cars outside the hairdressers, one minivan has bumper stickers reading GOD BLESS AMERICA and UNITED WE STAND.

Geek-Speak: When Andrew sees the Invisibility Ray he says that he'd pictured something cooler. 'More ILM, less Ed Wood.' Industrial Light and Magic are a division of George Lucas' production company, and are mainly responsible for creating state-of-the-art special visual effects. Ed Wood was a director who made notoriously cheap and campy movies including the legendary *Plan 9 from Outer Space*. Warren calls Jonathan Frodo, the vertically-challenged hobbit from *The Lord of the Rings*. Also, Superman's nemesis Lex Luthor.

Bitch!: Willow knows that she deserves 'the wrath of Dawn' over the events of **110**, 'Wrecked', but she's uncertain as to why Buffy is getting cold-shouldered too. 'Because I let it happen,' notes Buffy, sadly.

Xander, to Spike: 'Still trying to mack on Buffy? Wake up already. Never gonna happen. Only a complete loser would ever hook up with you. Unless she's a simpleton like Harmony, or a nut-sack like Drusilla.'

Awesome!: Buffy and Spike's fumbling performance in front of Doris, the officious Social Services lady and, subsequently, Buffy's delicious invisible revenge on her. Spike, trying to hold a conversation with Xander while Invisible-Buffy plays sexy games with his ears. Warren's incompetent declaration of the *troika's* identity to Buffy: 'We're your arch-nemesis ... ses.' And, the *troika's* dreadfully poor subsequent escape attempt.

'You May Remember Me From Such Films and TV Series As . . .': The great Susan Ruttan gained a cult following as Roxanne in *L.A. Law*. She also appeared in *Love Kills*, *The Sure Hand of God*, *Popular* and *Take My Daughters, Please*. Daniel Hagen was in *The Deep End of the Ocean*, *Roswell*, *Party of Five*, *Friends*, *Wilder Napalm*, *Mad About You* and *Bonfire of the Vanities*.

Valley-Speak: Jonathan, to Warren: 'You *penis*!'
  Xander: 'I'm less with the why and more with the how.'
  Buffy: 'Lame.' And: 'You know kids today and their buggin' street-slang.'

Cigarettes and Alcohol: Spike's cigarette lighter plays an important part in the plot. He has a glass of whisky while having a serious post-coital talk with Invisible-Buffy.

Sex and Drugs and Rock'n'Roll: The *troika* are planning to turn themselves invisible so they can get into a women-only bikini-wax spa.

Logic, Let Me Introduce You to This Window: When Buffy and Spike are talking in his crypt, Spike tells her to find her clothes if she can and push off. As her clothes are also invisible (and scattered all over the crypt), it's probable that Buffy couldn't find some and/or all of them, but when Willow restores her visibility Buffy's fully dressed. In Buffy's kitchen there are rays of sunlight and Spike seems to be in their direct influence. Buffy tosses Spike's lighter into the box of magic stuff to be thrown out. Next time we see it, Spike's fishing it out of the pocket of Buffy's jeans.

Motors: Willow hacks into the Department of Motor Vehicles to find out the details of the mysterious black van that has been stalking Buffy since **105**, 'Life Serial'.

Quote/Unquote: Xander: 'Kidding aside, Spike, you really should get a girlfriend.'
  Buffy: 'For the first time since . . . I'm free. Free of rules and reports. Free of this life.' Spike: 'Got another name for that. Dead.'
  Warren: 'You haven't won yet, Slayer.' Buffy: 'No, that part comes after I beat the snot out of you.'

Notes: 'Kind-of fits the day I've had. Willow's still a wreck, Dawn's mad at both of us, and the Social Services lady put me through a wringer. Says she's gonna watch me. I'd like to see her try now.' Metaphors are funny things. Like London buses, you wait for ages for one to turn up, then two come along at once. On the surface, 'Gone' is little more than a remake of **11**, 'Out of Mind, Out of Sight', with the plight of the invisible girl in this case being Buffy herself. Normally, when a series starts remaking its own previous episodes, it's usually in trouble. But 'Gone' is much more than a revisitation of the past. In vanishing, Buffy is given exactly what she wants – a chance not to be herself. She has fun with her new gift at first: she can shag Spike without conscience or regret because, hey get this, *it's not really her* doing it. Spike, in what is becoming a regular part of the show these days, is required to talk some sense into her. 'Gone' reflects the changing nature of *Buffy* by presenting us with the kind of episode they used to make – funny, thoughtful, and with a metaphor at its heart – but in a much more schizophrenic and dark world that season six inhabits. For those who prefer Chicken Tikka to a Mars Bar.

When Invisible-Buffy is leaving the social services centre she whistles a few bars of 'Going Through The Motions' (see **107**, 'Once More, With Feeling'). Xander asks Buffy if she has been ignored lately, referring to the cause of Marcie's invisibility (see **11**, 'Out of Mind, Out of Sight'). In discussing the seating arrangements for their wedding, Anya tells Xander that she's invited her former vengeance-demon boss, D'Hoffryn (see **50**, 'Doppelgängland'; **65**, 'Something Blue'). Xander's Uncle Rory is mentioned (see **20**, 'The Dark Age'; **47**, 'The Zeppo'; **60**, 'Fear Itself'; **116**, 'Hell's Bells'). Among the magic stuff that Buffy is throwing out to help Willow avoid the temptation are tarot cards, a crystal ball and lots of candles. The hairdressers that Buffy uses is called Continental Hair Design.

Soundtrack: 'I Know' by Trespassers William.

Did You Know?: Adam Busch told *zap2it.com* that the *troika*'s anorakish squabbles were wholly inspired by fights between the Buffy writers. '[Joss] said the arguments they have in the writing room they put directly in the script – about who's the best James Bond, that kind of stuff,' he claimed. Despite the evil threesome's internecine wrangling and substantive comic potential, however, Marti Noxon indicates that they are a serious threat. 'They're not simply meant for comic relief, and we throw some surprises out in all of those characters,' she noted. 'They're definitely villains. Maybe not "super" – I think they're kind of sub-par villains.'

Joss Whedon's Comments: 'My plans every season extend a year past where I am,' Joss told Dana Meltzer, 'but I don't have a giant, overriding plan. It's the journey of life. There are certain points I want to make about female empowerment and the pain of growing up but, beyond that, every episode is an opportunity to explore how I feel about the world. I only learn that day to day.' So what's Joss's plan for the upcoming season? He promises more sin and debauchery. 'We have horrible misery and sex in store for everybody,' he notes. 'It's not a bad combination.'

112
Doublemeat Palace

US Transmission Date: 29 January 2002
UK Transmission Date: 21 March 2002

Writer: Jane Espenson
Director: Nick Marck
Cast: Pat Crawford Brown (Wig Lady),
Brent Hinkley (Manny the Manager), T Ferguson (Gary),
Douglas Bennett (Phillip), Andrew Reville (Timothy),
Kevin C Carter (Mr Typical), John F Kearney (Elderly Man),
Sara LaWall (Housewife Type), Victor Z Isaac (Pimply Teen)

Strapped for cash, Buffy gets a job at a fast food restaurant where the weird manager and high turnover of employees has her more than a little suspicious. When co-workers end up in pieces, the mystery behind the burgers' 'secret ingredient' comes into question.

Dudes and Geeks: Xander says he understands Warren being the supervillainy type (see **93**, 'I Was Made to Love You'), but he thought Jonathan had learned his lesson from the events of **73**, 'Superstar'. Willow describes their headquarters as 'the nerd natural habitat.' Buffy found spell books, parchments, charmed objects and a conjurer's harp at the *troika*'s headquarters.

Authority Sucks!: Manny, the humourless and horribly clothed manager of the Doublemeat Palace seems to be a sinister corporate murderer for most of the episode, but ends up being eaten by the monster which leaves only his foot behind.

A Little Learning is a Dangerous Thing: One of Anya's ex-demon colleagues, Halfrek, shows up after getting a garbled message concerning the wedding (she notes, rather chillingly, that vengeance-demons spend much of their time maiming the wrong man). She thinks she's been summoned by a scorned woman to wreak a terrible vengeance upon Xander.

Mom's Apple Pie: Dawn's friend Janice (see **106**, 'All the Way') has a sister who's a lawyer. Dawn sadly notes that Buffy's never going to be either a lawyer, or a doctor. She's the Slayer, says Xander, she saves the world. But this means that she's going to have crappy minimum wage jobs her entire life to fit in with her Slayer duties, Dawn adds. Maybe Dawn will get a job with a massive salary, Xander suggests. Then she can use her money to support her deadbeat sister.

Denial, Thy Name is Anya: Anya's entire conversation with Hallie is a fascinating example of peer pressure and in showing how far removed she is from the character she presented when first becoming human (see **50**, 'Doppel-gängland'). Hallie suggests this is quasi-domestication and that Xander's little habits, like criticising Anya's lack of tact (see **109**, 'Smashed'), should be a source of annoyance to Anya herself. Cleverly, however, she never actually criticises Xander directly, merely questioning each point in his favour that Anya highlights in a seemingly reasonable, but really pointed, way.

The Conspiracy Starts at Home Time: The Doublemeat Palace is one of California's biggest fast-food chains. Their speciality, the Doublemeat Medley, made from 'the harvesting of two special meats' includes a closely guarded secret ingredient which, Buffy speculates, due to a few circumstantial bits of evidence, is actually *people*. It isn't. It's a blend of vegetable products. The company, nevertheless, are keen that their customers don't discover they're actually eating veggie burgers. Buffy, having been sacked for her outburst in the restaurant, gets her job back by promising to keep the secret.

Work is a Four-Letter Word: When Anya was a vengeance-demon, she caused pain and mayhem. 'But I put in a full day's work, and I got compensated appropriately,' she notes. 'Welcome to today's episode of *Go Money Go*,' replies Xander. 'I hear it daily.'

It's a Designer Label!: A strange bunch, with Xander's horrible shirt falling deep into the fashion victims column (he wears a much more sartorial red one later when meeting Halfrek). Anya's white top and crimson velvet pants, Willow's ill-fitting jumper, Dawn's red jacket and Buffy's cute black 'star' T-shirt.

References: Visually, *Alien*. Conceptually, *Society* and *Eat the Rich*. Also, Jolene Blalock (Willow noting that the *troika* had numerous 'pictures of that Vulcan woman on *Enterprise*'), *Sleepless in Seattle* and its stars Meg Ryan and Tom Hanks, *Friends* ('hey, standing right here'), Disneyland and the Lollapalooza tour. Buffy's 'variety is the spice of bad' is a paraphrase from *The Timepiece* by William Cowper (1731–1800).

Awesome!: Xander's reaction to the *troika*'s taste in Vulcan sex symbols. The dreadful company training video that Buffy watches – so *Simpsons*esque that the only thing missing is a Troy McClure narration. Xander's startled expression when Halfrek appears, and then at the sudden transition to girlie-talk when Anya walks in. Buffy clearly having sex with Spike against the wall outside the diner.

Willow angrily ending her friendship with Amy in a staggering metaphor for the inherent problems of abuse recovery when you are surrounded by junkie friends. And, of course, the giant penis-shaped monster that squirts liquid at Willow, who screams and runs away. No intended Freudian symbolism there, clearly.

'You May Remember Me From Such Films and TV Series As . . .': Brent Hinkley was in *The Silence of the Lambs*, *The West Wing*, *Bob Roberts*, *Carnival of Souls*, *Falling Down*, *Say it Isn't So* and *Ed Wood*. Pat Crawford Brown's CV includes *Jack Frost*, *Moonlighting*, *Sister Act*, *The Rocketeer*, *The Wonder Years*, *Johnny Skidmarks*, *Reality Bites* and *Coach*. Kirsten Nelson played Lani in *Three Women of Pain* and the young Dolores Landingham in *The West Wing*, and appeared in *The Fugitive*. Kali Rocha was in *Meet the Parents*, *When Billie Beat Bobby* and *Autumn in New York*. John Kearney appeared in *Giro City* and *Judgement*. Kevin Carter's movies include *Ripple* and *Stonewashed*. Sara LaWall was in *The Cable Guy*. The director/producer of *Hungry*, Douglas Bennett was also in *Gone in Sixty Seconds* and *Crime Scene Investigation*.

Don't Give Up the Day Job: Puppeteer Pons Maar previously worked on *Phantoms*, *Return to Oz* and *Theodore Rex*. He was also the voice of Roy in *Dinosaurs*.

The Drugs Don't Work: When Gary gives Buffy a soda cup and tells her to fill it she replies, cheekily, that she wasn't aware they'd be drug testing on the job. Amy says that she understands Willow is working on 'this whole cold turkey thing'.

Valley-Speak: Buffy: 'Holy crap!' And: 'Yay, it's Manny.'

Sex and Drugs and Rock'n'Roll: In the alley outside the Doublemeat Palace, a tired and depressed Buffy lets Spike have his way with her.

Logic, Let Me Introduce You to This Window: Whose was the finger and how did it get into the grinder? This is never made clear. How does Anya know, just after she's arrived

at the Magic Box after her reunion with Halfrek, that the
chemistry Willow is performing concerns the ingredients of
the Doublemeat Palace burgers? What, exactly, are the
opening hours of the Doublemeat Palace? Gary was said
to be coming in early, around 7 a.m. to open up, so we can
probably assume it opens around 7.30 or eight o'clock
(albeit, Buffy is shown clocking-in for her shift a few
minutes after nine, and she's not alone). More problematic
is closing time. Most fast-food chains close around midnight. While Willow is working on the contents of the
burger, with Xander and Dawn, Buffy goes to the Doublemeat which is now closed. So if it's, say, just after
midnight, and it was Sunday the day before (the only
explanation as to why both Anya and Xander would be at
home in the middle of the day when Halfrek arrives, and
why Willow's at home and not at college) then why is Buffy
not bothered about Dawn still being up in the early hours
of the morning with school the next day? When Willow
arrives, even though the interior is in darkness, the exterior
is lit up as though the store is still open, and the drive-thru
intercom is still working. Did Buffy tell Spike she was
working at the Doublemeat Palace? If so, why? And if not,
then how does he know? Not illogical *per se*, but certainly
a crime against all laws of God and man: what the hell is
up with Willow's hair? She looks like she's had an accident
with an electrical implement. Why does Buffy, who has
always been so keen to keep Dawn away from Slayer
business (see **122**, 'Grave'), show her the severed finger?

Cruelty to Animals: The company video, telling the story of
how a cow and a chicken come together to form the
Doublemeat Medley was, according to Buffy, 'kinda
graphic with the slaughter'. Manny: 'Curiosity killed the
cat.' Buffy: 'Theory number five. Cat burgers.'

Quote/Unquote: Spike: 'What's in the Doublemeat nug-
gets?' And: 'This place'll kill you.'

  Buffy: 'That's just great. I try to do the simplest thing in
the world, get an ordinary job in a well-lit place, and look,
I'm back where I started. Blood and death and funky smells.'

Notes: 'We have a lot of turnover here.' If the old saying is true and we are what we eat then *Buffy*, by way of its constantly healthy diet of horror pastiche, wry social comment and cunning observational comedy is in far better shape than most of the competition. Ah, Magic Jane, where would we be without her? A witty parody on some of the more disturbing aspects of the processed food industry and, of the awful realities of the minimum wage lifestyle which many viewers will be able to identify with, 'Doublemeat Palace' has more jokes per-square-inch than the Edinburgh Comedy Festival. Much of the delightfully queasy subject matter centres on the secret ingredient in a Fast Food chain's burgers and whether it has anything to do with the high turnover of staff. Comedically obvious? Certainly. But it's done with such clever, knowing glances that you can't help but be impressed at the sheer nerve of the thing. *Buffy* usually works best when it's making you laugh at the same time as making you think. 'Doublemeat Palace' does both. With fries.

Buffy mentions waitressing 'that summer in LA' in a diner, referring to the events between **34**, 'Becoming' Part 2 and **35**, 'Anne'. Xander too has been employed in the fast-food industry (at Hot-Dog-On-A-Stick, see **64**, 'Pangs' and as a pizza delivery boy, **67**, 'Doomed'). Amy asks Willow if she can have the rat cage she lived in for three years citing sentimental reasons, and Willow agrees. In reality, she probably just wants to sell it and use the money to get another fix from Rack.

Soundtrack: Warren Bennett's 'The Twist' and Austin and Hughes's 'Pow!' and 'Power Play' play during the Double-meat Palace Training video.

Critique: 'It may seem strange to see a gruesome tale about a burger bar run by a parasitic monster, as welcome light relief,' wrote John Binns. 'The first two thirds remind us how good *Buffy* can be at lampooning the horror genre. Inevitably, perhaps, the resolution is more disappointing: other than the slight wry smile raised by the idea that a burger chain's secret might be that its products are vegetable-based.'

'The episode never sold a real threat,' noted Sharon Goodman on *FanboyPlanet.com*. 'The idea that there was something fishy going on was easily explained by Buffy's boredom. By the time we find out there was evil afoot, we stopped caring. I have to think the writers are saving up the good stuff for February sweeps.'

Did You Know?: The exterior location used for the Doublemeat Palace diner in this and future episodes is a hot dog restaurant called Hipperty Hopperty Dog which can be found on Sepulveda Blvd close to Los Angeles airport. 'Doublemeat Palace' is the only *Buffy* episode to have caused advertisers to pull out of supporting the series. 'They did *not* like us making fun of fast food,' Joss Whedon told *DreamWatch*.

Cast and Crew Comments: Sarah Michelle Gellar reveals her tips for staying healthy. 'I carry a bottle of water with me all the time,' she told the *National Post*. 'I don't really drink anything except water and iced tea.' Vitamins play a part in the Gellar health regime too. 'I really believe vitamins can fix almost anything: skin and hair problems, energy problems, colds. I always take my vitamins, usually a multi and a vitamin C.'

When asked by *FHM* if she'd heard about a *Buffy* drinking game where, every time the viewers catch a glimpse of Buffy's bra-strap, they have a drink, Sarah noted: 'In the first season they always made me wear tank tops. I was about 15 pounds heavier and a full cup size bigger and I wasn't going to wear tank tops without a bra, so you *always* saw the straps. I was thinking, "Great, I'm adding to the drunk-rate in America." But for the second season I discovered strapless bras and it ruined the whole game.'

Jane Espenson's Comments: Was the Doublemeat Palace demon's symbolism deliberate, asked the Succubus Club, and if so what's it a metaphor for? 'It was an enormous penis,' Jane replied candidly. 'We didn't know it was going to look like that. It wasn't intentional. Would we have a lesbian cut off a giant penis? That's icky and unpleasant and very strange. However, once it had happened, we felt free to comment on it.'

'[All of the writers] had fast food experiences except me,' Jane noted in the same interview. 'Marti had worked at McDonald's and had a lot of insight. My boyfriend worked at some dreadful fast food places in Ohio. Really awful-sounding places so he had all the information about the buttons and the grill. We almost backed away from having her in fast food when Joss remembered she had waitressed before. But, fast food is a whole different kind of job than working in a diner. You wouldn't believe the amount and length of the conversations about what Buffy should do for a living. It needed to be something awful we and finally decided that fast food was about as awful as we could think of.'

Joss Whedon's Comments: Ever since John Ritter appeared in **23**, 'Ted', *Buffy* has been lacking in celebrity guest stars. Hasn't anyone famous asked if they could do a cameo? 'I heard a rumour that R.E.M. wanted to be on the show,' Joss told *Maxim*, 'but I haven't confirmed that. Famous people aren't going, "I want to be on the show!" Which is OK, because this isn't *Friends*.'

113
Dead Things

US Transmission Date: 5 February 2002
UK Transmission Date: 28 March 2002

Writer: Steve S DeKnight
Director: James A Contner
Cast: Rock Reiser (Desk Sergeant), Bernard K Addison (Cop #1),
Eric Prescott (Cop #2)

The *troika*'s latest riotous escapade is to turn Warren's ex-girlfriend Katrina into their 'willing sex-slave'. Inevitably, it goes horribly wrong when Warren kills her. They use sorcery to make Buffy believe that *she* killed Katrina – and it works as Buffy's world begins to fall apart.

One Freudian Guilt Trip Coming Right Up: Believing, as Buffy herself does, that she's killed an innocent girl in the forest, Spike manages to get Buffy home. There, she suffers a terrifying, erotic nightmare full of lesbian overtones, penis and bondage metaphors (the stake, the handcuffs) and guilt with a capital G. For the psychology student this has got, literally, *everything*. Subtext: Buffy is so appalled by her continued involvement in an abusive tryst with a vampire unredeemed by a soul, and by her shame that, after two essentially noble boyfriends, she's been reduced to *this*, she is seeking some pretty severe punishment for it. As her mom's dead and a spanking's probably out of the question, what better than a long stretch in prison? It's the best bit of the episode by a mile, but it also highlights everything that's, conceptually, wrong with 'Dead Things'.

Dudes and Babes: Unable to confide in Willow, Buffy tells Tara that Spike can hurt her and asks about the resurrection spell. Does this mean she came back as a demon? Tara uses numerous texts including *The Brekenkrieg Grimore* to check and ultimately tells Buffy that there's nothing wrong with her. She *is* slightly different as, when her essence was funnelled back into her body, it subtly altered Buffy on a molecular level – probably just enough to confuse the sensors in Spike's chip. Tara compares it to nothing worse than a bad sunburn. Buffy then, tearfully, confesses to Tara that there *must* be something wrong with her otherwise she wouldn't let Spike do these things to her (there's that subtext again). Buffy suggests that while Spike stands for everything she hates, the only time she *feels* anything since she returned from Heaven is when she's with him. Tara sympathetically asks Buffy if she loves Spike, stressing that, despite his less-than-admirable qualities, he *has* done a lot of good and, in his own way, he very definitely *does* love Buffy. However, Buffy finally realises that she's been using him.

A Little Learning is a Dangerous Thing: Anya notes that human perception is based on a linear chronology. Being exposed to the Rwasundi (the demons that Jonathan seemingly summoned) for more than a few seconds can cause vivid hallucinations and a slightly tingly scalp. However, Buffy has regained enough of her awareness by this point to realise that Warren *must* have had something to do with Katrina's death. And, thus she herself didn't.

Denial, Thy Name is Buffy: She's got it as bad as her mom ever did. 'You don't have a soul,' she screams at Spike. 'There's nothing good or clean in you. You are dead inside.' Denial transference, anyone? This is, in many ways a pivotal episode for Buffy, character-wise. She finally climbs out of the hole of denial into which she's been sinking since **103**, 'After Life' in the closing moments, weeping on Tara's knee. At least now she's admitted that she's been using Spike, but it's been a long slow process to get to this point. She's also very bloody-minded about going to the police, and is seemingly oblivious that this will really mess up Dawn's life (even if Buffy could convince the authorities that killing Katrina was an accident, Dawn would still be put into care immediately). Of course, this isn't the first time Buffy has believed she's killed someone human (see **23**, 'Ted'). The part of her that isn't a Slayer is still a bewildered 21-year-old woman who knows she's done something appalling and needs to atone for it to rid herself of the guilt. Nevertheless. Dawn is correct when she says that Buffy's unhappiness since she came back from Heaven is partly the reason she's so keen to go to the police. Prison, in many ways, is an ideal place for people who don't want to deal with their more complex issues. Buffy *has* responsibilities – both as a surrogate-mum to Dawn and as the Slayer to the world at large – neither of which can she walk away from no matter how tempting that solution may be. And, really, she *knows* that.

The Psychology Starts at a Dramatically Appropriate Time: This whole season, in a way, can be viewed as a subtextual essay on both personal and social perceptions, and this episode is the key to that locked door. Both Buffy, post-resurrection, and, especially, Warren have a real problem in seeing other people as distinct entities (Buffy's treatment of Spike is frequently appalling; with Warren it's an almost sociopathic disregard for anything other than an abstract concept of life as a kind of hedonistic toyshop; we saw this in **93**, 'I Was Made to Love You' and it's even more evident here). His friends don't seem immune to this either: after Katrina's death note how Jonathan refers to Warren's dead girlfriend as 'her' once and then, looking at the body, notes 'we have to get rid of *it*.' Andrew merely seems intoxicated at the end of the episode that they have, in effect, gotten away with murder (something that will grow fatter and more rancid as the season progresses). Spike, for his part, has the same problem that many serial killers do: an inability to view humans as anything other than mere lumps of meat. Katrina is only real to him in the sense that she's a dead body the discovery of which will get Buffy in trouble. Spike dumps her in the river and genuinely can't understand why Buffy is willing to give up everything because of this faceless girl's death.

Work is a Four-Letter Word: Buffy's still putting in long hours at the Doublemeat Palace, to the extent that Dawn is becoming even more distanced from and intolerant of her.

It's a Designer Label!: Warren's urban pimp pickup suit. *Nice threads*. Also, Xander's purple shirt, Buffy's green strapless top, Willow's suede jacket and Tara's lumpy green sweater. Anya is a pure vision in red at the Bronze.

References: The title may be an oblique reference to the movie *Very Bad Things* which is also about an elaborate cover-up of the accidental death of a woman. Buffy refers to cult movie director David Lynch *(Eraserhead, Twin Peaks, Wild at Heart, Mulholland Drive)* and claims to have some New Kids on the Block posters. Also paraphrases from *The Wacky Races* ('And, she's off'), *The Simpsons* ('quit it!', 'Gentlemen, to crime'), *I Dream of*

Jeannie ('I love you, Master'), *The X-Files* ('this isn't happening'), and allusions to *Soul Train*, *Rosemary's Baby* (Buffy's dream sequence) and The Mills Brothers' 'You Always Hurt The One You Love'.

Geek-Speak: Jonathan steals Andrew's copy of Peter Frampton's *Frampton Comes Alive*. Later, the pair spar with plastic *Star Wars* lightsabers.

Awesome!: While there *is* something inherently amusing about Jonathan and Andrew chanting "BAZOOMBAS!", the fact that this occurs in a scene where they are aiding Warren to procure an intended rape victim renders this somewhat tacky. Whatever one may think of Spike, his love for Buffy in this episode is demonstrably clear. When he says he loves her and Buffy replies that he doesn't, Spike's response is particularly impressive: 'You think I haven't tried *not to*?' The final scene, with Buffy tearfully begging Tara *not* to forgive her for having sex with Spike *is* cathartic and *almost* cancels out some of the episode's less savoury aspects.

'You May Remember Me From Such Films and TV Series As . . .': Amelinda Embry was in *Romy and Michele's High School Reunion*, *Scrubs* and *Two Guys, a Girl, and a Pizza Place*. Rock Reiser appeared in *Never Been Kissed*, *Gideon's Crossing*, *Melrose Place* and *Space: Above and Beyond*. Eric Prescott was in *Days of Our Lives*. Bernard Addison's CV includes *Frasier* and *Celebrity*.

Don't Give Up The Day Job: Producer John Perry previously worked on *Midnight Caller* and *Falcon Crest*.

The Drugs Don't Work: Willow has been spell-free for 32 days (presumably that was how long ago the events of **110**, 'Wrecked' took place). She did some involuntary magic in **112**, 'Doublemeat Palace', but it was Amy who cast that spell, against Willow's wishes so she's probably not counting that.

Valley-Speak: Andrew: 'This sucks.' And: 'Dude, *that* is messed-up.'

Cigarettes and Alcohol: When the Scoobies are planning to go to the Bronze, Xander promises 'tall glasses of frosty relaxation on me; nectar of the working man'. In the bar, Katrina is drinking red wine. Warren dumps his earpiece into a cocktail. The *troika* toast the initial success of their cerebral dampener with champagne (which Andrew thinks tastes funny). Spike smokes while drinking his blood in the crypt.

Sex and Drugs and Rock'n'Roll: Yet another torrid episode opening full of grunting and nakedness with Spike and Buffy going at it on the floor of his crypt. 'The way you make it hurt in all the wrong places,' notes Spike. 'I've never been with such an animal.' Buffy angrily replies that she's not an animal. Spike asks her if she'd like to see his bite-marks. Sexually, at least, they *do* seem to have a good time ('you're amazing,' 'you get the job done yourself'). Nevertheless Spike remains concerned about what, exactly, is going on between them and asks Buffy if she even likes him. 'Sometimes,' she replies, honestly. Then, holding up a pair of handcuffs, Spike asks Buffy if she trusts him. 'Never,' is the obvious reply.

Warren's latest deranged plan, aided by Jonathan's bone-magic, involves a cerebral dampener which will make any woman the *troika* desire into their slave. Of course, it all goes horribly wrong when Katrina, dressed inevitably in a sexy black-and-white French-maid's outfit straight out of *The Benny Hill Show*, suddenly throws off her conditioning, realises what's going on, gives a dramatic little 'rape' speech, and then gets murdered with a blunt instrument. Jonathan, who otherwise comes out of the episode fairly well (certainly better than Andrew and Warren), nevertheless says he could have used a cerebral dampener in high school. As opposed to, say, a gun (see **52**, 'Earshot')?

Logic, Let Me Introduce You to This Window: At one point Buffy turns her head to reveal her neck. Since she's been bitten on at least three occasions in the series (**12**, 'Prophecy Girl'; **56**, 'Graduation Day' Part 2; **79**, 'Buffy vs Dracula') shouldn't she have scars as shown in previous episodes (notably the one Parker comments upon in **59**, 'The Harsh Light of Day')? Buffy and Spike have a huge fight beside a police building and yet aren't spotted or arrested for affray. Principal Snyder's line about the police of Sunnydale being deeply stupid (**34**, 'Becoming' Part 2) is something the writers – not unjustifiably – keep on coming back to (see **122**, 'Grave'). What's Katrina doing back in Sunnydale? In **93**, 'I Was Made to Love You' she came from out of town. It's difficult to imagine that, after the horrors she went through in that story, she would have any reason to come back. Katrina is wearing mainly black clothes in the bar. Next time we see her, the *troika* have changed her into the French-maid outfit. After her death, the scenes in the woods have both her and Jonathan impersonating her wearing a short blue skirt and a blue sweater – where did *those* come from? The whole deal with the Rwasundi is rather confusing. Who summoned them? Jonathan, seemingly, since he's the one interacting with them, though isn't Andrew normally the *troika* member with responsibility for the demony-type stuff? Additionally, if the Rwasundi cause the time distortion then why isn't Jonathan (who's impersonating Katrina) affected by this along with Buffy and Spike?

I Just *Love* Your Accent: Tired of talking bollocks (see **110**, 'Wrecked'), seemingly, Spike uses another British variant: 'Oh, balls!' And, also 'wonky'.

Quote/Unquote: Spike, on Buffy's friends: 'You try to stay with them. But you always end up in the dark places. With me.'

  Andrew: 'What happens now?' Jonathan, bitterly: 'The night's young. Gotta be some more girls we could kill.'

Notes: 'This isn't some fantasy. It's not a game, you freaks, it's rape . . . I'm going to make sure they lock you away for this.' There are many laudable things in this episode's story of shallow desire versus mature needs. Unfortunately, a thoroughly sick, venal aberration within the presented characterisation (particularly of the *troika*) and a series of

highly unsavoury BDSM-gags in the Buffy/Spike relationship that seem to be there purely to get up the noses of The
Parents Television Council, drag a promising script into
some murky depths. A *Buffy* episode including rape and
bondage allusions? How desperately grown-up. Watching
113, 'Dead Things', frankly, is like wading through a
cesspool in search of a diamond. Like **49**, 'Consequences'
(which, on more occasions than is truly healthy, this episode
greatly resembles), 'Dead Things' plays with the idea of the
Slayer equivalent of collateral damage. Only this time,
Buffy, rather than Faith, is the central figure. All of this
occurs as she's getting a depressing dose of victim-culture
concerning her continuing morbid fascination with Spike.
Sadly, elsewhere, the episode plays dangerous, disturbing
games with what this season seems to have as the central
theme. It's all very well to say 'oh, grow up' to fat immature
fanboys who live in the basement with their comic
collection and *Star Wars* figures. But when that growing up
process turns them into Jeffrey Dahmer, is it really such a
good idea to pick at this raw scab? This is, by no means, the
first time that a *Buffy* episode has disturbed me. Unlike **66**,
'Hush' or **94**, 'The Body', however, what's disturbing about
'Dead Things' is what it says rather than the way it says it.

Spike says he ate a decorator once. Katrina mentions
Warren's 'wind-up slut,' and 'when Little Miss-Nuts-and-
Bolts tried to choke me to death,' (see **93**, 'I Was Made to
Love You'). Dawn is staying at Janice's (**106**, 'All the
Way') where Janice's mom intends to teach her how to
make tortillas. The coroner who reports on Katrina's death
is called Willard Batts. Dated 1 February 2002, the report
states: 'Victim sustained injuries consistent with a fall.
Twenty-one-year-old Katrina Silber's death appears to
have been caused by an accidental drowning or suicide.'

Soundtrack: 'Boo Wah Boo Wah' by Red & the Red Hots
plays at the Bronze when Anya, Xander and Willow are
dancing. Also, 'Sleeping Beauty Waltz' by Piotr
Tchaikovsky, 'Out of this World' by Bush (the highly
charged scene in which Buffy almost-but-not-quite enters

Spike's crypt) and 'Fingersnap' from the Non-Stop Music Library.

Did You Know?: Two British teenagers who tried to push a girl over a cliff and threatened to bite her after watching a *Buffy* video escaped a custodial sentence in March 2002. Nicola Millar and Kelly Brannigan, from Stevenston, Ayrshire, carried out the attack on their victim and left her on waste ground, an Edinburgh court heard. Both pleaded guilty to charges of assault. The judge took into account that they were first-time offenders, placed both on probation for three years and ordered them to do 240 hours' community service.

Joss Whedon's Comments: Which movies does Joss say to himself 'Damn. I wish *I'd* written that?' '*The Matrix, Magnolia, Three Kings, Casablanca, South Park, Sense and Sensibility* and *Firestorm* with Howi Long,' Joss told the *BtVS Posting Board.* As for television: 'If I could write for any show, it would be *The Simpsons* or *Twin Peaks*,' Joss said in an interview with the *Buffy* magazine. 'As much as you could say that *Buffy* is a cross between *90210* and *The X-Files*, you could also say it's a cross between *The Simpsons* and *Twin Peaks*. Also, I want to kill Aaron Sorkin, eat his brains and gain his knowledge because I love *The West Wing* so much. His stuff is just amazing.'

114
Older, and Far Away

US Transmission Date: 12 February 2002
UK Transmission Date: 4 April 2002

Writer: Drew Z Greenberg
Director: Michael Gershman
Cast: Ryan Browning (Richard), Laura Roth (Sophie),
Elizabeth Cazenave (Teacher)

Friends, new and old gather at 1630 Revello Drive for Buffy's 21st birthday party and (for once) it all seems to go off without a hitch. However, feeling neglected by Buffy, Dawn's wish to keep people from leaving her is answered by Anya's former colleague Halfrek, who binds the attendees of the party to the house. When Tara tries a spell to free them, she only makes the situation worse by accidentally releasing a demon.

Dudes and Babes: Tara suggests that Richard – the proposed date that Anya and Xander have set Buffy up with – is cute, although she admits she's not a very good judge of cuteness in boys. However, Clem agrees with her. Spike just scowls at them both.

A Little Learning is a Dangerous Thing: Amusingly, after all the grief the Scoobies have given Willow, it's Tara's magic that goes disastrously wrong on this occasion.

Mom's Apple Pie: Despite having to run out on Dawn, yet again, in the opening scene (see **113**, 'Dead Things') Buffy does find the time to tell Dawn to finish dinner, do her homework, and not to stay up too late.

Denial, Thy Name is Dawn: Proving, not for the first time, that when the mood takes her she can be a stroppy, attention-seeking drama queen, Dawn accidentally sets in motion the events of the episode. Not that she doesn't have some legitimate grievances in her life (Glory, Joyce's death, Buffy's death) *and*, to be fair, she's handled herself with great maturity for much of the time. It's hard for the girl, especially as even the one member of Buffy's crowd that she really likes and that everyone else can't stand, Spike, has been more interested in shagging her sister than hanging out with her like he used to. But she's been dealing with many of these insecurities through kleptomania, perhaps hoping that when she gets caught she'll finally receive some attention. Even before Halfrek's intervention, Buffy's birthday present (see **Presents**) was an incredibly blatant cry for help, literally demanding that Buffy ask questions about its purchase. Hanging out with the people she does, it's reasonable to assume Dawn should know better than to make a wish to a stranger, but the phrase 'sometimes I wish ...' is a part of every teenager's vocabulary. Buffy's sense of just how lonely Dawn is may, indeed, help her with her own disassociation complex (see **113**, 'Dead Things'). Still, the theft thing finally comes home to roost and Anya, the owner of most of the trinkets in Dawn's secret stash, *is* in the mood for forgiveness, but at a price: 'We're gonna talk about payment,' she notes. 'There are two words I want you to get used to. Punitive damages!'

The Allergies Start at Party Time: Sophie, Buffy's seemingly school-age friend (last name unknown) is allergic to chocolate, egg yolk and peanuts. And, sometimes, dairy products. And alcohol (because of the barley).

Presents: Buffy's birthday gifts include a battery-operated back massager (probably from Willow), a gorgeous black leather jacket (which Dawn shoplifted) and a weapons chest (which Xander built and Anya 'offered helpful suggestions' about).

It's a Designer Label!: Dawn's red top (which also appears in **115**, 'As You Were'). Loads of cool party clothes including Buffy's strapless black top, Willow's gorgeous see-through blouse and Tara's crimson skirt.

References: Witty allusions to *Children of the Corn* ('only thing missing is a cornfield') and *Night of the Living Dead*. The title is a quotation from the novel *Empire of the Sun*. There's an issue of Neil Gaiman's *The Sandman* ('24 Hours') about a group of people trapped in a diner that's conceptually similar to this episode. Also, *Moonlighting* (Buffy and Spike's argument, and especially both repeating 'fine' to each other is *very* Maddy/David), *Stargate SG-1* ('well, *this* can't be good'), *The Simpsons* ('that was sarcasm by the way') and *The Addams Family* ('you rang?').

Awesome!: Xander gets most of the good lines, and Spike most of the pithy ones. Tara suggesting Spike put some ice on his 'muscle cramp'. Sophie noting that she'd sooner stay trapped in the house than do a shift at the Doublemeat.

Anya's hilarious claustrophobic panic attack (and, '*Our friend is better!*') and Halfrek's dramatic little *deus-ex-machina*-style arrival before being trapped in her own curse. Also, Clem's closing line: 'Cool party!'

'You May Remember Me From Such Films and TV Series As . . .': Ryan Browning appeared in *Stealing Sinatra*, *Losing Grace* and *Baywatch*. Laura Roth was in *Once and Again* and *Malcolm in the Middle*. Elizabeth Cazenave appeared in *The Mothman Prophecies*.

Don't Give Up The Day Job: Visual Effects creator Randy Goux's talents can also be seen on *The Rage: Carrie 2*, *X-Men* and *Lord of the Rings: The Fellowship of the Ring*.

Valley-Speak: Dawn: 'We should *totally* have a slumber party.'

Buffy: 'Hey, Mister Passive-Aggressive Guy.'

Richard: 'You have some weird friends.' Xander: 'News from the file marked *duh*.'

Cigarettes and Alcohol: Spike arrives at the party with a six-pack of beer.

Logic, Let Me Introduce You to This Window: Buffy's birthday has been established as being mid-January (see **25**, 'Surprise', **36**, 'Helpless'). Yet for the last two seasons the episode that contains her birthday have been broadcast in February. When Buffy pulls Spike away from the group after he jokes about eating Richard you can see Spike's reflection in the hall mirror. When Tara casts the release spell, why is Spike getting ready to rush the door, into broad daylight, without a blanket or any other form of protection from the sun? Also, how can Spike be in Dawn's room where there is sunlight pouring through the open windows without bursting into flames? Moving someone with a heavy stomach wound up a flight of stairs isn't recommended emergency medical treatment, and would most likely make the victim's condition worse. When Richard is stabbed, it appears that the blade went deep enough to rupture a major organ, yet he lives for several hours while trapped in the house, and the Scoobies don't even bother to put on a bandage (although Tara does dab at the wound with something). How did Dawn get the jacket out of the store with the security tag still attached? Anya claims that only a vengeance-demon can break his or her own vengeance spell. She, of all people, should know better. Giles destroying her amulet in an alternate reality broke Anya's spell for Cordelia, and trapped Anya in human form (**43**, 'The Wish'). If Halfrek can't get out of the house due to her own curse then how did she get *in*? If Willow and Tara have classes in the morning then shouldn't Dawn, also, have to go to school? She certainly doesn't seem like she's getting ready to go.

I Just *Love* Your Accent: Spike calls Richard a 'stupid git.'

Cruelty to Animals: When Xander suggests the boys play poker, Clem says it's 'weird without kittens' (see **105**, 'Life Serial').

Quote/Unquote: Spike: 'I had a muscle cramp. Buffy was helping.' Tara: ' . . . In your pants?'

Notes: 'People have a tendency to go away . . . Sometimes I wish I could make them stop.' Buffy's birthday parties always seem to end with some catastrophe for her friends. 'You ever think about *not* celebrating?' asks an exasperated Spike at one point. The pain of her perceived and constant rejection by Buffy and a craving to be the centre of attention for just once forces Dawn into her own, private version of **43**, 'The Wish'. Thus, we get a classic bottle-show in the tradition of all good slasher movies (and some very bad ones), with ten characters trapped in a house. Drew Greenberg's previous script, **109**, 'Smashed', hinted at a real talent emerging and, while 'Older, and Far Away' isn't a patch on *that* riotous collection of comedy highjinks, it does show a writer developing a unique and interesting new voice in the *Buffy* oeuvre. Well directed and as sharp as a needle when it's going for the joke-shock-joke-joke two-step (let's pretend a thoroughly slovenly ten minute middle section without a laugh in sight never

happened) once again *Buffy* proves that even when it's
taking shortcuts, it can produce innovation.

Spike still has a black eye from the beating Buffy gave
him in **113**, 'Dead Things'. Tara says she thought that
cursing unfaithful men was all that vengeance-demons did.
Halfrek says that was Anya's *raison d'être* but they all have
different specialities. And they prefer the more ideologi-
cally sound term 'justice-demon'. Halfrek's main area of
work is protecting neglected children and punishing their
parents and she originally came to Sunnydale because she
heard Dawn's cries for attention ('Daddy issues' says
Anya, bitchily). In one of the most clever pieces of
continuity the series has ever done, when Halfrek sees
Spike she calls him William and then, embarrassed, they
both try to pretend that they don't know each other (Kali
Rocha played the then-human William's unrequited love
interest, Cecily, in **85**, 'Fool For Love'). The Magic Box's
range of 'Essence of Slug' candles are mentioned again (see
105, 'Life Serial'). Willow appears to be attending a group
of like-minded witches who are trying to give up magic.
They're called 'Spellcasters Anonymous' though they're
looking for a better name. Richard works with Xander at
the construction site. Dawn refers to the events of **50**,
'Doppelgängland' (telling Willow 'you want me to ask
your other self?'), while Xander alludes to his invocation
of the musical amulet in **107**, 'Once More, With Feeling'.

Soundtrack: Mint Royale's 'Rock and Roll Bar', 'The
Race' by Gwenmars, 'California Calling' by Opus 1,
'Seconds' by Even, 'Down, Down, Down' from the Extreme Music Library, 'Pictures of Success' by Rilo Kiley
and Aberdeen's 'Clouds Like These'.

Did You Know?: James Marsters appeared naked in his first
acting job – a Chicago stage production of *The Tempest*.
But having to get his kit off regularly on TV necessitates
some discipline, as he told *Sci-Fi Wire*. 'Luckily, Sarah and
I have built up trust and friendship, so we lean on each
other. She taught me that love scenes are much like fight
scenes. You're going to a level of unreality that's beyond

normal acting. We did like eight takes. Finally Sarah said, "OK, James just don't do anything. Do the worst acting in your life. Think about breakfast." We did it again, and that's the take you see.'

Cast and Crew Comments: Michelle Trachtenberg, according to *CT Now* website, had previously set her sights on going to Yale and studying theatre and English. However: 'I realised I wanted to consider other colleges and decide what subjects I really wanted to study,' she says. 'I know what to do before the cameras. Now I want to learn what to do behind them. I'm even thinking of taking a year off after I graduate and maybe making a movie in a place like Italy. That would give me a chance to travel and work at the same time. Education is important to me. So is work. But the most important thing in my life is my family – my mother, my sister, my father and my cat, Casey.'

Joss Whedon's Comments: When *Buffy* actors get questions concerning future developments in interviews, they always seem to answer with horrific threats like 'I can't tell you; Joss will rip out my tongue and feed it to wolves.' So, does he actually say things like that? 'I'm a very gentle man, not unlike Gandhi,' Joss told Tasha Robinson. 'I don't ever threaten them. There is, sort-of hanging over their head, the thing that I could kill them at any moment. But that's really just if they annoy me. They know that I'm very secretive about plot twists, because I think it's better for the show. But anybody with a computer can find out what's going to happen, apparently even before I know. So my wish for secrecy is pathetic.'

115
As You Were

US Transmission Date: 26 February 2002
UK Transmission Date: 11 April 2002

Writer: Douglas Petrie
Director: Douglas Petrie

Cast: Ivana Milicevic (Sam Finn), Ryan Raddatz (Todd),
Adam Paul (Skanky Vamp), Marilyn Brett (Lady),
Alice Dinnean Vernon (Baby Demon Puppeteer)

Riley Finn pursues a demon to Sunnydale and seeks Buffy's help in capturing it. He also comes with a surprise: he's happily married. His wife, fellow military demon hunter Sam, befriends the Scooby Gang. But Buffy's own relationship with Spike comes into question when her ex's perfect romance shows her what she, herself, no longer has.

Dreaming (As Blondie Once Said) is Free: Xander says he's starting to have dreams of gardenia bouquets and is glad his manly co-workers can't hear him confess this to Anya.

Dudes and Babes: Sam gives Willow a sweet little pep talk over her bravery in facing up to her addiction. Riley's team, Sam notes, had two hard-core shamans working dark magics for them. Both got addicted and neither survived the ordeal. Sam tells Willow that she's never met anyone with enough strength to quit. Before now.

A Little Learning is a Dangerous Thing: In a pointed moment, Doublemeat Palace know-all Todd reminds Buffy that she dropped out of college. Todd, himself, is attending night classes working for his MBA so he doesn't have to spend all his life flipping burgers. Later, Buffy receives a rejection letter for her application to re-enrole at UC☉D from Surrinda Blackmaster, the assistant to the dean.

Denial, Thy Name is Buffy: Shaken by Riley's return, and the fact that he's managed to get over Buffy by marrying (in effect) a female clone of himself, Buffy goes to Spike, ostensibly for information, but actually, so that he can comfort her. Tell me that you love me, she demands before they go to bed. After the discovery that Spike *is* responsible for obtaining the demon eggs, Riley offers to kill Spike if Buffy would like him to. Buffy asks Riley if he deliberately waited until his life was absolutely perfect before returning to find her sleeping with a repulsive vampire. Despite Buffy's self-proclaimed incredible patheticness, none of

that means anything because it doesn't touch the real
Buffy, he notes. She's still the first woman Riley ever loved.
Buffy admits that on the night he left Sunnydale (**88**, 'Into
The Woods') she never had the chance to tell you him how
sorry she was about what happened between them. 'You
never have to,' replies Riley.

After Riley's departure, Buffy returns to Spike and tells
him that their relationship is over: 'I *do* want you,' she
reveals, sadly. 'Being with you makes things simpler.' But,
she admits, she's using him. 'I'm just being weak and
selfish. And it's killing me.'

The Conspiracy Starts at Home Time: Riley and Sam are
tracking a Suvolte demon which is rare, lethal and nearly
extinct. They've been following it through every jungle
from Paraguay. Suvoltes start to kill from the moment they
hatch and reach full maturity around three months. Sam
believes the demon's eggs are being sold on the black
market. There are foreign military powers who would love
to have their own Suvolte. You could never train it, but
drop it on an urban population and it would cleanse the
area (as Dawn notes, that's a nice way of saying it kills
people). When they approach the demon, Riley clears the
area by telling bystanders that he's from the National
Forestry Service and there's a wild bear on the loose.

It's a Designer Label!: Buffy's disgusting yellow duffel coat.
Much better is the 'ninja-wear' lightweight Kevlar state-of-
the-art combat gear that Riley provides.

References: Allusions to Niccolò Machiavelli (1469–1527,
Italian political and military theorist), *Thunderbirds*
('m'lady'), Lyndon B Johnson (1908–73), the 36th president of the United States, and his successor Richard Nixon
(1913–94), golfer Arnold Palmer, the character of James
Bond, *GoldenEye* ('boys with toys'), the June 1944 allied
invasion of Normandy (as portrayed in movies as diverse
as *The Longest Day* and *Saving Private Ryan*), the Broadway showtune 'If I Knew You Were Coming I'd Have
Baked a Cake' most associated with Ethel Merman

(1908–84), although the hit version was by Eileen Barton, The Small Faces' 'Tin Soldier' and Neil Armstrong's 1969 moon-landing speech ('that's a first big step'). Riley paraphrases 2Unlimited's 'Get Ready For This'. Xander's description of Riley and Sam as 'Nick and Nora Fury' is a reference to Nick and Nora Charles, the sophisticated sleuths of Dashiell Hammet's *The Thin Man*, and to Nick Fury, the cigar-chomping Marvel comic hero.

Geek-Speak: When Riley describes the Suvolte's breeding habits, Buffy notes: 'So they're like really mean tribbles? Sorry, I've been dealing with these geeks ...' Later, she asks Riley if he's got a jet-pack (see **119**, 'Seeing Red').

Bitch!: Being hyper-supportive of her best friend, Willow tells Buffy she's prepared to hate Sam in any way Buffy wants. 'I don't wanna seem petty,' says Buffy who, it turns out, rather likes Sam. 'That's the beauty,' replies Willow. 'Let me carry the hate for both of us!' Willow subsequently gets on really well with Sam too, and they swap e-mail addresses. But, as the chopper carrying Sam and Riley leaves, having waved them off, Willow turns away scowling and tells Buffy, brilliantly: 'What a bitch!'

Awesome!: The vampire refusing to eat Buffy once he realises she's been eating Doublemeat burgers. Buffy's dim-witted response to Riley's surprise arrival: 'My hat has a cow.' All the Buffy/Riley/Sam scenes.

'You May Remember Me From Such Films and TV Series As ...': A former professional basketball player with the Manchester Giants, Marc Blucas played the basketball hero in *Pleasantville*. He was also Buddy Wells in *The 60s* and Billy in *Undressed* and, since leaving *Buffy* in early 2001, has appeared in *Jay and Silent Bob Strike Back*, *We Were Soldiers*, *Prey for Rock & Roll* and *A View From the Top*. Bosnian-born Ivana Milicevic was Emma in *Vanilla Sky* and Roxana in *Head Over Heals*. She also appeared in *Postmortem*, *The Devil's Child*, *The Nanny*, *Felicity* and *Jerry Maguire*. Marilyn Brett was, memorably, in *Ameri-*

can Pie 2, *Going Nomad* and *Girl, Interrupted*. Adam Paul's movies include *Biohazard* and *The Pentagon Wars*.

Don't Give Up The Day Job: Key Grip George Palmer worked on *Titanic*, *Independence Day*, *Tales from the Crypt* and *Cutting Class*. Chief Lighting Technician Chris Strong's CV includes movies such as *Alien: Resurrection*, *Nixon*, *Se7en*, *Speed* and *Twins*.

Cigarettes and Alcohol: Xander has a beer with his nachos at the Bronze as he and Anya argue about the wedding arrangements.

Sex and Drugs and Rock'n'Roll: Spike suggests to Riley that Buffy always had a little thing for Spike, even when she and Riley were together.

Logic, Let Me Introduce You to This Window: As with Spike in **112**, 'Doublemeat Palace', how does Riley know Buffy works at the diner? Riley notices Buffy's new haircut, but he doesn't question further her comment that she died (nor, the fact that Joyce is absent – presumably all of this was done off-screen in one big catching-up session. He knows, for instance, that Xander's getting married). When Buffy stakes the vampire, the stake clearly doesn't go through his heart, but rather the middle of his chest yet he still explodes. Wasn't Xander supposed to be at Buffy's house watching Dawn while Buffy, Sam and Riley were out? Instead he was at *his* house with Anya hiding from his relatives. More queries about the Doublemeat Palace's opening hours: Buffy was 'working till close', then she did a quick patrol, had sex with Spike, and finally goes home and tells Dawn, who is going to the Bronze with Willow, to be home 'by eleven'. Wouldn't it already be well past eleven by the time she got home (assuming a late shift is just that, see **112**, 'Doublemeat Palace')? Riley says that The Doctor is 'a man', yet it turns out to be Spike who isn't even human. If as soon as one Suvolte is killed, a dozen take its place, as Riley suggests, then how is the race nearly extinct? Spike is now an international criminal mastermind, seemingly. Despite Buffy and Riley's low opinion of his intelligence ('incompetent' and 'an idiot' respectively), Spike's a sharp enough kiddie to be unlikely to store anything potentially valuable without making sure he knew how to keep it in good condition. And why would he use the street name 'Doctor'? Everybody in the Sunnydale underworld who matters knows exactly who he is. Plus, more importantly, a demon with a very similar name was involved in the worst night of Spike's life (see **100**, 'The Gift') – he might be evil but he's not a masochist. Sunnydale's zip code is 95037 which is actually a code for the town of Morgan Hill at the southern end of the Santa Clara Valley south of San Francisco.

I Just *Love* Your Accent: Spike is the first person to use the phrase 'it's a fair cop,' on TV since around 1971. He tells Riley that Buffy isn't 'your bint anymore' (see **59**, 'The Harsh Light of Day'; **82**, 'Out of My Mind'). Dawn suggests Willow is 'awfully chipper' tonight. Must be Spike's influence rubbing off.

Quote/Unquote: Buffy, to Sam and Riley after their revelation: 'Husband? Wife? Those aren't code names like Big Dog or Falcon?'
  Riley: 'I'm taking this place apart until I find that nest.' Spike: 'Over my dead body.' Riley: 'I've seen enough of your dead body for one night, thanks.'

Notes: 'You want me to say that I liked seeing you in bed with that idiot? Or blinding orange is your best colour? Or that burger smell is appealing?' The prodigal returns. Riley Finn, fresh from a glut of demon slaughtering in South America, comes back to Sunnydale. And, guess what, he's brought the wife with him. 'As You Were' neatly ties up the loose ends left from Riley's sudden departure (see **88**, 'Into the Woods'). Like why it happened, for instance. In offering up Riley to the sacrificial alter of fandom, Joss Whedon stated that such a Gary Cooper-like character could not function in the Buffy universe, except, perhaps, as a comic feed, which is the role Marc Blucas gets to play here and, credit to the lad, he pulls it off very well. Amid the torrid and sandblasted emotional lives of the Scooby Gang, we also have the most *Buffy*-like episode of this season thus far: a story about tracking a demon nasty in which Xander and Willow keep out of the way and say funny things, Buffy and Riley (plus Mrs Finn) get proactive with the demon-murdering and Spike's actually evil for a change. There are lots of throwaway comedy gems in Petrie's script (Spike's delight at Riley finding him *in-flagrante* with Buffy is particularly noteworthy). Very much as you were, then, with just a hint of what is yet to come.

When Willow was little she spent many hours imagining what her eventual wedding to Xander would be like. Anya and Xander are going to the airport to pick up Xander's often mentioned alcoholic uncle, Rory (see **116**, 'Hell's Bells'). Xander says he hates him and, indeed, his whole family. Riley and Sam have been married for four months. Sam asks Buffy if she has a safehouse. Buffy replies she has a house and it's usually safe; sometimes you can't even leave (see **114**, 'Older, and Far Away'). Riley mentions Willy's Bar (he was last seen there in **86**, 'Shadow' getting some vampire-love from Sandy). Sam went to Central America with the Peace Corps where her whole infirmary was slaughtered by something supernaturally horrid. She subsequently joined the government's latest version of The Initiative (see **63**, 'The Initiative') which she calls 'the Squad' and, in her first firefight, met Riley.

Soundtrack: 'Sound of the Revolution' by Lunatic Calm and 'Washes Away' by Trespassers William.

Critique: 'The bleakness of the themes puts the series closer to Philip Roth, even Samuel Beckett, than Anne Rice,' noted Robert Hanks in the *Independent*. 'All this makes it sound pretentious and heavy-going. But the other point to make about *Buffy* is that it is deliciously competent. The dialogue [is] unvaryingly slick and witty, up there with the best Hollywood screwball comedies ... This is what attracts the intellectuals.'

Did You Know?: An average episode of *Buffy* only requires two days on location away from the Mutant Enemy lot in Santa Monica which has increased in size dramatically over the last five years. That's a big difference from the early days where the production will be on the road for up to six days per episode. Filming at Torrance High School, which doubled for Sunnydale High in the first three seasons was an interesting logistical challenge. 'The school were helpful to us and everyone was very nice until the end of season three,' notes producer Gareth Davies. 'We'd told [the local population] that we were going to blow up the school, unfortunately we neglected to tell them *when.*' So, when the massive explosion in **56**, 'Graduation Day' Part 2 happened at 5 a.m. one morning in 1999, many residents were less than impressed. 'We recently went back to the area,' Davies told Rob Francis, 'and as soon as we announced it I got a series of irate letters from people over something that happened three years ago.'

Head On: 'When a record company said they were interested in doing an album with me. My first reaction was "Actor in his 40s releases album. Put it on the shelf between William Shatner and David Hasselhoff,"' Tony Head wryly notes. 'But I figured it was safe enough if I made it working with people I respect and love. So, Joss has contributed a song, James is on the album and so are Amber and Alyson.' The fruit of his labours, *Music for Elevators* was released early in 2002. The record was made in collaboration with noted dance producer George Sarah of THC (who had previously appeared **61**, 'Beer Bad' and **62** 'Wild at Heart' as part of Veruca's band). A mixture of ambient-trance and folk, the CD includes a startling reworking of Lennon and McCartney's 'We Can Work it Out' and the Joss Whedon written 'Last Time'. James Marsters provides backing vocals on the CD's standout song, 'Owning My Mistakes'.

Joss Whedon's Comments: 'It's going to get worse,' Joss noted, concerning the levels of misery in season six. 'We have a lot of humour in store, and a lot of goofy, crazy stuff, but are we bringing on the pain? We *love* pain. But, there's happiness. There's always hope.'

116
Hell's Bells

US Transmission Date: 5 March 2002
UK Transmission Date: 18 April 2002

Writer: Rebecca Rand Kirshner
Director: David Solomon
Cast: Casey Sander (Tony Harris), Lee Garlington (Jessica Harris),
Steve Gilborn (Uncle Rory), Jan Hoag (Cousin Carol),
George D Wallace (Old Xander), Daniel McFeeley (Warty Demon),
Rebecca Jackson (Tarantula), Mel Fair (Tentacle Demon),
Nick Kokich (Demon Teen), Robert Noble (Night Manager),
Julian Franco (Young Bartender), Susannah L Brown (Caterer Girl),
Joey Hiott (Josh Aged 10), Abigail Mavity (Sara Aged 8),
Chris Emerson (Josh Aged 21), Ashley-Ann Wood (Sara Aged 18),
Megan Vint (Karen)

Xander and Anya's wedding day arrives. While Xander's dysfunctional family go head to head with Anya's mostly non-human friends, an old man approaches Xander to warn him that his future life may not turn out to be a bed of roses.

Dreaming (As Blondie Once Said) is Free: The old man, claiming to be Xander from the future, shows him an orb in which Xander sees visions of what his life will allegedly be like if he marries Anya. They will have two children, Josh and Sara (the little girl will inherit aspects of her mother's genes and grow up with strangely deformed ears) both of whom will have a strained relationship with their father. Xander will injure his back fighting demons along-side Buffy (who is, seemingly, killed in this fight) and will be unable to work, thus putting pressure on Anya as the family's breadwinner. Xander and Anya's relationship sours after this and, although they stay together, they're never intimate or happy. Some thirty years after they're married, Xander will kill Anya during a blazing row, by smashing her in the face with a frying pan. The only way to stop all of this from happening, the old man tells Xander, is to abort the wedding.

No Fat Chicks: Xander's cousin, Carol, is a nervous plump middle-aged woman – seemingly married on more than one occasion – with a young daughter, Karen. She asks Xander about one of Anya's guests, Krevlin, a cheerful (if rather warty) demon. Carol wonders if he could clear up the skin problem does Xander think he'd be willing to date a woman with a kid? 'I really can't afford to be very picky!'

Dudes and Babes: Buffy tells Xander that he and Anya give her hope; they're proof that there's light 'at the end of this very long, nasty tunnel' (see **89**, 'Triangle').

A Little Learning is a Dangerous Thing: The old man pretending to be future-Xander is really Stewart Burns, a philanderer whom Anyanka cursed in Chicago in 1914 by sending him to another (seemingly hellish) dimension.

Denial, Thy Name is Spike: He arrives at the wedding with a skanky goth girl. It's a clear and obvious attempt to make Buffy jealous. 'Is it working?' he asks desperately. 'Yes,' Buffy replies, 'a little.' Spike, in one of the episode's best scenes, apologises and tells Buffy that it's good to see her happy for a change. Then he takes his date and leaves, having assured Buffy that the goth chick won't be going home with him.

The Ceremony Starts at Home Time: The location of the wedding is the Sunnydale Bison's Lodge. Willow notes that the rehearsal dinner last night was like a zoo without the table manners. It's not entirely clear whether she's referring to Anya's demon friends or Xander's family. On the latter, Willow suggests she hasn't seen them so badly behaved since her bar mitzvah (Mr Harris got drunk the previous night and threw up in Buffy's purse). Buffy can't believe that the Harrises bought the cover story about Anya's people being 'circus folk'.

Anya, practising her vows, intends to stick pretty much to the traditional Christian wedding ceremony, promising to cherish and honour her husband. But not to obey, of course, 'because that's anachronistic and misogynistic and who do you think you are, like a sea captain or something?' By later in the episode, she's adding stuff like a pledge to be Xander's friend, confidante, and 'sex poodle', much to Tara's alarm.

In the end, even once he realises that the visions were a lie, Xander still decides not to go ahead with the wedding. He isn't ready and, believing that the visions were his own worst-case-scenario perceptions of how the marriage could turn out (possibly based on his own parents' disastrous relationship), Xander tells Anya that he can't go through with it.

It's a Designer Label!: Aside from the horrors of the bridesmaids' dresses, look out for Buffy's I SURVIVED T-shirt at the end. A witty summation of the episode and, ultimately, the season.

References: Allusions to actress and cabaret singer Marlene Dietrich (1904–99), *Henry V* ('into the breach with you'), *Stargate SG-1*'s 'Window of Opportunity' (the juggling), the Athenian legend of the Minotaur, *The Godfather* ('I mean no disrespect') and The Beatles' 'Yesterday' ('I'm not the man I used to be'). Elements of the plot may have been inspired by a *Hammer House of Mystery and Suspense* episode called 'A Distant Scream', the *Back to the Future* trilogy and *The Outer Limits*' 'Demon With a Glass Hand'.

Awesome!: The opening, with the dresses. Buffy's increasingly desperate excuses to Anya for the delay, and her entertaining of the wedding guests. And, especially, the moment when it all kicks off and descends into a brawl.

'You May Remember Me From Such Films and TV Series As . . .': Lee Garlington was Natalie's Mom in *American Pie 2* and Kathy Donovan in *Townies*, and appeared in *Boys and Girls*, *The Babysitter*, *Shame*, *Field of Dreams*, *In the Mood* and *Virtual Obsession*. Steve Gilborn's CV

includes *Evolution, Nurse Betty, Doctor Doolittle, The West
Wing, The Brady Bunch Movie, Ellen, The Practice,
Blossom* and *He Said, She Said.* In a career stretching
almost sixty years, George Wallace can be seen in *Bicen-
tennial Man, Multiplicity, Child of Rage, Postcards From
the Edge, The Towering Inferno, The Six Million Dollar
Man, Forbidden Planet, Radar Men From The Moon,
Kojak, Bonanza, Perry Mason* and *Rawhide.* Casey Sander
was Rock in *Home Improvement* and appeared in *Dynasty,
Knight Rider, Body Double, Grace Under Fire, Crosscut,
Predator 2* and *Dragnet.* Jan Hoag played Bambi in *The
Parlor* and was in *Murphy Brown, Silk Stalking, The Last
Dance, 976-WISH, Armed and Innocent* and *Murder, She
Wrote.* Daniel McFeeley appeared in *Hunter's Blood.*
Robert Noble was in *Robin Hood: Men in Tights, Bill &
Ted's Bogus Journey, Stir, Mail Order Bride, The West
Wing* and *Love, Cheat & Steal.* Nick Kokich played
Kevin in *The United States of Leland.* Ashley-Ann Wood
appeared in *From the Earth to the Moon* and *Beyond
Reality.* Andy Umberger (D'Hoffryn) can be seen in
Dragonfly, Angel, The West Wing, NYPD Blue, The X-Files
and *Tempting Fate.* Abigail Mavity was in *100 Mile Rule*
and *Strong Medicine.* Chris Emerson appeared in *What
Women Want* and *Boston Public.* Joey Hiott was in *That
'70s Show, Super Jesus* and *Family Law.*

Don't Give Up The Day Job: Musical editor Tim Isle also
worked on *Bring It On, Whatever It Takes* and *Watching
Ellie.* Rebecca Jackson was a scenic painter on *Just a Little
Harmless Sex.*

Valley-Speak: Buffy: 'Did you see the guy with the
tentacles? What's he supposed to be? Inky the Squid Boy?'
  Dawn: 'Spike's here and he brought a total skank. A
manic-panicked freak who he's like totally macking with
right in the middle of the room.'

Not Exactly A Haven From The Harris Family: Nick
Brendon's perceptive 1999 comment to *Entertainment
Weekly* about Xander's family background ('He was

abused as a child. I've got two people in mind for his dad – George Hamilton or Steven Seagal') seems remarkably apt when we finally get to meet the dysfunctional, proudly Episcopalian, Harris family. Mr Harris senior is a sarcastic, short-tempered, foul-mouthed, nasty drunk. His wife, Jessica, is a bag of nerves, insecure over her weight and constantly self-deprecating and belittling herself. Xander's list of jobs for Buffy at the wedding is:

- 1. Don't let Mr Harris near the bar.
- 2. Don't let Mrs Harris near the bar.

The oft-mentioned Uncle Rory finally shows up. Most of what Xander had previously alleged about him is confirmed. He likes booze (he's trying to make himself an Irish coffee for breakfast), is an ex-taxidermist ('it was my trade, I used to stuff things. I still do, but only for fun') and also a lecherous old raver whose target group seems to be girls half his age. He also claims to have invented Velcro and isn't half as funny a practical joker as he thinks he is.

Cigarettes and Alcohol: During Xander's first vision he's got a beer in his hand. In his second, he's drunk on red wine. Tony Harris drinks copious amounts of Jack Daniel's during the wedding.

Sex and Drugs and Rock'n'Roll: As Buffy leads a violently drunk Tony Harris away from a confrontation, he looks at her ass and comments: 'Nice chassis, what's under the hood?' After another couple of lewd suggestions, Buffy threatens him and he goes very quiet.

Logic, Let Me Introduce You to This Window: It appears to be a reasonably bright day outside throughout most of the episode, albeit it's raining. How, therefore, does Spike get into (and out of) the wedding? Burns says he was a victim of one of Anyanka's curses. In **43**, 'The Wish' when Giles destroyed Anyanka's amulet, he specifically said that this would return her to human form and reverse *all* of the wishes she had granted.

What A Shame They Cut . . .: A scene from the draft script
in which we learn that Giles couldn't attend the wedding
because he's fighting daemons (Willow is specific about the
spelling) in England. Instead he paid for all of the wedding
flowers. Also, in the same scene, Dawn describes her dress
as 'the colour of snot'.

Cruelty to Animals: D'Hoffryn shows up with Halfrek
bearing the greetings of Hyman, the god of matrimony. He
gives Dawn his gift and tells her to be careful with it. 'Is it
fragile?' asks Dawn, taking the box. 'Squirmy,' he replies
as tentacles burst out of the box and Dawn looks terrified.
Later, Dawn tells a startled Xander that 'one of Anya's
presents got loose'.

Quote/Unquote: Old Man: 'You'll hurt her less today than
you will later. Believe me. Sometimes, two people, all they
bring each other is pain.'

Notes: 'I, Anya, want to marry you, Xander. Because I love
you and I always will.' I personally hate weddings. Most of
those I've attended resemble that funeral in *Steptoe and Son*:
bitter, incestuous and always ending in a huge fight. I'm not
sure if Rebecca Kirshner's seen any Galton and Simpson,
but she's clearly been to a few such horrorshows. 'Hell's
Bells' is one of the least amusing and most emotionally
draining *Buffy* episodes ever. This is *really* tough going. The
plot lurches from one extreme of misery to the next – like
sitting through twenty-four hours nonstop of the Jesus and
Mary Chain, the Smiths and Radiohead. You'll wonder
how you made it out alive. At heart, there's a really nihilist
core to 'Hell's Bells' which, despite strong material (much of
which is eloquently played by the regulars and the excellent
guest cast) renders the episode somewhat arch compared to
more emotionally involving pieces. Future-imperfect riddles,
racism allegories and lots of fear battle for prominence. But
in the last few moments we get a scene that is among the
most touching, lyrical and saddest of all *Buffy* climaxes.
    Willow tells Xander 'It's a good thing I realised I was
gay because here we are in formalwear,' a reference to

Willow and Xander's romantic 'fluke' in **39**, 'Homecoming'. After Xander decides not to go through with the wedding, D'Hoffryn suggests to Anya that she has become domesticated and needs her demon powers back (see **118**, 'Entropy').

Critique: 'Some fans have felt that the momentum of the sixth season was lost in the mid-season repetition of controversial issues and themes,' noted John Mosby. 'Others felt that this was a clear sign that the show was reflecting the confused journey of teenagers into the adult world where their safety nets are gone, the mistakes greater and the consequences higher.'

Did You Know: It was revealed at the Academy of Television Arts and Sciences *Buffy* event in June 2002 that the *Buffy* cast has frequent get-togethers at Joss's house. The first time they did this (prior to filming the untransmitted pilot episode in 1996), the actors were very nervous and ill-at-ease so, according to Joss, they all 'drank a bit to get comfortable'. At this point Nick Brendon pointed towards the very pregnant Marti Noxon and said 'and look what happened'. What *did* happen at a later get-together, Joss noted, was that everyone wound up around a piano, singing. Surprised at how well his actors could sing, Joss says it was at this point that he realised he had a group who could actually pull off a musical episode. Alyson Hannigan confirmed that when Joss first wrote the musical, he and his wife, Kai, sang all of the songs on to a tape for the actors to learn. Alyson said this was rather intimidating as Kai has a fabulous voice. The Whedons' demo version of 'Something to Sing About', included as a bonus track on the *Once More, With Feeling* soundtrack CD, confirms this. Michelle Trachtenberg told Joss that while she wasn't too comfortable with her voice, she loved to dance and had studied ballet and tap. So she asked for a production number. He duly obliged, choreographing the sequence himself. Joss said he wrote each song for the actor and their strengths. He wrote a rock number for James, because 'it had to be,' and a ballad for Amber because she's a wonderful ballad singer. The 30s-pastiche number for Anya and Xander was based, in part, on the art-deco style of their apartment set. When asked whose musical talent had surprised him the most, Joss responded Emma Caulfield's: 'We'd never heard her sing before. She was amazing.'

Joss Whedon's Comments: He has two shows on the air, two more in preparation and a comic to write. So, how does Joss Whedon cope with it all? 'One trick is to be behind in everything all the time,' he told *TV Guide*. 'I have such great crews working on *Buffy* and *Angel* [that] I know they can get a lot done without my supervision. A lot of the machine can run without me now.' Variety helps to spice things up too. 'Every now and then, I work on the animated series, or *Angel* ... You get juiced up and you actually get more creative.'

117
Normal Again

US Transmission Date: 12 March 2002
UK Transmission Date: 25 April 2002

Writer: Diego Gutiérrez
Director: Rick Rosenthal
Cast: Michael Warren (Doctor), Sarah Scivier (Nurse),
Rodney Charles (Orderly), April Dion (Kissing Girl)

As an apparent result of the *troika*'s latest attempts to mess with Buffy's mind, she suffers horrifying hallucinations, imagining herself to be a mental patient in a Los Angeles hospital watched over by distraught parents and puzzled doctors. Sunnydale has been a figment of her psychotic imagination. But now, seemingly, the walls are crumbling, the villains have become more mundane, the friends she has depended upon are less reliable. It's not *fun* anymore.

Dreaming (As Blondie Once Said) is Free: Either in reality or a demon-induced hallucination (it's up to the viewer to choose, seemingly, since the episode ends without definitive resolution), Buffy has been an inmate at the hospital for six years, the victim of an undifferentiated type of schizophrenia. The doctor tells Joyce and Hank that Buffy's delusions are multi-layered. She believes that she's some kind of superhero, the Slayer. But this is only one level. She's also created an intricate latticework to support her primary delusion. In her mind, she's the central figure in a fantastic world surrounded with friends, some with their own superpowers. Together they face grand overblown conflicts against an assortment of monsters both imaginary and rooted in myth. Every time the doctors think they're getting through to her, yet more fanciful enemies and allies magically appear. Like Dawn – a literal key – that Buffy inserted into her delusion, actually rewriting the entire history of it to accommodate her need for a familial bond. But this pressing of the cosmic reset button, of course, created inconsistencies. Buffy starts to ask *obvious* questions. Why, exactly, *does* she sleep with a vampire that she hates? And what's with Dawn – a ball of energy created by monks to fight a god?

The doctor convinces Buffy that the only way for her to get out of her delusion is to kill the things that are keeping her in it: Dawn and her friends. Buffy tries, and is tempted by the offer of being an only child again, having her mother (and father) back in her life, and not having the responsibilities of being the Slayer. But, ultimately, she decides that Sunnydale is, for better or worse, *her* reality.

Dudes and Babes: Willow nervously practises asking Tara if she'd like to meet for 'coffee, food, kisses and gay-love,' but just as she's about to ask for real, she spots Tara in the university corridor kissing another girl (see **118**, 'Entropy'). Xander says that Anya's suitcase is gone and that there's a closed sign on the Magic Box, which chills him to the bone. She left a couple of days ago, Willow confirms. Xander still loves Anya (see **118**, 'Entropy'). He knows that he's a better person with her in his life, but things got too complicated with the wedding (see **116**, 'Hell's Bells').

Mom's Apple Pie: Buffy angrily tells Dawn that she must try harder with her grades, and to stop the stealing thing (see **114**, 'Older and Far Away').

Denial, Thy Name is Buffy: Buffy tells Dawn that, in her hallucination, their parents were together, like they were before Sunnydale. She wonders why it is that Dawn's taller than her despite Buffy being older. Drifting back and forth between realities, Joyce asks Buffy to say out loud that she doesn't have a sister. Back in Sunnydale, hearing this, Dawn is upset: 'It's your *ideal* reality. And I'm not even a part of it.'

Buffy tells Willow that even before the demon injured her and induced the hallucinations, she was detached. 'Every day I try to snap out of it. Figure out why I'm like that.' She confesses that when she saw her first vampires (presumably 1996, see **33**, 'Becoming' Part 1) she told her parents and they freaked out. They thought there was something seriously wrong with Buffy and sent her to a clinic. She was only there for a couple of weeks, and, eventually, her parents simply forgot about the incident.

'I hope you don't think this antidote's gonna rid you of that nasty martyrdom,' Spike tells her, suggesting that Buffy is addicted to the misery. He alleges this is why she won't tell her friends about him. She might be happy if she did. They would either understand and try to help her, or ostracise her. Either way she'd be better off than she is now.

Denial, Thy Name is Spike: Spike hadn't heard about the wedding debacle. He notes 'some people can't see a good thing when they've got it,' which seems to be as much about Buffy breaking up with him as about Xander and Anya. Having agreed to help Xander track the demon with the unpronounceable name (Glarghk Guhl Kashmahnik) to obtain the antidote for Buffy, Spike says that if everything in their lives really is a product of Buffy's twisted brain it might explain a few things. Like the chip in his head, making him soft and turning him into 'her soddin' sex-slave'.

Denial, Thy Name is Xander: He clearly *hears* Spike's 'sex-slave' line (he alludes to it later when talking to Buffy). But he convinces himself that it's part of Spike's obsession with her, and not real – despite the evidence of his own eyes in **111**, 'Gone'.

It's a Designer Label!: We see Buffy's first two woolly hats of the season. Also, Willow's red blouse and Buffy's suede jacket.

References: Allusions to *Taxi Driver* and *Blue Velvet* ('you lookin' for me?'), *Julius Caesar* ('friends, Romans'), *Supergirl* and *One Flew Over the Cuckoo's Nest*. The music is, in places, highly reminiscent of Bernard Herrmann's celebrated score for *Psycho*.

Geek-Speak: *Ocean's Eleven* ('I still say we're gonna need at least eight other men to pull this off,' notes Andrew. 'I never should have let you see that movie,' replies Warren). Jonathan mentions Jack Torrance, the hero of Stephen King's *The Shining* (as played by Jack Nicholson in Stanley Kubrick's film adaptation) and the DC superhero comic *Legion of Doom*. Warren says Andrew's demon has the Slayer 'tripping like a Ken Russell film festival.' Also, *The Hitch-Hiker's Guide to the Galaxy* ('don't panic').

Bitch!: Warren, to Jonathan: 'Midgetor, get back to the monitors.'

Xander: 'Just run along.' Spike: 'I guess you know all about that, don't you? The king of the big exit.'

West Hollywood: Xander calls Spike a 'pathetic poof'.

Awesome!: Jonathan's increasing paranoia that Warren and Andrew are plotting against him (completely correct as it turns out). Spike and Xander's testosterone-fest in the graveyard. Buffy making her decision and saying goodbye to her mother for the last time.

'You May Remember Me From Such Films and TV Series As . . .': The great Kristine Sutherland was Matt Frewer's wife in *Honey I Shrunk the Kids* and appeared in *Legal*

Eagles, *California Dreams*, *Remington Steele* and *Providence*. Dean Butler is best known as Almanzo in *Little House on the Prairie* and was in *The Final Goal*. Michael Warren was Bobby Hill in *Hill Street Blues* and appeared in *Cleopatra Jones*, *S.W.A.T.*, *Cold Steel*, *A Passion to Kill* and *Buffalo Soldiers*.

Don't Give Up The Day Job: Rick Rosenthal directed *Halloween: Resurrection*, *Roar*, *Witchblade*, *Nasty Boys* and *American Dreamer* and, as an actor, worked on *Better Off Dead*, *Video Vixens* and *Johnny Dangerously*. Joss Whedon's former assistant, Diego Gutiérrez has also written for *Dawson's Creek*.

The Drugs Don't Work: Lorraine, Buffy's supervisor (see 112, 'Doublemeat Palace') suggests that if she didn't know better she'd swear Buffy was on drugs.

Valley-Speak: Warren: 'It's just stuff, big man. You'll be in the know just as soon as you stop being all freakazoid.'

Logic, Let Me Introduce You to This Window: Why doesn't Tara knock before she enters the basement? Spike, seemingly, leaves the house in the middle of the day. It seems strange that Buffy in the alternate reality has perfectly cut and streaked hair, even though she has been in an asylum for six years. If Joyce is alive in an alternate reality, why would Buffy kill her off in her fantasy world? That's *very* Freudian. Perhaps Spike's right and she does just enjoy misery and pain. Despite all the research she does on the demon, Willow never tells Buffy exactly what the demon's poison is supposed to do. A doctor expecting a delusional schizophrenic patient to will herself back into reality isn't standard medical practice or anything remotely like it, although that inaccurate view of schizophrenia might be further evidence that the sanatorium is the fantasy since Buffy isn't a psychiatry expert. Alternatively, the explanation that the entire series has been the fevered imaginings of a teenage girl might help to explain a few things, like Angel's dreadful Irish accent (presumably Buffy's never heard a real one to base it on).

Quote/Unquote: Xander: 'You think this isn't real just because of all the vampires and demons and ex-vengeance demons and the sister that used to be a big ball of universe-destroying energy?'

Joyce: 'I know the world feels like a hard place sometimes, but you've got people who love you.'

Notes: 'All the people you created in Sunnydale. They're not as comforting as they were ... You used to create grand villains. Now what is it? Not gods or monsters. Just three pathetic little men.' An unexpected lurch into existentialism, 'Normal Again' plays an interesting game with the audience, casting a weary eye on recent critical analysis. A risky move. This isn't just knocking down the fourth wall and winking (the series did *that* in **47**, 'The Zeppo' three years previously), rather it appears to be full-blown artistic comment. 'Normal Again' is clever and radical and imaginative, can't say that often enough. With a Byzantine complexity, its defiance of traditional dramatic signposts is to be applauded. The episode is really funny in places and also *very* scary – in the way that padded cells are. A primal fear for many people is that madness is simply one bad day away. For all these reasons, Diego Gutiérrez's debut should have been the season's crowning jewel. Sadly, 'Normal Again' is also, whether consciously or by coincidence, a conceptual parallelogram to the *Star Trek: Deep Space Nine* episode 'Far Beyond the Stars'. And this unoriginality renders the episode's climax a crushing disappointment. How tragic that, seemingly, we've all spent our lives watching too much TV.

- According to Jonathan it has been 'weeks' since the events of **113**, 'Dead Things'. When Buffy looks at the photograph of herself as a little girl, it's Alexandra Lee, who portrayed young Buffy in **99**, 'The Weight Of The World'. In one asylum scene, the doctor tells Buffy that she had a 'momentary awakening' during the summer and it was her friends who pulled her back into the delusion, a reference to Buffy's death and resurrection (see **100**, 'The Gift'; **101**, 'Bargaining' Part 1). Dawn's friend Janice is mentioned again (see **106**, 'All the Way'). The musical wind instrument Andrew uses to summon the demon is a didgeridoo (a deep-toned native Australian instrument also, briefly, seen in **105**, 'Life Serial').

Critique: 'The cleverness here lies in how a potentially disastrous dislocation is dovetailed into Buffy's emotional state,' noted the doyen of British *Buffy* critics, Mark Wyman. 'Weak points are sparse. Mostly, it's another sterling example of advancing core character arcs within the most outlandish of stories.'

Did You Know?: 'We get along really well,' Tom Lenk told Matt Springer about the *troika*'s off-screen activities. 'We watch Eddie Izzard videos in Adam's trailer. We're friends outside of work, too. I think our senses of humor all click. The three of us have our own geeky interests, but they're different from the sci-fi stuff. We're theater geeks. I have to admit that I do have a couple *Star Wars* T-shirts from when I was in high school. And I have an autographed picture of Carrie Fisher.'

Cast and Crew Comments: In *Steppin' Out*, Amber Benson talked about a glamour shoot she was about to undertake and noted that 'I'm a big prude and I don't want to wear anything revealing, but you need to do it [to get ahead in Hollywood] and that's sad. And what's sicker is that Hollywood encourages it. "Oh, she was on the cover of *Maxim*! So if she's in my movie, people will come see it!"' Despite her reservations, however, Amber concedes 'If they want me to do something I'm not comfortable with, then I'm going to say "Screw you". I'm not a size 0. I'm a 6 or even an 8 on a bad day. You don't want to see me in a thong.'

Joss Whedon's Comments: Concerning his now-legendary running battle with Donald Sutherland on the set of the *Buffy* movie, Joss told Tasha Robinson: '[Sutherland] was just a prick. People always make fun of Rutger Hauer. Even though he looked kind of goofy in the movie, I have to give him credit, because he was *there*. He was into it.

Whereas Donald would rewrite all his dialogue, and the director would let him. He was incredibly rude to everyone around him. Some people liked him in the movie because he's Donald Sutherland. He's a great actor. He could read the phone book and I'd be interested. But he acts well enough that you don't notice, with his little ideas about what his character should do, that he was actually destroying the movie more than Rutger was.' On the other hand Joss has nothing but kind words for another co-star of the film, Paul Reubens: 'He is a god that walks among us. He's one of the sweetest, most professional and delightful people I've ever worked with. He was my beacon of hope in that whole experience. He was such a good guy, and *so* got it. Paul was a delight to be around.'

118
Entropy

US Transmission Date: 30 April 2002
UK Transmission Date: 2 May 2002

Writer: Drew Z Greenberg
Director: James A Contner
Cast: Edie Caggiano (Mother)

Having become a vengeance-demon again, Anya attempts to curse Xander for all the pain that he caused her. Unable to do this herself, she attempts to enlist the help of some old friends. But it doesn't work out as expected. The Scooby Gang discover that the *troika* have been watching their every move with hidden cameras. And what's currently being captured on video proves to be devastating for everyone.

Dudes and Babes: Tara confirms that the girl Willow saw her kissing in **117**, 'Normal Again' was just a friend. During their conversation with Anya, Tara says that neither she nor Willow hate men; 'We're more centred around the girl-on-girl action,' adds Willow helpfully.

The first sign of Andrew's emerging confused sexuality occurs when the *troika* tune into Spike and Anya copulating. 'He is *so* cool,' says an impressed Andrew, before hurriedly adding, 'The girl's hot too.'

A Little Learning is a Dangerous Thing: Spike lies, cheats, steal and manipulates, Buffy notes, but she agrees with him that he doesn't hurt her. He tells her that his feelings for her are real and Buffy acknowledges this. But, she says, they aren't feelings *she* shares and that he must move on for both their sakes. However, it's noticeable that, after he has sex with Anya, Buffy looks at him sourly and suggests that it, seemingly, didn't take Spike very long to move on.

Mom's Apple Pie: Trying desperately to make up for her attempts to murder Dawn in the last episode, Buffy suggests all sorts of stuff they can do together (hiring a movie, having pizza). Not, she stresses, that this is guilt; she just wants to spend some time with her sister. But then, she realises: 'I'm cramping your teenage style. I'm the embarrassing mom who tries too hard. When did this happen?' Dawn suggests that, rather than Buffy hanging out with Dawn, they could patrol together. Buffy is less than impressed with this idea saying she works very hard to keep Dawn away from that side of her life. However, as Dawn rightly points out this would be a perfectly reasonable argument, if Buffy was protecting the world from tax audits. But, with her sister being the Slayer, dangerous things that want to kill Dawn seem to find her anyway.

Denial, Thy Name is Buffy: When Spike again threatens to reveal his relationship with Buffy to the Scooby Gang if she doesn't, Buffy notes that she tried to kill her friends last week (see **117**, 'Normal Again') and they still don't hate her. So, she believes, they'd also be able to deal with the fact she's been sleeping with Spike. She's very wrong, as Xander proves at the climax of the episode (see **Denial, Thy Names Are Anya and Xander**).

Denial, Thy Names Are Anya and Xander: Xander is horrified that Anya would go out and have sex with the first person she could find, dead or alive. Anya suggests that Xander is in no position to be judging her. The mature solution, she argues, would be for him to avoid spending his life telling jokes in the hope that no one will notice that he is scared and insecure. His reaction to finding out Buffy and Spike were intimate is angry denial: 'I don't wanna know *any* of this.'

The Confessions Start at Home Time: Dawn has returned all of the stolen goods that she still had to various stores, and she's paying for the rest. Seemingly, she's been banned from entering these stores. She tells Buffy that she can't go into one as she shoplifted three pairs of earrings, a coin purse and a toothbrush. The latter item amuses Buffy: 'As rebellious teenagers go, you're kinda square.' Dawn offers to work off her debt to Anya at the newly reopened Magic Box.

It's a Designer Label!: Lots of red clothes dominate this episode, which may be an unconscious comment on the state of mind of the characters. Willow's deep red Chippewa Guy, New York sweatshirt, Anya's tight scarlet top, matching skirt and leather boots. Also, Spike's tasty black shirt, Andrew's hilariously 'mommy's-boy' jumper and Buffy's flower-embroidered jeans.

References: 'Things fall apart,' says Tara, quoting *The Second Coming* by Irish existentialist poet WB Yeats (1865–1939). Xander tells Anya 'you had to do it cos he was *there*. Like Mount Everest,' paraphrasing a quote attributed to George Leigh Mallory (1886–1924) before his fatal expedition to the Himalayas. Also, International House of Pancakes, The Who's 'Pinball Wizard' ('he'd have to be deaf, dumb and blind not to'), *Friends* ('how *you* doin'?'), *Diamonds Are Forever* (the mini bike chase sequence) and a possible allusion to The Smiths' 'I Don't Owe You Anything'.

Geek-Speak: *Star Wars* (Warren calls Jonathan 'Padawan', a term for a trainee Jedi) and *Indiana Jones and the Temple of Doom* (Short Round). Andrew says Jonathan has the same look on his face as he did 'that time I highlighted in his *Babylon 5* novels'.

Bitch!: When Tara and Willow ask Anya if there's anything they can do to help: 'There is an eensy something ... You're lesbians, so the hating of men will come in handy. Let's talk about Xander ...'

Spike says that he can't stand any of the Scoobies except Anya, because she speaks her mind. He respects forthright women, he says, citing Drusilla as an example. 'Didn't have a single buggering clue about what was going on in front of her, but she was straight about it.'

Halfrek tells Anya about a man she recently cursed who hadn't paid any child support in eleven years. So now, every time he picks up a piece of paper that isn't a cheque for the child, he gets a paper cut.

Awesome!: Anya incompetently trying to get Tara, Willow, Dawn and Buffy to wish all manner of horrors upon Xander only to find that, ultimately, that isn't what she really wants. Also, Anya needlessly complicating her options. Spike's an ideal candidate, but he's not a woman, so all she had to do is get someone to wish Spike *were* a woman, and then ... As Hallie notes, Anya still has a 'female power, Take Back the Night-thing' about vengeance which is very sweet. But she also states that men have need of vengeance too. Willow averting Dawn's eyes from her computer screen as she focuses on Spike and Anya having sex. Spike's denial that he has a 'sexy dance'. And, the moment when Spike says: 'You know, I wish ...' and Anya, quietly, replies: 'Don't.'

You May Remember Me From Such Films As ...': Edie Caggiano played Tina in *The Brothers Grim*.

Cigarettes and Alcohol: Xander is drinking and feeling sorry for himself as the episode opens. Later, Anya and Spike get drunk on Giles's Jack Daniel's at the Magic Box.

Sex and Drugs and Rock'n'Roll: Hurt by their rejections (by Xander and Buffy), Anya and Spike get bladdered at the Magic Box and talk about their respective lovers. How weak, uptight and repressed they both are – it's no wonder they couldn't deal with the likes of us, Spike notes. They should, after all, have been dead hundreds of years ago. Then they seek mutual solace in some meaningless sex.

Logic, Let Me Introduce You to This Window: Anya's haircut varies from scene to scene. What, exactly *is* the disc that the vampires have that the *troika* are so desperate to acquire? It's given huge focus early in the episode, then never mentioned again. Also, the disc that Warren recovers in the opening scene, is a completely different colour to the one Jonathan is working on later. Dawn tells Anya that, since the events of **114**, 'Older, and Far Away', she never uses the word 'wish', spelling it out to be on the safe side. Yet, she uses it in the very next sentence.

I Just *Love* Your Accent: Spike calls Xander a ponce and a wanker.

Cruelty to Animals: Dawn, jokingly, claims she stole goldfish by hiding them in her pockets. She dislikes pet shops as they keep animals in cages and people poke them.

Quote/Unquote: Anya: 'I wish your intestines were tied in knots and ripped apart inside your lousy gut.' Xander: 'They are.' Anya: 'Really? Does it hurt?'

Tara: 'Trust has to build again . . . You have to learn if you're even the same people you were . . . It's a long and important process. Can we just skip it? Can you be kissing me now?'

Notes: 'You could try getting someone to make the wish for you.' An inevitable universal constant, entropy is the thermodynamic quantity that measures disorder and, as a concept, can be seen as a metaphor for a long-running TV series reaching the point where it all comes to pieces. Except in the case of 'Entropy', the episode of *Buffy*, which is a taut and beautiful thing. Never cynical in its targets or execution, 'Entropy' understands that love is a double-edged sword, and that pain is an equal part of the game to all the good stuff. Anybody who has been involved in a relationship that has stalled, or died, will find themselves nodding their heads in sympathy at this episode's depiction of the bewilderment of rejection and the remorse that follows. A bittersweet essay on an inexplicable part of human frailty, 'Entropy' is a clear light shined on an awful part of everyone's life. Cherish it.

This isn't the first time Spike and Anya have comforted each other due to their mutual frustrations. In **74**, 'Where the Wild Things Are', they talked about getting revenge on Drusilla and Xander. Subsequently Anya took Spike as her date to the college party to make Xander jealous. Anya says she hasn't been scorned by a man in a thousand years (the last would have been Olaf, see **89**, 'Triangle'). Willow tells Tara about some of the events of **112**, 'Doublemeat Palace' (asked what the monster in the wig lady's head looked like, she notes: 'let's put it this way, if I wasn't gay before . . .'), **111**, 'Gone' and **115**, 'As You Were'. Tara is back living in the dorms at UC Sunnydale. When Anya suggests that men have been riding roughshod over Buffy for years, Buffy says there have only been four of them. Then, realising she's including Spike, she quickly amends it to three (Angel, Parker and Riley).

Soundtrack: 'Sao Paulo Rain' by Tom McRae accompanies Xander's moody introspection. The beautiful 'That Kind of Love' by Alison Krauss is heard at the end of the episode.

Did You Know?: Does Danny Strong get any of the nerd references that the *troika* deal in? 'Where they called me "Frodo", a Jane Espenson moment, I asked, "Jane, is this supposed to be Fredo from *The Godfather*?" She's like, "No! *Lord of the Rings*! It's a short reference!"'

Cast and Crew Comments: It may be like filming a mini-movie each week, but for Sarah Michelle Gellar, TV beats the big screen. 'Films still don't afford me the opportunities that *Buffy* does,' she told *Cult Times*. 'Until I'm a little older, I'll never get the opportunities in feature films [that] I can do every week on the show.'

Joss Whedon's Comments: While Joss himself established the overall look of Sunnydale, he is quick to credit production designer Carey Meyer and set decorator David Koneff. 'These guys are extremely talented,' he told Bob Blakey. 'They created this world. They've been to all the warehouses. They'll find furniture you couldn't conceive of. Sometimes I have to pull them back because they want to have too much fun.'

119
Seeing Red

US Transmission Date: 7 May 2002
UK Transmission Date: 9 May 2002

Writer: Steven S DeKnight
Director: Michael Gershman
Cast: Amy Hathaway (Blonde Woman),
Nichole Hiltz (Beautiful Woman), Garrett Brawith (Frank),
Tim Hager (Administrator), Stefan Marks (Guard #1),
Christopher James (Guard #2), Kate Orsini (Girl at Bronze)

The *troika* initiate their plan to steal a pair of mystical orbs which render the wearer invulnerable. A battle between Buffy and Warren goes badly for the Slayer until Jonathan reveals the secret of Warren's power. Buffy manages to defeat Warren but he escapes to take a terrible revenge on the Slayer and her friends.

No Fat Chicks: The blonde in the bar is seeking vengeance on her boyfriend, Carl, who apparently slept with her 'fat ugly sister'. Anya asks if he likes them fleshy. She bets the woman wishes Carl would bloat up a couple of thousand pounds and pop like a 'meat zeppelin'.

Dudes and Babes: Willow guesses that Buffy and Spike have been involved and Tara confirms this. Willow asks how Buffy could hide something like that from her best friend. 'I think she was afraid of the look you'd get on your face. Kinda like the one you're wearing now,' suggests Tara.

Andrew's repressed love for Warren finally bubbles to the surface, first through innuendo ('can't wait to get my hands on his orbs') then, when he and Jonathan are arrested, when he finally realises that Warren has been using him. 'He promised we'd be together. He never really loved ... hanging out.'

Abuse Sucks!: Warren confronts Frank who, along with his jock buddies, used to make Warren's life a misery in gym class ('that thing with the underwear? I thought I'd never stop crying'), and takes his revenge in a suitably violent way.

A Little Learning is a Dangerous Thing: Spike's no longer part of the team, Buffy tells Dawn. Later, Dawn asks Spike if he really loves Buffy and he is unable to answer. That, in itself, tells Dawn everything she needs to know. Forcing his way into Buffy's bathroom, Spike apologises for hurting her. He tells Buffy he's tried everything to rid himself of these feelings and that he wishes she had let Xander kill him. Then he tries to force himself on her. Suitably horrified at what he's done, he realises he's lost every chance he ever had of getting Buffy to like him.

After a chance remark by Clem gives him an idea, he leaves Sunnydale on a motorbike vowing to return a changed vampire.

Denial, Thy Name Isn't Xander: The lone sane voice left in Sunnydale, Xander tells Buffy that he understands why Anya slept with Spike (see **118**, 'Entropy'), but not why Buffy herself did. Buffy suggests that Xander has no idea how hard it has been for her since she was resurrected. 'You could have *told* me,' suggests Xander, with the unspoken implication that, once upon a time, she *would* have. Buffy suggests that Xander's decision-making skills haven't exactly been world class recently. I've made mistakes, Xander confesses, 'but last time I checked, slaughtering half of Europe wasn't one of them'.

The Conspiracy Starts at Home Time: Xander enters into the soul-vs-chip debate concerning Spike (see **92**, 'Crush').

It's a Designer Label!: Willow's nightshirt. Buffy's cool leather jacket. Dawn's fluffy ice-blue sweater. Warren's 'Ace of Spades' T-shirt. Spike's excellent black sweatshirt.

References: *The Fall and Rise of Reginald Perrin* ('great', 'super'), *High Society* ('true love'), Frank Sinatra's 'Love and Marriage', *Psycho* (the shower scene), *Thunderball* (the jet-pack), Sherlock Holmes, *The Wizard of Oz* (allusions to flying monkeys), *HR Pufnstuff*, illusionists Siegfried and Roy (see **55**, 'Graduation Day' Part 1), Mahatma Gandhi (see **35**, 'Anne'), Bob Dylan's 'Blowin' in the Wind', The Beatles' 'She Loves You', Charles Atlas, *Bring It On*, *Mighty Mouse*, *Knight Rider*, Jiminy Cricket, *The Burns and Allen Show* ('say goodnight, bitch'), Elton John's 'Rocket Man' and *Empire of the Ants*.

Geek-Speak: The *troika*'s buzzsaw-trap for Buffy is outrageously ripped off from *Indiana Jones and the Last Crusade*. They have a (semi-naked) Xena action figure in their lair. *Star Trek: The Next Generation* (Andrew tells Jonathan that Warren is 'Picard. You're Deanna Troi. Get used to the feeling, Betazoid'). Among the items Buffy recovers from the *troika* lair are some love poems written in Klingon. Xander recognises them.

Bitch!: Blonde Woman: 'He said he loved me.' Anya: 'Gee, then I guess he must have meant it, cos guys never say anything they don't really mean.'

Andrew, to the now-dead Nezzla demon: 'You want a piece of this? Huh? Not so tough now, are you?'

Awesome!: The opening post-sexual-indulgence shot of Willow and Tara. Buffy's reaction to Warren's jet-pack ('oh, come *on*!'). Dawn's joyous little giggle as she realises Tara and Willow are back together. Anya getting distracted from her vengeance work by her own problems. Dawn confronting Spike. Jonathan giving Buffy the information with which to beat Warren. Xander and Buffy's touching reconciliation.

Surprise!: Tara's death (unless you'd been reading certain Internet spoiler pages).

'You May Remember Me From Such Films and TV Series As . . .': Amy Hathaway played Shelby in *My Two Dads* and Tanya in *Joyride*, and appeared in *In God's Hands*, *Last Exit to Earth* and *The Wonder Years*. Nichole Hiltz was in *Scorched* and *Shallow Hal*. Garrett Brawith appeared in *Black Hole* and *The Invisible Man*. Christopher James was in *Thursday the 12th*. Stefan Marks appeared in *The Sky is Falling*.

Don't Give Up The Day Job: Lead Person Keith Cuba wrote *The Dark Ride* and also worked on *Tremors 2: Aftershock* and *Dangerous Indiscretion*.

Valley-Speak: Dawn: 'I'm totally not here.'
    Andrew: 'Dude, unholy hairgel.'

Cigarettes and Alcohol: Spike drinks vodka and blood in his crypt when Dawn comes to see him. Xander's got several bottles and cans of beer on the go when Buffy calls. He thinks there might be another one in the fridge. Andrew's drinking something with lots of fruit in it at the Bronze while Anya shares a Martini with the blonde girl.

The Magic Bullet: When Warren fires the shots they all appear to go reasonably horizontally. If Tara and Willow are on the first floor, the shot that kills Tara would, therefore, have had to be at more of an angle for the bullet to have struck her. When Tara is shot, she's facing away from the window. After she sees the blood on Willow's shirt, and falls there is clearly an exit wound. Wouldn't the bullet, therefore, have also hit Willow who was standing directly in front of her?

Logic, Let Me Introduce You to This Window: When Warren is trying to overturn the armoured car, the sun has not fully set. But when the camera cuts back to Jonathan and Andrew, it's completely dark. Other shots in this sequence fluctuate between twilight and night-time. Also, two men carrying brushes appear in the background in several shots when Buffy is fighting Warren but in others they're nowhere to be seen. When Warren activates his jet-pack, two long poles sticking out of the back are clearly visible. How did Warren and Andrew hide their jet-packs from Jonathan? Wouldn't he notice something bulkier than usual under their jackets? They're not exactly unobtrusive. How did Warren's jet-pack survive the vicious pummelling that Buffy gave him without something malfunctioning, or short-circuiting? Both Xander and Willow barge into Buffy's bathroom unannounced – we know it's an open house at Revello Drive, but that's *ridiculous*. When Spike and Buffy are in the bathroom, the reflection of Spike's foot can be seen in the mirror. There's now a Verizon pay phone outside the Magic Box that's never been seen previously.

I Just *Love* Your Accent: Spike refers to the *troika* as wankers.

Quote/Unquote: Spike: 'Trust is for old marrieds, Buffy. Great love is wild and passionate and dangerous. It burns and consumes.' Buffy: 'Until there's nothing left. That kind of love doesn't last.'
    Warren: 'You know who I am?' Buffy: 'You're a murderer.' Warren: 'That too. But more to the point, I'm the guy that beat you.'

Notes: 'Tara? Come, on baby. Get up.' At the risk of sounding like a broken record, definitive evidence that someone who is bullied and emotionally abused in childhood will, as a consequence, turn into a megalomaniac rapist is rather compelling by its absence. And, that's just Spike: wait till you see what it's supposed to have done to Warren. 'Seeing Red' is the, literal, living end of an awkward, at times unbearably close-to-home plotline that's weaved its way through this season. In tying several seemingly frayed loose ends, DeKnight does a remarkably mature job of changing the series' focus. But, there's something darkly unsatisfying about the 'little men, and

you *know* you are' riff that marbles this episode. 'Seeing
Red' is clever, funny and dangerous, and, in its shocking
final scene, as emotionally spot-on as *Buffy* has ever been.
It's just not very likeable, that's all.

Dawn is sleeping over at Janice's yet again (see **106**, 'All
the Way' and **113**, 'Dead Things'). Xander suggests he's
part-fish (see **32**, 'Go Fish'). Buffy, Clem notes, is a sweet
girl, but she has issues. Clem has a cousin who once got
resurrected by a kooky shaman.

Part of this episode was filmed at Six Flags Magic
Mountain theme park in Valencia, 35 miles north of Los
Angeles. Shooting took place on Thursday 28 February,
and Friday 1 March, beginning late in the afternoon on
both days, with the second day of filming lasting until the
early hours of Saturday morning. The Cyclone Bay section
of the park featured as the backdrop. For the first, and
presumably last, time Amber Benson is credited in the
series' opening titles. The portrait photo of Dawn seen in
this episode is one of the official publicity shots from
season five.

Soundtrack: 'The Leaves' by Daryl Ann, 'Stranded' by
Alien Ant Farm and 'Displaced' by Azure Ray.

Critique: 'Reacting to this accomplished, hugely symbolic
drama based on Warren's lone gunmen actions, or the
horrific bathroom scene, would misrepresent the episode,'
wrote Mark Wyman in *TV Zone*. 'There are pure comedy
moments, introspection, action, horror. Uneasy viewing,
but unforgettable.'

Did You Know?: According to a report in the *Sun* in early
2002, audiences for the *Scooby Doo* movie were likely to
see both more and less of Sarah Michelle Gellar than they
might have expected. A scene in the movie, it stated,
involved Daphne baring her bottom. However, fans would
be disappointed to learn that a body double was used for
the scene as Sarah is said to be 'embarrassed by her bum'.
When the movie premiered, of course, it contained no such
scene or anything even remotely like it.

Jane Espenson's Comments: 'I love Spike,' Jane notes. 'I was very worried about the attempted rape because that's not something you play around with. It's very hard to come back from. I think we have to be very careful that we are not saying anything about humans. When we say that Spike looked into his soul, at that moment, and saw the demon in him, that's what made him want to go get a soul.'

Marti Noxon's Comments: What does Marti think about the fans who still want Buffy and Angel to get together? 'They call themselves shippers,' she told an online interview. 'These are the people who still have their high school sweetheart's picture in a frame on the wall. They can't seem to let things go. I think Buffy and Angel's relationship was idealised. It was like a fairy tale, in the way young girls dream about – to have this perfect, unattainable man. But you have to throw curve balls. We gave Buffy and Angel a barrier they couldn't surmount. This locks it into a romantic ideal, because they never fought over who has to do the laundry. They were stuck in the first beautifully passionate stage of love, and that's where it will be forever.' Conversely, some fans want Buffy and Spike together. Does that surprise her? 'Sometimes, things don't go the way we intend. It seemed very obvious to us that the Buffy-Spike relationship couldn't work in the long run, so now we need to reiterate why. We need to show people the difference between loving someone who is good to be around and loving someone who is good.'

Joss Whedon's Comments: Within hours of this episode's broadcast, Joss appeared on the *BtVS Posting Board* to tell fans: 'I killed Tara . . . because stories, as I have often said, are not about what we *want*. I knew some people would be angry with me for destroying the only gay couple on the show, but the idea that I *couldn't* kill Tara because she was gay is as offensive to me as the idea that I *did* kill her *because* she was gay. Willow's story was not about being gay. It was about weakness, addiction, loss . . . the way life hits you in the gut right when you think you're back on your feet.'

120
Villains

US Transmission Date: 14 May 2002
UK Transmission Date: 16 May 2002

Writer: Marti Noxon
Director: David Solomon
Cast: Tim Hodgin (Coroner), Michael Matthys (Paramedic), Julie
Hermelin (Clerk), Alan Henry Brown (Demon Bartender), Mueen J
Ahmad (Doctor), Jane Cho (Nurse #1), Meredith Cross (Nurse #2),
David Adefeso (Paramedic #2), Jeffrey Nicholas-Brown (Vampire),
Neson Frederick (Villager)

While the paramedics work on Buffy, Willow desperately
tries a spell to return Tara to life. She is unsuccessful and
goes to the Magic Box, drawing dark power from the
books. After saving Buffy by removing the bullet from her
shoulder, Willow heads off to find Warren. When he
discovers that Buffy is not dead, Warren seeks Rack's help
against the Slayer but he is informed that Willow's wrath
is a more immediate concern. Willow finds Warren and
unleashes her full awesome power on him, torturing him
with the ghost of Katrina and eventually ripping the skin
from his body. 'One down . . .'

Dudes and Babes: Spike now appears to be in Africa,
striding through the native village like he owns the place.
He enters a forbidden cave where he seeks a demon who
knows about the Slayer. The demon asks if Spike wishes to
return to his former self. 'Look what she's reduced you to,'
it notes. 'You were a legendary dark warrior and you let
yourself be castrated. And you have the audacity to crawl
in here and demand restoration?' Spike is told that he will
be unable to endure the trials required to grant this
request. 'Do your worst,' Spike snarls. 'But when I win, I
want what I came here for. Bitch is gonna see a change.'

A Little Learning is a Dangerous Thing: Xander and Buffy
finally learn that Anya has regained her vengeance-demon
powers.

Mom's Apple Pie: Despite Xander's protestations, Buffy is prepared to let Dawn stay with Spike while the Scoobies search for Willow. But, when they get to Spike's crypt they find him gone and Clem crypt-sitting while his friend is out of town.

Denial, Thy Name is Willow: In one of the best scenes of the season, Buffy, Xander and Dawn discuss the rights and wrongs of what Willow wishes to do. Xander suggests that Warren is as bad as any vampire Buffy has destroyed, but being the Slayer doesn't give Buffy a licence to kill, she notes. More importantly, Warren is human and the human world has its own rules for dealing with such people. Xander suggests that those rules don't seem to work very well. Buffy thinks they do sometimes, but it's impossible to control the universe. If they could, they would be able to bring Tara back. And Joyce, Dawn adds, sadly. According to Buffy, there are limits to what can be done, and there should be. Willow, seemingly, doesn't want to believe it.

The Psychology Starts at Home Time: Katrina asks how Warren could say he loved her and then kill her. Because you *deserved* it, Warren replies. Because you *liked* it, Willow dares to suggest. She concludes that Warren never felt like he had any power with women until he killed Katrina; now he gets off on it. Hence his attack on Buffy.

It's a Designer Label!: Highlight of the episode – Anya's hilarious spotty pants.

References: Country Time Lemonade (a staple of Americana and the innocence of summer), *Puppet Master* (a series by Full Moon about puppets who come to life), *The Wedding Planner*, *Dragnet*, gritty prison drama *Oz* and *The Andy Griffiths Show* ('this isn't *Oz*, it's Mayberry,' see **37**, 'Faith, Hope and Trick'). Also allusions to French philosopher, physician and (alleged) seer Michel Nostradamus (1503–66), goth-punk band The Damned, a paraphrase of Psalms 8:2 ('out of the mouths of babes'), *Licence to Kill* and *Monty Python's Flying Circus* ('you take the comfy chair'). Willow giving Warren a vision of the dead Katrina owes a debt to Dostoyevsky's *Crime and Punishment*.

Geek-Speak: Andrew is a fan of Matthew Broderick (*War Games, Godzilla, Inspector Gadget, Glory, Election*), in particular his teen comedy *Ferris Bueller's Day Off*. He's less enthusiastic about Broderick's more recent work ('Broadway-Matthew, I find him cold'). Andrew wonders if the police will let his aunt bring him his Discman in jail.

Bitch!: Rack: 'You're new.' Warren: 'I come bearing dead presidents. Think we can skip the small talk?'

'You're *My* Little Puppy Now': Jonathan nervously notes that a guy in the next cell has been looking at him and, he believes, wants to make Jonathan his butt monkey. 'Don't flatter yourself,' says Andrew who heard him talking to the guard. He's in for parking tickets. Jonathan, nevertheless, has heard that prison changes a man, and that sex-starved inmates prefer 'the small ones, with little hands like their girlfriends ...'

Awesome!: Jonathan sarcastically describing Warren as 'a nice murderer'. Dawn finding Tara's body. And, subsequently, Buffy discovering Dawn sitting in the dark with the body because 'I didn't want her to be alone.' Many of the performances that Michelle Trachtenberg has put in over the last year and a half, are worthy of considerable praise, this included. Willow draining the knowledge from the books, sending her eyes and hair black. Anya making the decision to ignore her demon responsibilities and help Buffy and Xander (and, thus, Willow). And, the closing line.

'You May Remember Me From Such Films and TV Series As ...': Steven W Bailey (Cave Demon) played Cyrus in *Phantasmagoria* and appeared in *Nash Bridges*.

Valley-Speak: Jonathan: 'Oh yeh, that was *rad*.'

Cigarettes and Alcohol: Warren goes into the demon bar and orders a whiskey, straight up, and a round for everyone in the house to celebrate killing the Slayer.

Logic, Let Me Introduce You to This Window: The blood splatters on Willow's neck and blouse and Xander's shirt are different in several shots. Why do the medical staff leave the operating theatre when Willow tells them to without so much as an objection when their patient appears to be flatlining? There's no channel ID on the programme on crocodiles that the vampire in the bar is watching. Willow finds the time to change her clothes after absorbing the black books before setting out to save Buffy and bring down her wrath on Warren. Xander changes his blood-stained shirt while at Buffy's after the discovery of Tara's body. So, where did he get these new clothes from? In the woods, Warren is running with nothing in his hands. Then, suddenly, he has an axe. As Willow chases him creating a psychic path, the cables pulling the trees away from her are visible. It took Warren months to build his first robot (see **93**, 'I Was Made to Love You') and a few weeks to build the second (the Buffybot in **96**, 'Invention'), yet he builds this replica of himself in less than a day. Willow summons Osiris through willpower; in **101**, 'Bargaining' Part 1, she had to use a magical urn. Why doesn't she attempt to get one of the Gora demon eggs for a resurrection spell as Dawn did in **95**, 'Forever'? The process of entry into the body that a bullet takes, which Willow demonstrates while torturing Warren, is the reverse of what happened to Tara – she was shot in the back and the bullet exited from the front. Buffy's gun-wound looks lower in the hospital than where she was initially shot (see **119**, 'Seeing Red'). How did Spike get all the way to a specific location in Africa in the timespan shown, and do so while avoiding direct sunlight (of which, there's quite a bit in Africa)? The bullet that killed Tara, and that we see Willow extract and later put in Warren's chest, seems oddly intact. Dare one suggest, again, *magic* (**119**, 'Seeing Red')? The emergency-room scene with Buffy makes no sense. The doctors are working on her 'left ventricle' but haven't removed her shirt. There's no oxygen mask or sterile covering, and she's seemingly not hooked up to an IV or any medical sensors (although an assistant seems to be reading off a machine giving her heart rate).

Quote/Unquote: Xander: 'I've had blood on my hands all day. Blood from people I love.'

Willow: 'One tiny piece of metal destroys everything . . . It took her light away from me. From the world. The person who should be here is gone. And *waste* like you gets to live.'

Notes: 'The magic's too strong. There's no coming back from it.' What is it about *Buffy* and rad-fem revenge agendas? Is there something contractual that says this subject has to be tackled once per season or it's a betrayal of the Sisterhood? We've both been there and done that (**38**, 'Beauty and the Beasts'). That this episode is *much* better than previous forays into this field, is significant however. 'Villains' is confused, confusing, touching and truly dreadful (in every sense of the word). Often all at the same time. As with some of the best episodes of this season (and all of the worst) it's unbearably intense and, at times, almost unwatchable. There's a viciousness to the points it has to make that matches the bovver-boot nature of the visual presentation. It's like watching somebody being repeatedly punched – is it horribly fascinating, or fascinatingly horrible? The aftermath of Tara's death sends Willow on a mystical bender; a grief-stricken lust for vengeance. Despite this, Buffy, Anya and Xander, still try to stop her. Because she's their friend and what she's doing is *wrong*. And, in that one line, is the reason why 'Villains' works at all. Essentially, it's about trying to do the right thing even if it's not the easy thing. Ultimately, 'Villains' is a little like biting into a Cadbury's Creme Egg and finding no yummy bit in the middle – hollow, but not entirely unpleasurable. There are lots of things that are wrong with this episode, occasionally trite and ham-fisted dialogue not least among them. And much that's shocking. But, there's also hope for redemption, this series' *raison d'être*.

Willow's 'bored now' was the catchphrase of her vampire alter-ego in **43**, 'The Wish' and **50**, 'Doppelgängland'. The destination of the bus the Warrenbot boards is San Diego. The scenes of Xander, Buffy and Willow and the

Warrenbot are rumoured to have been filmed in Joshua Tree National Park east of Los Angeles.

Soundtrack: Aptly, The Misfits' 'Die, Die My Darling' plays in the scene where Warren is in the demon bar.

Critique: While many lesbian critics saw dark and offensive overtones in Tara's death (see **122**, 'Grave'), Jennifer Greenman was more charitable: 'Despite my feelings of anger, betrayal and sadness, I am grateful for almost three years of an honest, beautiful lesbian relationship,' she wrote. 'I respect Whedon for staying true to his own vision even if I don't agree with it . . . Part of me is sad that I can't see this story the way Whedon must have intended it, where all the characters really are treated the same in death and in life.' Contrasting this was a piece by Emily Almond on *scifidimensions.com* entitled 'Lesbians, Where Art Thou?': 'If they're not dead, they're evil. Why are lesbians denied a sane reflection of themselves in today's media?' noted Almond, and concluded: 'I want a full and unconditional promise of compensatory damages for havoc wreaked. I don't want to have invested what I have in this story . . . It's back to the beginning: Bad lesbians. Bad girls.'

This was also the position taken by Hillary Clay who wrote that: 'The fact is that Willow and Tara are the only couple even trying to portray a healthy and loving relationship between two people of the same sex. You can't claim equal treatment when you are talking about the only example of its kind. Anything that happens to Willow and Tara is necessarily excluded from equal treatment because they are the only lesbian couple on television. The only equal treatment that Willow and Tara received was [that of] all of the other lesbians in Hollywood. Dead. Evil.'

Did You Know?: Despite failed attempts to feature Britney Spears in an episode of *Buffy's* fifth season, several sources continue to report that the Princess of Pop is set for a major role. *Sky News* recently claimed that Britney is planning to take the part of a baddie who will face-off against the Slayer. A *Buffy* insider is reported as having claimed: 'This will be an amazing sight. Millions will tune in to see them fighting in their trademark figure-hugging outfits.' Yes, that sounds like *just* the kind of thing someone on the *Buffy* staff *would* say. Not. Although never officially confirmed, Britney was alleged to have had the part of April in 93, 'I Was Made to Love You' written with her in mind before scheduling problems forced her to drop out. If Sarah Michelle Gellar has her way, however, Britney won't be featuring any time soon on *Buffy*. She told the *Sun*, 'our producers [said] she was gonna do it and I was saying, "I don't think so."' Mia-ow!

We Read Dickens When I Went To School: According to a freelance journalist studying the Slayer for her MA in English Literature at Sussex University, Buffy is much more than just a superhero. Jac Bayles wrote a 17,000 word dissertation – *Drop Dead Monstrous* – which dealt with how the women in the series are more dangerous than the vampires they hunt. She says the programme empowers women and girls with its depiction of strong female role models. 'Quite a few academics are now writing about Buffy,' notes Jac. 'Lots of people see the monsters as allegorical for the teenage condition.'

Another academic to recognise the artistic value of *Buffy* is Rhonda Wilcox, an English professor at Georgia's Gordon College. 'The title invites simplification,' she told the *Globe and Mail*. 'But *Buffy* is the opposite of simple. It has extraordinary writing and acting. It recognizes the complexity of art and life. It has a wonderful balance of mythic power and postmodern self-consciousness. It *is* art. Like Shakespeare. Like Dickens,' she declares with enthusiasm. '*Buffy* is an example of a *Bildungsroman*, (a German term for a novel of growth).'

Cast and Crew Comments: 'This season starts out really dark and heavy,' costume designer Cynthia Bergstrom told style website *katrillion.com*. 'Buffy's wardrobe is rather reflective of that. It's jeans and T-shirts, but as each episode progresses she does change somewhat.' Hello Kitty couture is big on *Buffy* too. 'I saw the Hello Kitty rhinestone T-shirt at Fred Segal, and they were so popular I was only able to get two for Michelle Trachtenberg,' Bergstrom revealed.

Marti Noxon's Comments: Having been quoted as saying that she thought it important that parents know they can turn *Buffy* off because of the occasionally excessive violence, Marti told Andy Mangels: 'I feel parents should watch with their kids, and they should be aware that not every episode is appropriate for young children. We write to an adult sensibility with a lot of stuff that kids enjoy, but I worry about the violence and, moreso, the sexual content. Sometimes the shows get pretty sophisticated sexually, and we do a lot of equating sex and violence.'

Joss Whedon's Comments: Continuing an annual tradition, Joss Whedon announced his plans for season seven even before season six was completed. 'I always like to get on the net and reveal everything that's going to happen next year,' Joss told the *BtVS Posting Board*. 'That way, you don't spend all summer stressing.' Spoiler fans, don't worry. These alleged teasers are from the man who once promised Zeppelin battles over Neptune and an 'all naked, all gay episode'. 'Buffy will become a "vampire slayer"' notes Joss. 'I can't really explain what that means yet, cause Doug [Petrie] hasn't explained it to me. But it seems to point towards adventure. Format change: from now on, the first half hour will be about Buffy figuring what the monster is, and the second half hour will be about Sam Waterston [*Law & Order*] prosecuting the monster. We're easing back on the goats. There've been complaints.' Also, 'because of the coincidental movie name, we will no longer refer to the kids as the Scooby Gang. They will now be known as the "*Scooby-Doo*, The Film, Coming This Christmas To Your Local DVD Store" gang.' Plenty to look forward to then?

Tales of the Slayer: With many of the *Buffy* writers contributing scripts to Dark Horse's hugely impressive monthly *Buffy* comic series (and numerous one-off and limited edition spin-offs), early 2002 saw the release of the graphic novel anthology *Tales of the Slayer*. This featured seven stories of Slayers of the past and a coda featuring Joss Whedon's futuristic Slayer, Melaka Fray. Written by Whedon, Jane Espenson, David Fury, Rebecca Kirshner, Doug Petrie and Amber Benson, the beautifully illustrated book became a 'must have' for all *Buffy* fans.

'I chose my period impulsively,' Jane Espenson told the Dark Horse website. 'I like Jane Austen, so when Joss said that everyone who was contributing had to pick a time period, I said, "I want Jane Austen." I realised later that it's not a very comic-book era. It's not about action; it's about words.' The other writers, particularly Joss and Doug Petrie started writing comics because they grew up as comics fans and loved the medium. Is the same true for Jane? 'Not at all,' she added. 'It started out just being another challenge, but Joss and Doug introduced me to the world of comic books, and I get it now. It's an amazing medium.'

121
Two To Go

US Transmission Date: 21 May 2002
UK Transmission Date: 23 May 2002

Writer: Douglas Petrie
Director: Bill Norton
Cast: Jeff McCredie (Officer), Damian Mooney (Patrol Cop),
Michael Younger (Truck Driver)

Willow goes after Jonathan and Andrew, forcing Buffy into the unlikely role of protector to criminals. Buffy, with some help from Anya, frees Jonathan and Andrew from jail, then they all return to the Magic Box to try and find a protection spell to slow Willow down. Meanwhile, Spike undergoes the torrid challenge of an African demon to become what he once was.

Dudes and Babes: Anya tells Xander that, despite what he may think, she *does* care whether he lives or dies. She's just not sure which. When Xander speculates that things could get ugly with Willow, Anya wonders if he'll choose that moment to propose again (see **100**, 'The Gift'). Xander says he needs to know if Anya intends to use Willow as an excuse for revenge. Anya replies that, while there's nothing that would give her greater satisfaction than reaping vengeance upon him, she cannot. She says he should be happy: she can't hurt him, so she'll just have to settle for hating him. Xander notes that she *has* already hurt him when she had sex with Spike (**118**, 'Entropy'). That wasn't vengeance, says Anya, it was solace. It's got to be said that, as a demon, Anya, in dealing with Xander in an honest and composed manner, makes an impressive, compassionate human.

Denial, Thy Name is Willow: Her death-count is now two: Warren and Rack. But Buffy and Xander are still trying to stop her before she kills someone anybody actually cares about. However, her callous and downright nasty treatment of Dawn goes far beyond what one would expect from someone suffering from grief-stricken loss. How much of this is Willow and how much is the magic is a very interesting question, of course. Willow disassociates herself, by talking in the third person (and in very unflattering terms), but ultimately she is self-aware enough to use 'me' on at least a couple of occasions. 'Let me tell you something about Willow,' she notes at her most depersonalised. 'She's a loser.' Everyone picked on Willow in junior high and high school. Now, she tells Buffy, 'Willow's a junkie.' The only thing Willow was ever good for, she continues, were those moments when Tara would make Willow feel that she was wonderful. Buffy suggests that Willow has always had an addictive personality. Kind of makes one wonder why Buffy didn't say something sooner. Like two years ago when Willow first started dabbling casually with the dark mojo.

References: Spike gleefully quotes from Nirvana's 'Smells Like Teen Spirit' ('Here we are now. Entertain us'). The 'truck-chasing-car' sequence may be a tribute to Steven Spielberg's *Duel*. Also, Elizabeth Barrett Browning's *Sonnets from the Portuguese* (see **3**, 'The Witch'), R.E.M.'s *Out of Time*, *Gladiator*, *Sabrina, the Teenage Witch*, *Wayne's World* ('we'll be worthy'), Jesus Jones's 'Right Here, Right Now' and *Shindig*. Willow says 'if at first you don't succeed,' a quotation apocryphally attributed to Scottish king Robert the Bruce (1274–1329). Possible allusions to *A Clockwork Orange*, *Christina F*, Neil Young's 'The Needle, and the Damage Done' and Julian Cope's 1992 poem *Hanging Out with Emma-Jane When Emma-Jane's a Junkie*.

Geek-Speak: Andrew says 'we've got seconds before *Darth Rosenberg* grinds us all into Jawa-burgers and not one of you has the midichlorians to stop her.' Midichlorians are micro-organisms which exist in all living things (*Star Wars: Episode 1 – The Phantom Menace*). Jedis have many midichlorians, hence their psychic and supernatural abilities. 'Darth' is the title given to a Sith Warrior (e.g. Darth Vader, Darth Maul); Jawas are the scavenger people who live on Tattooine. Also, *The X-Files* ('you're checking for implants?') and allusions to the *Uncanny X-Men* character Dark Phoenix (Jean Grey, formerly Marvel Girl, whose powers included telepathy and telekinesis. Psychically seduced by the Hellfire Club, she was transformed into a power-hungry goddess). Andrew says that Lex Luthor had a false epidermis escape kit in the *Superman versus the Amazing Spider-Man Treasury Edition*.

Bitch!: Anya notes that a witch at Willow's level can only 'go airborne. It's a thing. Very flashy, impresses the locals,' but it takes longer than teleportation which Anya herself has the power to achieve.

Xander: 'Warren was a stone cold killer of women just getting warmed up. You ask me? Bastard had it coming.'

Awesome!: Jonathan and Andrew's big girlie cat-fight. Anya failing to convince an officious police officer to let the boys out of their cell. Clem and Dawn's scene: here's somebody else who, like Spike, doesn't treat her as a little girl. What a shame all of her best adult friends are demons. Spike's reaction when the hands of the huge beefcake he has to fight burst into flames.

Surprise!: Giles's arrival at the climax.

'You May Remember Me From Such Films As . . .': Michael Younger appeared in *Crazy in Alabama*.

The Drugs Don't Work: Rack comments to Willow that the rehab obviously didn't take.

Don't Give Up The Day Job: Bill Norton's previous work includes *Daughters*, *False Arrest*, *More American Graffiti* (which he also wrote), *Bad to the Bone*, *Freaky Links*, *Angel*, *Roswell* and the memorable TV movie *Gargoyles*.

Valley-Speak: Andrew: 'This is major uncool.'

Logic, Let Me Introduce You to This Window: In **110**, 'Wrecked' it was established that only a witch or a demon could find Rack's house (specifically, Buffy couldn't find it without Spike's help). But Buffy manages to locate it here without any demonic assistance. Willow pins Anya against the wall. Why does Anya scream? Couldn't she merely have teleported away as she demonstrated earlier in the episode? Or, thrown Willow aside with her vengeance-demon powers (as Halfrek demonstrated in **114**, 'Older and Far Away'). Even if Anya couldn't, she's immortal now, so no matter how hard Willow strangles her, or projects magic at her, she's not going to die. If Anya *could* scream for help then she wasn't being strangled *that* hard. What happened to Clem? He was in the waiting room of Rack's house but wasn't teleported to the Magic Box with Buffy, Dawn and Willow. Jonathan says he's known Willow almost as long as Xander and Buffy. In actual fact, given that he talks about Willow packing her own school lunches (the implication is he's talking about junior high or before) then he's known her considerably longer than Buffy, who only met Willow six years previously. Both Alyson Hannigan and Sarah Michelle Gellar's stunt-doubles' faces are clearly visible during the Buffy/Willow fight. A general error in several episodes, but it's especially noticeable here: Willow is often referred to as 'a Wicca' when the dialogue is clearly talking about her magical prowess, rather than of her as a practitioner of a group of pagan traditions of which witchcraft is only a part. Not all Wiccas are witches and vice versa. It's ironic that a series which once so successfully lampooned trendy and inaccurate uses of Wiccan terms by 'Wanna Blessed-Bes' (see **66**, 'Hush') should be guilty of such errors itself.

Motors: Willow destroys Xander's car to delay Buffy getting to the jail and stopping her killing Jonathan and Andrew. So, Xander does what any law-abiding citizen would, and steals a police car. Which leads to the mother of all car chases.

Quote/Unquote: Xander, to Andrew: 'You haven't had even a tiny bit of sex have you?' Anya: 'The annoying virgin has a point.'
   Willow: 'There's no one in the world with the power to stop me now.' Giles: 'I'd like to test that theory.'

Notes: 'The only time you were ever at peace in your whole life is when you were dead.' Best episode of the season, by miles, 'Two to Go' forgoes much of the legacy that has occasionally stifled creative development in this odd, uneven of years, and delivers, instead, a precise and lyrical essay on human frailty. Buffy and Xander, bound by a friendship that they're determined not to see broken, embark on a mission to save a friend from herself. And fail miserably. Anya rediscovers the spark of humanity at her core, tells Xander how much he hurt her, and then puts her life at risk for him and Buffy because *it's the right thing to do*. Jonathan's sudden lack of moral ambiguity is beautifully fashioned and totally in character. And Willow? Willow's *gone*, baby! Willow's talking about herself in the third person. A disfigured, insane remnant of the girl we once knew, who makes Dennis Hopper in *Apocalypse Now* seem *normal*. A sneering Johnny Rotten-style ball of piss and anger, telling the home truths that Buffy doesn't want to hear. A critical nexus of the previous year, and a pointer, just, to the future. A dark, malevolent future devoid of many of the things that made *Buffy* great, maybe, but, in its own way, every bit as good as what's gone before. Some people will tell you this series is running out of ideas. Show them this episode, please.

Willow mentions that Dawn used to be mystic energy (see **83**, 'No Place Like Home'). Andrew says he likes following orders. The usual 'Previously on *Buffy the Vampire Slayer*' opening is replaced for this episode by a Nick Brendon voice-over stating 'this is what happened this year'.

Critique: 'Whether standing atop an 18-wheeler truck, or taunting Dawn and Buffy with her angsty yet calm diatribes, Hannigan's Dark Willow remains awesomely powerful,' noted *TV Zone*. *Impact*'s John Mosby added: 'It may have seemed that the "Three Wankers of the Apocalypse" were a small-time concern, but they too factored into the high drama. And, of course, there's *that* entrance from Giles. Superb!' The *Australian*'s Kate MacKenzie considered that: 'While this double episode doesn't save the season from being the show's worst so far, it's still a breath of fresh air in a world full of formulaic reality shows and courtroom dramas.'

You Sexy Things: *FHM*'s annual *World's 100 Sexiest Women* poll – published in May 2002 – saw the girls of *Buffy* and *Angel* once again dominating. After being narrowly defeated by Alyson Hannigan last year, the 1999 winner Sarah Michelle Gellar led the *Buffy* charge at number 11. Alyson slipped back from 10th place in 2001 to 21st, but did come third in a separate poll of the magazine's lesbian readers. Emma Caulfield was a new entry at 86, with former series regular Eliza Dushku taking 58th position. *Angel* fans also had cause to celebrate with Charisma Carpenter's impressive rise from 29 to 13.

Did You Know?: Anyone jittery about American policies in the vanguard of the war against terror may be relieved to learn about Anthony Cordesman, a professor at the Center for Strategic and International Studies, an influential Washington thinktank which helps to formulate US defence policy. His new treatise is entitled 'Biological Warfare and the Buffy Paradigm'. 'The US must plan its homeland defense policies for a future in which there is no way to predict the weapon that will be used, or the method chosen to deliver [it],' posits the professor. 'I would like you to think about the biological threat in terms of *Buffy the Vampire Slayer*; that you think about the world of biological weapons in terms of the "Buffy Paradigm"; and that you think about many of the problems in the proposed solutions as part of the "Buffy Syndrome".' For any three-star generals bemused by this, Anthony explains that *Buffy* is 'about a teenage vampire slayer who lives in a world of unpredictable threats where each series of crises only becomes predictable when it is over.' Aren't you *glad* you live in a world where Buffy helps the president decide who to bomb next?

Cast and Crew Comments: Nick Brendon described how he transformed Xander from a skinny high school wimp into a beefcake. 'I hired a trainer and started working out,' he told *YM* magazine. 'At first Joss really didn't want me to, because it wasn't part of the character, [but] we talked it over and decided I was out of high school and going into the workforce.' Nick also revealed a romantic side when asked what he would like to see more of on *Buffy*. 'Less blood, more love. You *can* quote me on that.'

Head On: Tony Head has admitted that despite his reduced role in Season Six, he'd like to be around more for *Buffy*'s seventh year. If Buffy does end, however, Tony believes that might not be such a bad thing. 'Personally, I think it would be good if the show finishes on a high,' he told *Entertainment Weekly*. Tony has been very busy since returning to Britain. After the success of his comedy drama series *Manchild*, filming of more episodes is likely to impact on production of the much-anticipated *Ripper* spin-off. The BBC wants to do it,' he noted. 'Fox is still interested, so it's ultimately about when Joss has the time.' Although he misses the *Buffy* cast and crew, returning to Britain meant plenty of action – not least in the bedroom. 'I did a love scene in a show called *Spooks*. I seem to be doing a lot of them for the first time in my life.'

Joss Whedon's Comments: Some *Buffy* and *Angel* fans seem to have been more openly critical than ever this season. 'It affects me,' Joss told *E! Online*. 'At the same time, I need to give them what they need, not what they want. They need to have their hearts broken. They need to see change. They hated Oz, then they hated that he left. These things are inevitable. If people are freaking out, I'm good.'

122
Grave

US Transmission Date: 21 May 2002
UK Transmission Date: 30 May 2002

Writer: David Fury
Director: James A Contner
Cast: Brett Wagner (Trucker)

Giles's return to Sunnydale may be the last hope of stopping Willow before she destroys the world in her thirst for vengeance. But is he too late?

Playing the Homophobia Card: The amount of Internet bandwidth used to discuss the possible subtexts surrounding Tara's death (**119**, 'Seeing Red') and Willow's subsequent actions, could have filled Wembley Stadium. The outrage that many fans (of all sexualities) felt over the death of a well-loved character was understandable. But that's no different to the emotional response that, for instance, **94**, 'The Body' achieved. This time, the fact that the character in question was gay made the situation more problematic. Firstly, and rightly, a bit of praise. For the past eighteen months *Buffy* has been near enough the only mainstream US series to feature two regular characters engaged in a loving same-sex relationship. That should *never* be forgotten. Willow and Tara, whether by accident or design, have been positive role models to gay teenagers everywhere. They've shown that you don't have to hide your sexuality or to be an outsider, that ridicule and homophobia are products of ignorance. The sudden death of one of those characters, while dramatically interesting, obviously raises the question of *agenda* and whether the reason behind this was not, at least in part, a decision that a mistake had been made. In a strongly worded piece on the website *xtremegames.com*, fan Robert Black wrote an essay entitled 'It's Not Homophobia but That Doesn't Make it Right' in which he argued that the killing of Tara showed a callous disregard for fans, and for the wider gay community. 'To a marginalized segment of the population,' Black notes, 'where there is a constant feeling that one's very existence is being denied, onscreen reflection can be priceless.' Very true. A counter-argument is that such attacks can be viewed as, at best misguided, and at worst, as offensively myopic as those postings on message boards and newsgroups which stated that *Buffy* had just lost a viewer now they had 'turned Willow queer'.

The *positive* presentation of lesbianism over three seasons on *Buffy* cannot be overstated and can only have done gay tolerance good in a wider context. *Buffy* was nominated at the 2001 Gay and Lesbian Media Awards, which honours 'accurate and inclusive representations of the lesbian, gay, bisexual and transgender community,' alongside groundbreaking shows such as *Queer as Folk* and *The West Wing*. Although generally praised for its sensitive handling of the issue, *Buffy* had, previously, come in for some mild (even amused) criticism from the gay community over the way that Willow's sexuality was referenced in both **89**, 'Triangle' (when Anya suggests Willow is attracted to Xander, Willow replies: 'Hello, *gay now*') and **96**, 'Intervention' (the Buffybot's information on Willow: GAY 1999–PRESENT). Character-wise, Willow certainly *seems* to be bisexual given that she had such an intimate and loving relationship with Oz before meeting Tara. It's therefore difficult to believe she is completely unattracted to all men. One theory put forward as to why Willow should describe herself as gay rather than bisexual is that the American public generally associate bisexual women with porn videos, jokes on *Friends* and *The Jerry Springer Show*.[10] They're simply not as comfortable with using the term as we are in Britain. Nevertheless, *Buffy* has featured, let's remember, two popular same-sex characters in a wholly positive relationship for nearly fifty episodes. Regardless of how it ended, one cannot wipe away the memories of that entire period.

But even after Tara's death, the arguments surrounding Willow didn't end. They run something like this: *Buffy* has always had a subtext that *sex is evil* – going as far back as Buffy's relationship with Angel (a literal 'I slept with my boyfriend and he turned into a monster'). It's one of the cornerstone metaphors of the show. Of all the Scoobies, Willow is one of only two who's ever had a partner killed. It's a bit of a stretch, but as fan-writer Susannah Tiller has theorised, this could be seen if one were looking for underlying themes, as a metaphor that lesbian sex is somehow worse than heterosexual promiscuity. Compare Tara's case with, for example, Buffy and Riley's break-up. Riley is 'rewarded' with a happy marriage. Tara gets a bullet. Another of *Buffy*'s few openly gay characters, Larry, also died (see **56**, 'Graduation Day'). Heterosexual characters, even if they're initially unlikeable, wickedly promiscuous or downright evil (Wesley, Harmony and Faith, respectively) all ultimately get a shot at redemption, Tiller notes. Gay characters, generally, don't. Tara was killed immediately after she and Willow had sex, making the 'lesbian sex is evil' metaphor even more obvious. So

---

[10] In an interview with *E! Online*, Joss noted: 'Marti and I debated about whether or not Willow was bisexual, experimenting, going back and forth. We thought, after Tara, it really would be disingenuous of us to have her be anything less than gay. So we decided that's pretty much final – that's who she is. To backtrack on that would make it appear as if Tara's death was something other than it was.'

ingrained is this negative portrayal that it has been well documented by film historians as the 'dead/evil lesbian cliché,' (most notably in *The Celluloid Closet* by Vito Russo). David Fury even admitted in an Internet interview in May that he believed this juxtaposition was a mistake: 'In retrospect, I can see the cliché. That was not our intent. We wanted to show them together and happy. It created the impression in a lot of people's minds that [Tara's] death was linked to them having sex.' To some fans, Tara's death also seemed gratuitous. If compared to, for example, Angel's death in **34**, 'Becoming' Part 2, which served a specific dramatic purpose. His was a *noble* death whereas Tara's felt like an afterthought, and does little but to act as a clumsy plot-device for Willow's actions in subsequent episodes.

It's also interesting to compare Willow's behaviour to Giles's reaction to Jenny's death in **29**, 'Passion'. While both are grief-stricken emotional responses, Giles's actions are much more instantaneous. By comparison, Willow's slow and calculated descent into vengeance-driven madness has the awkward potential to be viewed as another cliché: a lesbian who loses her partner becoming homicidal to the point of irrationality (or irrational to the point of genocide). From a psychological point of view, Willow's torture and murder of Warren (**120**, 'Villains') is where the entire plot threatens to fall into the murky world of Freudian stereotypes (perpetuated by popular culture) in which lesbians are frequently depicted as being inherently irrational, unstable man-haters. Perhaps, for some gay fans the ultimate slap in the face was that having decided to destroy the world, Willow is stopped from her apocalyptic designs when her best friend (a man, of course) tells her that he loves her. The Freudian stereotype is complete: a lesbian just needs the love of a good man to make her rational and 'normal' again.

Some of these charges have a degree of truth in them, though Marti Noxon used an interview with the gay publication the *Advocate* to present the production's proudly pro-gay credentials: 'We never meant for Willow to be a gay icon. Every character on *Buffy* is going to struggle with their dark side; that's the nature of our show. There are people who are unhappy Willow and Tara are not the poster-couple for gay relationships. But to my mind, that's not a fair representation of gay people.' However, Tara's death was, Noxon adds, 'the first time we've gotten public outcry where I can't even read some of the letters, they hurt so much.'

Joss Whedon defends the storyline and remains somewhat mystified by hostile reactions to it. Talking to *E! Online* he said: 'I wanted people to be upset – it's my *job* [to do that]. What was surprising was that there was a lot of hate toward us. It was an episode that was clearly about male violence and dominance, and suddenly I'm a gay basher. It's one thing when you piss off people you want wiped off the planet. It's different when it's people you care about like your audience. But it's frustrating when *they* treat you in the same knee-jerk manner.' It is certainly very strange to find articles such as one by author Rodger Streitmatter on *GayToday.com*, in which Streitmatter states: 'I was very pleased that I could finally recommend *Buffy* as a television program that provided a picture of young gay life that was both realistic and positive. I no longer can,' despite the fact that *Buffy* continues to include one proudly and openly gay character. That's one more than most TV series. Much of the anger directed towards Whedon seems to be not, specifically, because he killed Tara, but because Willow and Tara were the only positive lesbian role models on television. Ultimately, that's surely not Joss's fault, it's everyone else's.

This author remains open-minded and hopeful that the production team have a grand design in mind. Dramatically, if not emotionally, Tara's death made sense. But, let's put it this way, if in season seven, Willow's next relationship is with a man, then it will be difficult to escape the obvious conclusion that somebody chickened-out from one of the most innovative storylines that popular television has attempted. That would be a tragedy.

A Little Learning is a Dangerous Thing: Giles confirms what the audience already suspected from **90**, 'Checkpoint' – that the Watchers Council hasn't a clue about much of anything. There is, however, a powerful coven in Devon who sensed the rise of a dangerous magic in Sunnydale. A dark force, fuelled by grief. A seer in the coven told Giles about Tara and they imbued him with their powers and sent him to bring Willow down. Anya asks if Giles knew that Willow was going to take his powers to boost her own and that they were tainted, and he admits he knew there was a possibility. The gift he was given by the coven was the true essence of magic, which comes, in all its purity, from the Earth itself. Willow's magic, on the other hand, came from a place of rage and vengeance. That which she took from Giles tapped into the spark of humanity she had left within her. It allowed her to *feel* again, thus giving Xander the opportunity to reach her through love.

Denial, Thy Name is Xander: There are further references to the feelings of inadequacy that Xander mentioned in the previous episode. He was unable to stop the shooting of Buffy and Tara or to reason with Willow. Here, he sarcastically suggests to Dawn that some people always know what to do in a crisis, indicating that he isn't one of them. Later, he bemoans his inability to run away, and that's something, he notes, that he's had lots of practice at.

Yet, this is his finest hour, revealing a man who loses himself so easily in pity yet is still able to go to the, literal, ends of the earth to save a friend, and humanity along with it. A man who spends his life telling inane jokes and blurting out confidential information at inappropriate times (you can trust Xander with your life, but would you trust him with your secrets?), and yet will face down ultimate darkness. I've said it before (notably when he bought the prom dress for Cordelia in **54**, 'The Prom') but, when I grow up, I want to be Xander Harris.

Denial, Thy Name is Willow: Willow tells Giles he's a hypocrite, suggesting that he waltzed back to Sunnydale using borrowed magics so that he can chastise her. She says that she used to believe Giles had all the answers. Now she suggests he is really a fraud, jealous of her, unable to bear that she's become more powerful than him. Having subsequently been given insight into all the suffering of the world, Willow decides to summon the demon Proserpexa at a Satanic temple on Kingman's Bluff. She intends to drain the planet's life-force, funnel the energy through Proserpexa's effigy and burn the Earth to a cinder.

Denial, Thy Name is Buffy: Dawn asks why Buffy didn't tell her about Spike having attempted to rape her. She didn't need to know, is Buffy's reply, and she notes that she was trying to protect her sister. 'You *can't*,' Dawn explodes. People Dawn loves keep dying, even Buffy can't protect her from *that*. After their battle with the Earth Monsters, Dawn asks if Buffy is crying because the world *didn't* end. Buffy apologises to her sister and tells her that, from now on, everything is going to be better. Buffy wants to see her friends happy again, and she wants to see Dawn grow up into 'the woman you're going to become. Because she's gonna be beautiful. And powerful. I don't want to protect you from the world – I want to show it to you.'

The Hilarity Starts at Home Time: When Giles asks what's been going on in Sunnydale since he left, Buffy tells him that Willow is messing with dark forces, Dawn's a kleptomaniac, Xander left Anya at the altar, Anya became a demon again and Buffy's been sleeping with Spike. Giles does the only thing he can – burst out laughing. Buffy stares in disbelief, until his infectious amusement at the absurdity of what she's said hits her and she joins in. Between fits of giggles she tells Giles about the events of **117**, 'Normal Again', seemingly the most ludicrous of all that has happened.

References: *The Wizard of Oz* ('fly my pretty'), obliquely *Bill & Ted's Bogus Journey*, *Trading Places* ('it's a miracle!'), *The Mummy* (the insects attacking Spike), allusions to Van Morrison's 'Brown-Eyed Girl', *Alice Doesn't Live Here Anymore*, *Friends* (Xander uses Phoebe's occasional catchphrase 'whatcha doin'?), *Sleepy Hollow* and *Dead Men Walking*. Xander tells Willow: 'I was gonna walk you off a cliff and hand you an anvil, but that seemed too cartoony,' referring to a visual gag often used by Roadrunner on Wile E Coyote. Anya quotes Speedy Gonzalez ('*Holy frijole!*')

Bitch!: Willow asks Giles if he remembers the spat they had 'when you were under the delusion you were still relevant here,' (see **105**, 'Life Serial').

Xander, on Spike: 'Is this blind spot a genetic trait with you Summers women? The only useful thing that animal ever did was finally leave town.'

Awesome!: Buffy and Anya hugging the returned Giles. Giles asking Buffy how a recovered Willow will be able to live with herself, and Willow replying: 'Willow doesn't live here anymore.' Dawn turning into a fighting machine almost as impressive as her sister as she and Buffy battle the Earth Monsters that Willow brings forth. 'What? You think I never *watched* you?' Dawn asks as Buffy looks at her proudly, if somewhat incredulously. Jonathan and Andrew escaping, probably to Mexico, with a very scary-looking trucker. The completely unexpected finale, a demon hand reaching out to Spike's chest and telling him 'your soul is returned to you.'

'You May Remember Me From Such Films and TV Series As . . .': Brett Wagner appeared in *Finding Kelly*, *Sliders* and *Dark Skies*.

Valley-Speak: Willow: 'Uh-oh. Daddy's home. I'm in wicked trouble now.'

Andrew: 'Buttwipe.'

Logic, Let Me Introduce You to This Window: When Xander and Willow hug, in one angle Xander's left knee is drawn up but in another it's on the ground. During the scene where Willow is chasing the stolen car in the truck, parked police cars can be seen in the background, even though by this time they had all, apparently, been driven away from the station. It's easy to forget that the events of the last four episodes take place over such a short timescale. The final scene of **119**, 'Seeing Red' to the end of this episode, covers approximately 24 hours. It therefore seems unbelievable that Giles and Buffy would be laughing hysterically about the more ridiculous aspects of the season with Tara's body not even cold. Willow being given an insight into the suffering of all humanity is similar to the experience that Cordelia went through in *Angel*: 'To Shanshu in LA'. The main difference being that Cordy emerged wanting to help everyone. Willow, conversely, wants to end the world to make the suffering stop. The previous demonically perpetuated Sunnydale earthquake, mentioned in **2**, 'The Harvest', took place in 1937, not 1932 as stated here. Of course, this could refer to separate events, but even on a fault as active as the San Andreas, two major earthquakes within five years is highly unlikely. Giles refers to Devonshire, as opposed to Devon, which it has really been known as for many years in Britain. This could, of course, be an example of Giles being Giles, but it's still factually inaccurate. And Tony Head should have spotted this as he lives just a few miles away in Bath. A Wiccan performing a Satanic ritual is a contradiction in terms. Wiccans are pagans who don't believe in any Judaeo-Christian icons.

I Just *Love* Your Accent: Spike describes the tests set for him as 'a bloody doddle' and 'a piece of piss'. Willow calls Giles 'Jeeves', after the butler in PG Wodehouse's Bertie Wooster novels (see **43**, 'The Wish').

Quote/Unquote: Buffy: 'You were right about everything. It is time I was an adult.' Giles: 'Sometimes the most adult thing you can do is ask for help when you need it.'

   Xander: 'The thing is, I love you. I loved crayon-breaky-Willow and I love scary-veiny-Willow . . . You wanna kill the world you start with me. I've earned that.'

Notes: 'Is this the master plan? You're gonna stop me by telling me you love me?' So, we reach the end of a strange road. And a new theme emerges to compete with 'oh, grow up', as the core value of this disjointed, sometimes unsatisfying, occasionally hollow, but always fascinating year. Love redeems – *Buffy*'s final mission statement. The circular nature of the season, as with previous years, means that we end where we began: Buffy in the ground, surrounded by the dead; Willow knee-deep in dark magic through grief; Xander valiantly trying to keep his friends together in the face of terrible events; Spike, searching for meaning in a world that no longer allows him to be what he is; and Dawn trying to come to terms with what her sister was, and is, and what she, herself, will ultimately become. Buffy tells Giles about the events of the season and they laugh hysterically. Sometimes, that's the only answer to such darkness. 'Grave' *is* dark and hard to get a handle on, but its overall message, that nothing is ever so bad it can't be put right through love, is a wonderfully brave statement for a TV series to make in this day and age. In lesser hands, it could have been mawkish and risible. In these, it's staggeringly appropriate. *Buffy*'s been through a lot this year and, at times, it's been hard going, fractious, awkward, challenging TV. But, never less than extraordinary. The final four episodes pull the strands together and make it into a cohesive whole. What will we say in years to come when the next generation asks 'Daddy, what did you do in *Buffy* season six?' *I'll* say 'it depressed the hell out of me, son, but it was worth it at the end.'

On her first day in kindergarten, Willow cried because she broke the yellow crayon and was too afraid to tell anyone. Proserpexa is important in the hierarchy of she-demons. Her followers intended to use her effigy to destroy the world but they all died when the temple was swallowed in the earthquake of 1932.

Soundtrack: Series favourite Sarah McLachlan's version of 'The Prayer of Saint Francis' closes the season. The two McLachlan songs used in *Buffy*, interestingly, both include direct or indirect allusions to devotional prayers ('Full of Grace' to the *Hail Mary*. See **34**, 'Becoming' Part 2).

Critique: 'The finale belonged, unequivocally, to Willow,' noted Stephanie Zacharek on *salon.com*. 'It didn't have the queasy-making resonance of Whedon's finale last year. But this year, nevertheless, threw the show and its characters into yet another light; it has changed the shape of their shadows, showing us things in them – resources of unusual bravery and cruelty – that we couldn't previously have imagined.'

'Wasn't it cool to watch Willow get evil with her black hair and veiny face?' asked Sonia Mansfield. 'Finally Xander gets his day in the sun and saves the world. You can't ask for a better season-ender than that.'

Giving the episode a generally positive review, Robert Bianco felt that 'even when *Buffy* fails ... it fails in interesting ways. Most long-running series stumble because the writers ... exhaust their energy and interest. It's clear *Buffy* suffered from Whedon's reduced involvement – and ... from the absence of Anthony Stewart Head. But essentially, *Buffy* faltered because it charted a seemingly viable artistic course that simply didn't work. What the show was seeking was a metaphorical expression of real-world problems. Unfortunately, it's hard to sustain 22 weeks of character ennui without inducing the same in an audience.'

'The ending with Xander's defeat of bad Willow and Buffy's subsequent protestations that she now wants to live, to see her friends happy, seemed a bit contrived,' noted Thomas Hibbs. 'Indeed, the dialogue at times reduced the difference between good and evil to a sappy distinction between those who feel and those who don't. But, in a show that has always stressed the dire consequences of decisions and actions, we can be sure that earth will remain closer to Hell than to Heaven.'

Did You Know?: The mausoleum Xander attempts to enter is named Alpert, after producer Marc David Alpert.

Cast and Crew Comments: Sarah Michelle Gellar is keen that *Buffy* should go out on top. 'This was a little bit of a frightening year. A lot of shows that were very strong went out not with a bang but with a whimper,' she told reporters at a UPN end-of-season press event. 'It is very important to us that eventually when it is time to go, that we go out strong,' added Sarah. 'We don't want to be a show that got cancelled that people say, "Oh that should've been off three years ago."' Asked when she thought the show would end, Gellar added: 'I don't have an answer to that. I always say that if you would've told me in the beginning this show would have been on seven years, I would have laughed at you. You always want to challenge yourself. You want to constantly keep it fresh. If it's not fresh, exciting and something you passionately want to do, then the audience is going to know.'

The Buffy Novels

The Lost Slayer Part One: Prophecies

Writer: Christopher Golden
Published: August 2001
Tagline: Buffy's worst enemy is closer than she thinks . . .
Setting: November 1999 during season four

Buffy encounters Camazotz, the god of bats, and runs, leaving Giles at Camazotz's mercy. She's sent five years into the future to a Sunnydale overrun by vampires . . .

Authority Sucks!: Buffy falls foul of Professor Blaylock by failing to deliver a term paper.

Denial, Thy Name is Olivia: Buffy suggests that Olivia's scepticism would be cured by spending more time in Sunnydale.

References: Aerosmith, *The Matrix*, *Nosferatu*, *Jeopardy*, Kryptonite and Supergirl, Martha Stewart, The Who, Daffy Duck, action movie *God of Gambles* starring Chow-Yun Fat, The Rolling Stones, *Hill Street Blues* and *Mission: Impossible*.

Notes: Former Slayer Lucy Hanover (see **1**, 'Welcome to the Hellmouth') warns Buffy of an upcoming apocalypse. Giles is still dating Olivia (see **57**, 'The Freshman').

The Lost Slayer Part Two: Dark Times

Writer: Christopher Golden
Published: September 2001
Tagline: Buffy's most frightening nightmares have become a reality
Setting: November 1999 and an alternate 2004

Buffy learns about the horrifying vampire-controlled world of the future while her friends in the present deal with her now-posessed body . . .

Notes: A very grim tale, with not a single pop culture reference but loads of internal continuity. In 2004 Faith's successor as Slayer makes Buffy kill her so that another Slayer who isn't compromised will be called. Parker Abrams (see **59**, 'The Harsh Light of Day') is a vampire-sympathiser, Harmony is killed, Buffy stakes Drusilla 'for Kendra' (see **34**, 'Becoming' Part 2). Xander, Oz and Willow are freedom fighters (see **43**, 'The Wish'). There's no listing for Angel Investigations or for Wesley, but Cordelia has an unlisted number. And Giles? He's the Vampire King!

The Lost Slayer Part Three: King of the Dead

Writer: Christopher Golden
Published: October 2001
Tagline: Buffy faces an adversary who was once her most trusted mentor . . .
Setting: An alternate 2004

Buffy takes charge and leads an assault on Giles' head-quarters . . .

Authority Sucks!: Buffy has a run-in with future Watchers Council representatives. Some things never change.

Mom's Apple Pie: Buffy sees Joyce in a dream, making pancakes. Joyce reveals that Faith tried to save her.

References: Disneyland ('take a trip before the Mouse sprouts fangs,' Spike jibes), *The Wild Bunch*, *The Outlaw Josey Wales*, *Once Upon a Time in The West*, *Red River* and *Stagecoach*.

Notes: Another grim novel, prefaced with a 'Previously on *Buffy the Vampire Slayer*' catch-up: In 2004 Wesley has become a Watcher again, the Initiative was destroyed by the vampires, and Xander stakes Spike for killing Anya and Joyce.

The Lost Slayer Part Four: Original Sins

Writer: Christopher Golden
Published: November 2001
Tagline: Can Buffy defeat a foe who not only knows her techniques
– but helped her develop them?
Setting: An alternate 2004 and November 1999

After defeating Giles, Buffy goes back to ensure that time follows a different path ...

A Little Learning is a Dangerous Thing: Alchemy, apparently, only works if you're not using it for personal gain.

Denial, Thy Name is Everyone: Even in 2004, the best the authorities can come up with for five years' worth of Giles-led terror is 'biker gangs'.

References: John Wayne, *The Magnificent Seven*.

Logic, Let Me Introduce You to This Window: Buffy is told about the Initiative by the future Willow and is determined to retain all her memories of her stay in 2004. So why doesn't she mention the Initiative to anyone when she gets back? Nobody comments on the fact that Buffy is basically re-enacting the end of *Back to the Future* ...

Notes: Faith changed sides when Giles went bad; Angel is caught in a time-trap by Giles – Buffy kills Angel to save him. Again. Wesley and Xander are killed in the final battle against Giles, which sees Ripper staked as well.

Unseen: The Burning

Writers: Nancy Holder and Jeff Mariotte
Published: May 2001
Tagline: The first in a new crossover trilogy
Setting: Between *Buffy* Seasons Four and Five, and *Angel*
Seasons One and Two

Buffy tries to help a friend of Willow's find her missing brother. A secret Russian project is affecting reality.

Cordelia gets involved with some vampire wannabes. What's the connection?

Denial, Thy Name is Sunnydale: It's implied that Sunnydale residents make a deliberate choice to ignore things that go on there.

References: Sherlock Holmes, The Grateful Dead, *COPS*, *Adam-12*, *X-Men*, *Baywatch Hawaii*, *Starsky and Hutch*, *Miami Vice*, *The Exorcist*, *The Sound of Music*, *Sabrina, the Teenage Witch*, *The Simpsons*, *Cool Hand Luke* and Siegfried and Roy (see **119**, 'Seeing Red').

Cigarettes and Alcohol: The LA-based sections include lots of booze.

Logic, Let Me Introduce You to This Window: Willow vows never to use her powers to make someone love her. Later this is totally contradicted by **106**, 'All the Way'.

I Just *Love* Your Accent: The others think Giles is becoming more hip. Wesley 'pondered in his hmmming British way'.

Notes: The first proper *Buffy/Angel* novels-crossover. A lot of play is made throughout the trilogy of Riley and Angel's dislike for each other (see **76**, 'The Yoko Factor'). Cordelia makes sure she keeps up with her tetanus shots.

Unseen: Door to Alternity

Writers: Nancy Holder and Jeff Mariotte
Published: July 2001
Tagline: The second in a new crossover trilogy
Setting: Between *Buffy* Seasons Four and Five, and *Angel* Seasons One and Two

Sunnydale comes under attack from other-dimensional demons, and the disappearances in Los Angeles increase.

Mom's Apple Pie: Joyce offers everyone food while they're in the heat of battle.

References: Punk group the Plasmatics, *Miami Vice*, *Butch Cassidy and the Sundance Kid*, *The Sword in the Stone*, *Sex and the City*, *Home Beautiful* magazine, Michael Jackson's *Thriller*, *Snow White and the Seven Dwarfs*, James Bond, *The Lion King*, Humphrey Bogart (Wes tries to impersonate him), *The Addams Family*, *Conan the Barbarian* and Martha Stewart.

I Just *Love* Your Accent: 'The Queen Mum is an emotional topic for every Brit, Cordelia,' Wesley says. That's a matter of opinion. Giles greets Wesley on the phone with 'God Save the Queen.' Have the authors ever *met* any English people who do that?

Notes: There's a foreshadowing of Spike's obsession with Buffy in season five, and links to Christopher Golden's *Gatekeeper Trilogy*. The other dimension where Selma (and later Buffy, Angel and Spike) find themselves is very reminiscent of Pylea from *Angel*.

Unseen: Long Way Home

Writers: Nancy Holder and Jeff Mariotte
Published: September 2001
Tagline: The conclusion to the first crossover trilogy
Setting: Between *Buffy* Seasons Four and Five, and *Angel* Seasons One and Two

Buffy, Angel and Spike try to sort out what's going on in the other dimension – but they're going to need help from another Vampire Slayer. Will Faith join them?

Denial, Thy Name is Sunnydale: Everyone who didn't go to the alternate dimension forgets all that happened – a very convenient mindwipe to preserve continuity.

References: Madonna, *Cyrano de Bergerac*, the *Angel* episode 'I Fall to Pieces', *7th Heaven*, *Roswell*, *Dawson's Creek*, Robert Mitchum, *The Great Escape*, *Chicken Run*, *Los Tiranos*, Mickey Mantle, *The X-Files*, *Star Wars*, *The*

Shining, Lassie, The Wizard of Oz, Star Trek: The Next Generation, West Side Story, G.I. Joe.

Notes: Faith is broken out of jail, and agrees to go back at the end when she's done the necessary (see *Angel*: 'Sanctuary' and 'Judgment'). The Initiative headquarters are still standing, albeit derelict. There are loads of continuity references – even Spike tells the story of **32**, 'Go Fish'.

Tempted Champions

Writer: Yvonne Navarro
Published: March 2002
Tagline: The line between good and evil is thinner than Buffy thinks . . .
Setting: Circa 12 November 2000 (two weeks before Thanksgiving).
But, impossibly, after **95** 'Forever' (Joyce is dead and has been buried).
Where it fits into the *Angel* Season Two chronology is *anyone's* guess.

A Slayer-turned-vampire is after Buffy, and even Angel thinks she should be careful. At the same time D'Hoffryn offers Anya another chance to be a vengeance-demon . . .

A Little Learning is a Dangerous Thing: Five pounds of pressure is apparently enough to rip off a human ear. Now you know.

Mom's Apple Pie: Lots of references to Joyce's death, particularly from Anya, who is feeling vulnerably mortal.

References: *The Wizard of Oz, Judge Judy, Star Trek, The Jetsons*, Betty Boop, Joan Rivers, *Saturday Night Live, Kolchak: The Night Stalker, The Invisible Man, Ransom* (the Mel Gibson movie) and Sherlock Holmes.

Logic, Let Me Introduce You to This Window: There's no reference to the *Unseen* trilogy. Angel doesn't know who Anya is despite them having met in **50**, 'Doppelgängland' and **64**, 'Pangs'. The back cover's final question is unfortunately actually the climax of the book.

Notes: Some nice character interplay in this, but the book skews continuity to get everyone in the vulnerable position that the author needs them in. And it came out at almost the same moment that **116**, 'Hell's Bells' made it non-canonical anyway.

Sweet Sixteen

Writer: Scott Ciencin
Published: May 2002
Tagline: Buffy's not the only one chosen for a magical purpose . . .
Setting: Late Season Five, some time after Joyce's death in **94**, 'The Body'

Dawn befriends Arianna, an apparently helpless teenager – who is able to give Buffy a run for her money in a fight. Buffy needs to combine her Slayer skills with her new parenting abilities to sort Arianna out – and *really* doesn't need Spike trying to 'help' her by setting a load of demons on her case . . .

Denial Thy Name is Buffy: She's amazed that no one is attracted by the fight she has in the convenience store.

Bitch: Dawn and Arianna suffer from the latest version of the Cordettes' attacks.

References: Sylvester and Tweety Pie, *Shrek*, *This is Spinal Tap*, *Ghostbusters*, *Clue* (the board game and the movie), Britney Spears, Christina Aguilera, the Backstreet Boys, Julia Stiles, Charlie Brown, *Bloodsucking Freaks*, *Old Yeller*, Miss Piggy, *Carrie*, Jessica Alba of *Dark Angel*, *The Jerry Springer Show*, *Xena: Warrior Princess*, *Crouching Tiger Hidden Dragon*, Antonio Banderas, Gloria Gaynor, Elmer Fudd (Anya thinks the 'wabbits' really are attacking), Winnie the Pooh, *The Ed Sullivan Show*, the Three Stooges and *The Princess Bride*.

Notes: The first Dawn-centric novel is something of a throwback to the high school days of early *Buffy* with few appearances by the 'grown-ups'. And, as such, a possible prototype for season seven. Dawn makes comments about the hot guy in *Psycho Beach Party* – Nicholas Brendon, presumably?

Oz: Into the Wild

Writer: Christopher Golden
Published: June 2002
Tagline: Oz must find the balance between man and monster
Setting: In the immediate aftermath of **62**, 'Wild at Heart'

Oz travels to Fiji, Hong Kong and Tibet to find a cure to his condition – and learns that he must accept what he now is, even if that includes being hunted for his pelt.

A Little Learning is a Dangerous Thing: You can get enchanted cell phones that work inside mountains.

References: Antonio Banderas in *Desperado*, writer Jack London, *King Kong*, *Green Card*, *The Wizard of Oz*, Yoda from *The Empire Strikes Back*, *Mad Max 2: The Road Warrior*.

Notes: Featuring werewolf hunter Gib Cain (see **27**, 'Phases'), some good continuity with **75**, 'New Moon Rising', and lots of friends of Rupert Giles who aid Oz in various places. A great extrapolation of Oz's off-screen adventures that first appeared as a Dark Horse Comic.

Buffy and the Internet

Jenny: 'In the last two years, more e-mail was sent than regular mail. More digitised information went across phone lines than conversations.'
Giles: 'That is a fact that I regard with genuine horror.'

'I Robot . . . You Jane'

Buffy is, in many ways, TV's first *true* child of the Internet age. Even more than *The X-Files*, *Buffy* not only saw its fans embrace new technology to (articulately) spread the gospel, but the net itself quickly became a part of the series' iconography. Within weeks of *Buffy* beginning, flourishing fan communities had spawned newsgroups, posting boards and websites. As with most fandoms there is a lot of good stuff to have emerged as well as a little that's downright scary. This is a rough guide to the bewildering world of *Buffy* on the net.

Newsgroups: The usenet newsgroup, alt.tv.buffy-v-slayer, discusses the merits of new and old episodes and includes rumours, likely developments and other topics of interest. In the past it's been a stimulating forum with debate encouraged, however it has also, at times, attracted a distinctly aggressive and vocal contingent who are unhappy with the current direction of the show and want the world to know it. The group also features that curse of usenet, 'trolling' (people who send offensive messages to stir up trouble). Hell hath no fury, it seems, like a bunch of overgrown school children with access to a computer. When the last edition of *Slayer* was published, it was criticised by some posters because they regarded the above one-line description of trolling as a personal insult to them. This generated a thread with over 150 postings. All of which, kind-of, proves my point, that as with many fandoms, some of the users of a.t.b-v-s like talking about *Buffy* but they prefer talking about *themselves*. Still, it's always worth popping in to see what everybody thinks of the latest episode.

The newsgroup, alt.fan.buffy-v-slayer.creative is a fan-fiction forum and carries a wide range of 'missing adventures', character vignettes, 'shipper' (relationship-based erotica) and 'slash' (same-sex erotica stories), some of it of a very high standard. A UK newsgroup, uk.media.tv.buffy-v-slayer features gossip from the States, but has also in the past *starred* a number of obnoxious individuals, so readers are advised to approach with caution. There are also lively newsgroups in Europe (alt.buffy.europe) and Australia (aus.tv.buffy) where *Buffy* has big followings and also usenet groups devoted to both Sarah Michelle Gellar and Alyson Hannigan (although neither alt.fan.sarah-m-gellar or alt.fan.hannigan at present generate large numbers of posts).

Mailing Lists: More relaxed than usenet, at http:// groups.yahoo.com/ you'll find numerous *Buffy*-groups listed. Many are 'members only', like the impressive *JossBtVS* discussion list which also features daily news-flashes on the activities of the cast and crew, and *Buffy-Christian* a group who pride themselves on being 'Christians who love *Buffy*. No small-minded bigots. Positive talk only.' Among the public lists are *BuffyScripts* (which provides a 'unique look at *Angel* and *Buffy* including rarities such as early episode drafts, and special "written-but-not-seen" tidbits'), *skyonebuffythevampireslayer* (for UK viewers) and *BuffyWatchers* (basically a group of friends, including this author, who allow visitors to join us for after-dinner chats. A *Buffy* version of The Algonquin, if you will).

Posting Boards: www.buffy.com/bronze_home.jsp is where you can find The Bronze, the official *BtVS Posting Board*, which includes occasional contributions from Joss Whedon and other members of the production team (Jane Espenson, David Fury and Steven DeKnight have all posted).

This is an excellent forum, particularly as it features a direct line to the production office. The only problem is the sheer size of it. When asked about his Internet usage, Joss Whedon told *DreamWatch*: 'I came to it late. I'm still: "What's download"?'

Raven's Realm Forum (http://messageboard.cinescape. com/Buffy/cgi-bin/Ultimate.c gi) is a hotbed of fan activity, with lots of subsections. Readers who simply can't wait for future developments are advised to check out the 'rumours and spoilers' forum. Last February, you'd have known two months in advance that Tara was going to die.

Websites: There are literally thousands of sites on the Web relating to *Buffy the Vampire Slayer*. What follows is a (by no means definitive) list of some of the author's favourites. Many of these are also part of webrings with links to other related sites. An hour's surfing can get you to some interesting places.

Disclaimer: websites are transitory things at the best of times and this information, though accurate when it was written, may be woefully out of date after publication.

UK Sites: The BBC's *Buffy Online* (www.bbc.co.uk/cult/ buffy/index.shtml) has become a terrific resource with one of the most up-to-date *Buffy* news services on the net. Also features numerous exclusive interviews and video clips and a plethora of other goodies.

www.watchers.web.com/ (*The Watcher's Web*). An award-winning site and an invaluable source of information and analysis from a largely British perspective. Includes interviews, ratings figures, reviews and fiction. You can, literally, get lost in it for days.

Other UK sites include *Bonkers About Buffy* (www. geocities.com/bonkersaboutbuffy/index2.html), *Geoff's Comments* (www.cix.co.uk/~morven/buffy/index.html) and *Concrete Elephant* (www.concreteelephant.com/Telly/ buffy_guide/buffy_index.htm) which features in-depth episode commentaries (and lots of swearing).

US Sites: www.slayground.net/ (*Little Willow's Slay-ground*) is a delightful treasure trove of articles and reviews, plus all the latest news. Includes the VIP archive of the *BtVS Posting Board*, amusing subsections like 'The Xander Dance Club', filmographies and official web pages for Danny Strong and Amber Benson. It's also a useful link to the *Keeper Sites* (www.stakeaclaim.net/), a webring containing numerous associated pages. Again it's possible to find something new on each visit.

http://buffyguide.com/ (*The Complete Buffy the Vampire Slayer Episode Guide*) was one of the best general review sites, with excellently written, intelligent summaries of all the episodes, though it's now somewhat out of date.

www.angelicslayer.com/tbcs/main.html (*Buffy Cross and Stake*). This legendary page was one of the first major *Buffy* fansites and includes a huge range of material including character biogs, fiction, a weekly media update, an extensive episode guide, an impressive links page and its famous 'spoilers' section. While not always 100 per cent accurate, they often get the exclusives on hot *Buffy* news.

(www.slayage.com) *Slayage* is a fantastic media resource that's second-to-none. If you want to find out about *anything* that's happening in the world of *Buffy* and those associated with it, this should be your first port of call.

www.chosentwo.com/buffy/main.html (*Much Ado About Buffy the Vampire Slayer*) is another terrific site featuring an episode guide and extensive coverage of the comics. Fan-written transcripts and the shooting scripts of most *Buffy* and *Angel* episodes can be found at www.psyche. kn-bremen.de/.

www.buffymusic.net/ (*Buffy the Vampire Slayer: The Music*) Leslie Remencus's beautiful, frequently updated site is devoted to' the music on *Buffy*, and includes interviews, musical allusions, tour details etc. An absolute gem.

www.enteract.com/~perridox/SunS/ (*Suns – The Sunnydale Slayers*) was, according to the authors, set up by 'a gang of people . . . who wanted to talk about, lust after and discuss in depth *Buffy*.' It's great fun, and includes fiction and well-written reviews. Love the *FAQ* where they answer the question: 'So, this isn't just a women's drool fest over David Boreanaz, Anthony Stewart Head, Seth Green and Nicholas Brendon?' with 'Nope, we have male members too!'

www.alyson-hannigan.org (*Hannigan Online*) is dedicated to all-things-Alyson, and includes news, quotes and lots of photos. Well worth dropping-in. *The Sarah Michelle Gellar Fan Page* (www.smgfan.com) is the largest of hundreds of SMG fansites. *All For Anya* (http://members.tripod.com/anyanka/) is a smashing unofficial Emma Caulfield site, while *The Seth Green Megasite* (www.geocities.com/Hollywood/Land/1702) is a must-visit for the actor's many fans. *Anthony Stewart Head Shrine* (www.forbiddenwhisper.com/anthonyhead/shrine/) is the best of the Tony-sites, through *Risen From the ASHes* (http://risenfromtheashes.cjb.net) is also worth a look. Eliza Dushku's legion of fans should definitely bookmark the extraordinary *Everlasting Eliza* (www.edushku.com/). Many Dawn-related sites have recently been created, *Michelle Trachtenberg World* (http://geocities.com/marcburnard.home.htm) is a good example.

www.angelfire.com/wa/SpikesPrincess/ (*He's To Die For: The James Marsters Fan Page*) has amusing subsections like 'All I Needed to Know in Life I Learned from Spike' ('If you're going to hit a girl, make sure her mother isn't standing behind you with an axe') and 'Why Spike is Better than Angel'. www.jamesmarsters.com (*JamesMarsters.com*) is also highly recommended for Spike fans. 'I'd like to know what he was before being a vampire,' James says about his alter ego. 'I have a feeling he was pretty much an asshole. I don't think being a vampire is what made him evil. Perhaps Mommy didn't love him enough!'

www.amazingamber.co.uk/ (*Amazing Amber*) is a really good unofficial Amber Benson site.

http://slayerfanfic.com (*The Slayer Fanfic Archive*) is, as
the name suggests, a site dedicated to *Buffy* and *Angel*
fan-fiction with links to related pages. http://
badgirls.fishonastick.com/ (*Bad Girls*) is a *must* for those
adults yet to discover the joys of *shipper-* and *slash*-fic.
www.tdsos.com/ (*The Darker Side of Sunnydale*) and
www.geocities.com.willow_episodefanatic/mainpage.html
(*Eternal*) are excellent examples of the various different
kinds of fan fiction available. 'I love fanfic' Jane Espenson
told the *Posting Board*. 'I'm not really allowed to read
Buffy [stories] but I do read other fandoms. There's some
great stuff out there. Also some crappy stuff, but people
should feel free to read or write that as well.' On the same
forum, Joss Whedon has commented: 'On the subject of
fanfic I *am* aware that a good deal of it is naughty. My
reaction to that is mixed; on the one hand, these are
characters played by friends of mine, and the idea that
someone is describing them in *full naughtitude* is a little
creepy. On the other hand, eroticising the lives of fictional
characters you care about is something we all do, if only
in our heads, and it certainly shows that people care. So
I'm not really against erotic fic and I certainly don't mind
the other kind. I wish I'd had this kind of forum when I
was a kid.' Marti Noxon, meanwhile, is full of praise for
the genre: 'We're in a weird position,' she told the
Washington Post. 'It's flattering because a universe you're
part of has inspired people to continue imagining.' The
writers, however, have to be careful as a TV story with
similarities to previously published fiction could result in
accusations of plagiarism. 'Because of legalities, we have to
be judicious how much we read.'

Miscellaneous: Space prevents a detailed study of the vast
array of *Buffy* websites around the world, but a few deserve
to be highlighted.

Buffy's massive popularity in Australia is evidenced by the
large number of Aussie sites. These include:

- http://members.tripod.com/~sbia_becki/ (*Save Buffy in Australia*) which gives an excellent insight into the bewildering way in which *Buffy* is shown State to State down under.
- *Buffy Down-Under* (www.buffydownunder.com/) is a classy site described as 'the ultimate Australian resource for *Buffy* and *Angel*.'
- Danny Sag's *Episode Title Explanations* (www.geocities. com/glpoj/buffy/) is well worth a visit.
- *Slayer Sheila* (www.jenniferdudley.com/buffy/) promises '*Buffy* from an Australian perspective'.

For European readers, direct your search engines towards:
- *Buffy in Ireland* (http://bite.to/Buffy)
- Numerous French sites including *CyberBuffy* (www. ifrance.com/cyberbuffy)
  La Destinée de Buffy (http://destinbuffy.ifrance.com/destinbuffy/Sommaire.htm)
  Le Scooby Gang (www.scoobygang.ht.st/)
- *Dutch Buffy* (http://members.tripod.lycos.nl/dutchbtvs/)
- Germany's *BuffyMedia* (www.buffynews.k-babes.de/)
  Slayerweb (www.buffy-tv.de/)
- Italian site *Magic Shop* (http://digilander.libero.it/magicshop/)
- Iceland's *Blódsugubaninn Buffy* (http://oto.is/buffy/inngangur.htm)
- Portugal's *Buffy, a Caça Vampiros Page* (www.geocities. com/edilal/novaserie.htm)
- Sweden's *Totally Buffy* (http://medlem.spray.se/Totally_Buffy)
- *Buffy in Israel* (www.geocities.com/TelevisionCity/Station/9409/)

All of which offer impressive local coverage of the *Buffy* phenomena.

www.synapse.net/~dsample/BBC/ (*The Buffy Body Count*) contains 'an ongoing count of the number of dead bodies which have shown up on school property'. www.geocities.com/TelevisionCity/Loy/7330/index2.html

(*Beneath the Bronze*) has an impressive sound-archive. http://gurl/pages.com/jennifer-jcbuffyfan/IQuitMain.html (*I Quit*) is devoted to characters who have left the series. www.geocities.com/angeliklee/BandCandy.html (*Band Candy*) takes pride in being 'a site for *older Buffy* fans'. http://members.aol.cm/lostgiant/buffy/buffy.htm (*BtVS Series Timeline*) is an attempt to pull the entire backstory of *Buffy* into a chronology.

www.dymphna.net/loaded/ (*Loaded*) is the place for all Giles and Oz fans, whether your interest is their zenlike connection, a shared passion for highquality rock'n'roll or just some slash-fic, there'll be something here for you. http://pages.zoom.co.uk/kfantastico/frames/index.htm (*The Miss Kitty Fantastico Appreciation Society*) merits recognition for being so delightfully daft. Although it mainly concentrates on *Angel*, http://ljconstantine.com/doyle/ (*Doyle – Glenn Quinn*) is a beautiful celebration of both the series and the actor, with lots of *Buffy* crossovers. The regularly updated. www.fortunecity.com/lavender/rampling/271/ (*You Thought YOU Were Obsessed with BtVS*) assures all readers that, no matter how much you love *Buffy*, somebody out there *is* sadder than you are.

Finally, www.buffysearch.com ('your portal to the *Buffy* and *Angel* community') is an invaluable search engine that includes links to most of the above sites and hundreds more.

Select Bibliography

The following books, articles, interviews and reviews were consulted in the preparation of this text:

Adalin, Josef, '*Buffy* loss takes a bite of WB', *Variety*, 23 April 2001.

Adalin, Josef, 'Slayer shifts all the players', *Variety*, 10 July 2002.

Amatangelo, Amy, 'Taming her inner demons: Outspoken *Buffy* star Emma Caulfield makes peace with acting profession', *Boston Globe*, 4 March 2002.

'Angel Restores Faith', *DreamWatch*, issue 68, April 2000.

'. . . and finally', *Metro*, 12 July 2001.

Anthony, Ted, '12 Weeks After Columbine, Delayed *Buffy* airs', *Associated Press*, 12 July 1999.

Appelo, Tim and Williams, Stephanie, 'Get Buffed Up – A Definitive Episode Guide', *TV Guide*, July 1999.

Appelo, Tim, 'Buffy Slays. Now What? The least-watched great show on TV grows up', *Slate*, 5 November 2001.

Appleyard, Bryan, 'A teenager to get your teeth into', *Sunday Times* (*Culture* section), 10 December 2000.

Atherton, Tony, 'Fantasy TV: The New Reality', *Ottawa Citizen*, 27 January 2000.

Atkins, Ian, 'Homecoming' to 'The Zeppo', *Shivers*, issues 70, 71, October, November 1999.

Atkins, Ian, 'Superstar' to 'New Moon Rising', *Shivers*, issue 81, September 2000.

Baldwin, Kristen, 'Green's Day', *Entertainment Weekly*, May 1999.

Baldwin, Kristen, Fretts, Bruce, Schilling, Mary Kaye, and Tucker, Ken, 'Slay Ride', *Entertainment Weekly*, issue 505, 1 October 1999.

Barrett, David V, 'Far more than a teenage fang club', *Independent*, 3 January 2002.

Behr, Jason, 'Behr Essentials', interview by Paul Simpson and Ruth Thomas, *DreamWatch*, issue 68, April 2000.

Benson, Amber, 'Every Little Thing She Does . . .', interview by Matt Springer, *Buffy the Vampire Slayer*, issue 8, Summer 2000.

Benson, Amber, 'Is there life after death on *Buffy*?', interview by Alec Harvey, *Birmingham News*, 25 July 2002.

Benz, Julie, 'Little Miss Understood', interview by Ed Gross, *SFX Unofficial Buffy Collection*, 2000.

Bergstrom, Cynthia, 'Slaying With Style', interview by Matt Springer, *Buffy the Vampire Slayer*, issue 3, Spring 1999.

Betts, Hannah, 'And now, ladies, just for yourselves . . . When Harry met Garry', *The Times*, 7 July 2001.

Bianco, Robert, 'Holiday Ghosts Haunt the Vampire Slayers: A *Buffy* with a *Christmas Carol* bite', ('Amends' review), *USA Today*, 15 December 1999.

Bianco, Robert, '*Buffy* finale slays its fans', *USA Today*, 21 May 2002.

Bianco, Robert, '*Buffy* will rise from graveness', *USA Today*, 16 July 2002.

Bianculli, David, '*Buffy* Characters Follows Her Bliss', *New York Daily News*, 2 May 2000.

Bianculli, David, '*Buffy* fans to see more Giles', *New York Daily News*, 11 July 2002.

Billings, Laura, ' "Like , Duh," says Gen Y', *St Paul Pioneer Press*, 10 October 2000.

Binns, John, 'No Place Like Home' to 'Shadow', *Xposé*, issue 52, January 2001.

Binns, John, 'Listening to Fear' to 'Into the Woods', *Xposé*, issue 53, February 2001.

Binns, John, 'Smashed', to 'Doublemeat Palace', *Xposé*, issue 66, April 2002.

Binns, John, 'Where Do We Go From Here?' *TV Zone*, issue 153, July 2002.

Blakey, Bob, 'On *Buffy*'s Sunny Set', *Calgary Herald*, 16 July 2002.

Blucas, Marc, 'Slayer Layer', interview by Paul Simpson, *SFX*, issue 75, March 2001.

Boedeker, Hal, '*Buffy* to tap lighter vein, but be scarier too', *Orlando Sentinel*, 16 July 2002.

Bonin, Liane, 'Ripper van Winkle', *Entertainment Weekly*, 4 July 2002.

Boreanaz, David, Landau, Juliet, and Marsters, James, 'Interview with the Vampires', by Tim Appelo, *TV Guide*, September 1998.

Boreanaz, David, 'Leaders of the Pack', interview (with Kerri Russell) by Janet Weeks, *TV Guide*, November 1998.

Brendon, Nicholas, 'Evolving Hero', interview by Paul Simpson, *DreamWatch*, issue 53, January 1999.

Brendon, Nicholas, 'Only Human', interview by Keith Austin, *Sydney Morning Herald*, 25 April 2002.

Brendon, Nicholas, 'Just a Normal Everyday Hero', interview by James Abery, *Shivers*, issue 98, August 2002.

Britt, Donna, 'The Truth About Teen TV', *TV Guide*, 28 October 2000.

'Buffy in love? Checkout girls are over the moon', *Toronto Star*, 11 December 2001.

'Buffy move will alter little, creator says', *Indianapolis Star*, 18 July 2001.

'*Buffy* producer knows dyke drama', *Advocate*, 4 December 2001.

'*Buffy*: The Animated Series', *Starlog*, issue 14, June 2001.

'Buffy lives. And she sings too', *Chicago Tribune*, 5 August 2001.

'Buffy's practical joke backfires', *National Enquirer*, 18 July 2002.

'*Buffy* goes back to school', *DreamWatch*, issue 96, September 2002.

Bunson, Matthew, *Vampire: The Encyclopaedia*, Thames and Hudson, 1993.

Campagna, Suze, 'Bite Me: The History of Vampires on Television', *Intergalactic Enquirer*, October 2000.

Campagna, Suze, 'The World of Joss Whedon', *Intergalactic Enquirer*, February 2001.

Campagna, Suze, 'TV Tid Bits', *Intergalactic Enquirer*, June 2001.

Carpenter, Charisma, 'Charismatic', interview by Jim Boultier, *SFX*, issue 40, July 1998.

Carpenter, Charisma, 'Femme Fatale', interview by Mike Peake, *FHM*, issue 117, October 1999.

Carpenter, Charisma, 'Charisma Personified', interview by Jennifer Graham, *TV Guide*, 1 January 2000.

Carpenter, Charisma, 'In Step With ...' interview by James Brady, *Parade*, 5 March 2000.

Carrillo, Jenny, 'Buffy Round Table', *DreamWatch*, issue 80, May 2001.

Carter, Bill, '*Dawson's Clones*: Tapping into the youth market for all it is, or isn't, worth', *New York Times*, 19 September 1999.

Caulfield, Emma, 'Insider: She Hath No Fury', interview by Michael Logan, *TV Guide*, 25 December 1999.

Caulfield, Emma, 'Anya Horribilis', interview by John Mosby, *DreamWatch*, issue 70, June 2000.

Caulfield, Emma, interview, *Big Hit*, June 2001.

Cavallo, Jo, 'Buffy ready to give up her stake', *People*, 16 July 2002.

'Celebrity Shame', *Dolly*, October 2000.

Chan, Paul, '*Angel* faces do it all for laughs', *Huddersfield Daily Examiner*, 17 July 2002.

Chavez, Paul, 'Suspect's family "heartbroken" over son's role in UCSB deaths', *Los Angeles Daily News*, 28 February 2001.

'Cheers and Jeers' ('Hush' review), *TV Guide*, 1 January 2000.

'Cheers and Jeers' ('The Body' review), *TV Guide*, 17 March 2001.

Clapham, Mark and Smith, Jim, *Soul Searching: The Unofficial Guide to the Life & Trials of Ally McBeal*, Virgin Publishing, 2000.

Collins, Scott, '*Buffy* star goes to the woodshed over remark about sticking with the WB', *Los Angeles Times*, 30 January 2001.

Collins, Scott, '*Buffy* deal goes to heart of new net economy', *Hollywood Reporter*, 11 July 2002.

Cornell, Paul, Day, Martin, and Topping, Keith, *The Guinness Book of Classic British TV*, 2nd edition, Guinness Publishing, 1996.

Cornell, Paul, Day, Martin, and Topping, Keith, *X-Treme Possibilities: A Comprehensively Expanded Rummage Through the X-Files*, Virgin Publishing, 1998.

Cornell, Paul, 'Ally the Vampire Slayer', *SFX*, issue 60, January 2000.

Cornell, Paul, '20th Century Fox-Hunting', *SFX*, issue 63, April 2000.

Cornell, Paul, '*Buffy*: The Body', *SFX*, issue 80, July 2001.

Cortez, Carl, 'Bargaining Parts 1 and 2', *Cinescape*, 2 October 2001.

Darley, Andy, 'Waiting for Willow', *Science Fiction World*, issue 3, August 2000.

Day, Julia, 'Teen website renews *Buffy* sponsorship', *Guardian*, 11 May 2001.

DeCandido, Keith RA, *The Xander Years, Vol. 1*, Archway Paperback Publishing, 1999.

Denisof, Alexis, 'A Revival of Spirit', interview by Simon Bacal, *Xposé*, issue 43, February 2000.

Denisof, Alexis, 'Vogue Demon Hunter', interview by Matt Springer, *Buffy the Vampire Slayer*, issue 7, Spring 2000.

Denisof, Alexis, 'Half Price', interview by Paul Spragg, *Xposé*, issue 65, March 2002.

Donaldson, Andrew, 'Damsel in Distress', *Sunday Times* [South Africa], 30 June 2002.

Dougherty, Diana, 'Oh, Jonathan', *Intergalactic Enquirer*, April 2000.

Duffy, Mike, 'All Seems to be Rotating Perfectly on Planet *Buffy*', *TV Weekly*, October 1999.

Duffy, Mike, 'Brighter Days Ahead for Buffy and Gang, Creator Promises', *Detroit Free Press*, 15 July 2002.

Dushku, Eliza, 'A Little Faith Goes a Long Way!' interview by James G Boultier, *Science Fiction World*, issue 3, August 2000.

Dushku, Eliza, 'Keeping Faith', interview by Ed Gross, *SFX Unofficial Buffy Collection*, 2000.

Elz, Amy, 'Five Reasons Why *Buffy* May be the Best Thing On Television', *STL Today*, 11 December 2001.

Espenson, Jane, 'Superstar Scribe', interview by Joe Nazzaro, *DreamWatch*, issue 74, November 2000.

Espenson, Jane, 'I Journalist, You Jane', interview by Lisa Kincaid, *Xposé* issue 58, August 2001.

Ewing, Charles Patrick, *Kids Who Kill: Juvenile Murder in America*, Mondo Publishing, 1993.

Fairly, Peter, 'Last Night's View' ('The Puppet Show' review), *Journal*, 4 March 1999.

Ferguson, Everett, *Backgrounds of Early Christianity* [second edition], William B Eerdmans Publishing, 1993.

Francis, Rob, '*Buffy the Vampire Slayer* Season 4', *DreamWatch*, issue 71, August 2000.

Francis, Rob, 'TV Heroes', *TV Zone*, Special #45, March 2002.

Gabriel, Jan, *Meet the Stars of Buffy the Vampire Slayer: An Unauthorized Biography*, Scholastic Inc., 1998.

Gellar, Sarah Michelle, interview by Sue Schneider, *DreamWatch*, issue 42, February 1998.

Gellar, Sarah Michelle, 'Star Struck Slayer', interview by Jenny Cooney Carrillo, *DreamWatch*. issue 55, March 1999.

Gellar, Sarah Michelle, interview by Jamie Diamond, *Mademoiselle*, March 1999.

Gellar, Sarah Michelle, 'Staking the Future', interview by John Mosby, *DreamWatch* issue 61, September 1999.

Gellar, Sarah Michelle, 'Sing When You're Winning!'/'Buffy on Top', interview by Jenny Cooney Carrillo, *DreamWatch*, issue 89–90, February–March 2002.

Gellar, Sarah Michelle, 'Smile Sarah', interview by Linda Cardellini, *Seventeen*, July 2002.

Giglione, Joan, 'Some Shows Aren't Big on TV', *Los Angeles Times*, 25 November 2000.

Gilbert, Matthew, 'Teenage Wasteland', *Boston Globe*, 7 December 2001.

Gill, AA, 'A Teeny Pain in the Neck', *Sunday Times*, 24 January 1999.

Glover, Kelly, 'Buffy: The Musical Ones – How LA's rock scene can raise the dead', *Impact*, issue 127, July 2002.

Golden, Christopher, and Holder, Nancy (with Keith RA De-Candido), *Buffy the Vampire Slayer: The Watcher's Guide*, Pocket Books, 1998.

Golden, Christopher, Bissette, Stephen R, and Sniegoski, Thomas E, *Buffy the Vampire Slayer: The Monster Book*, Pocket Books, 2000.

'Good Deal for *Buffy* Fans', *NME*, 30 July 2002.

Goodman, Tim, 'Standing Ovation for Singing *Buffy*', *San Francisco Chronicle*, 6 November 2001.

Graham, Alyson, 'Today's Choice', *Radio Times*, 5 January 2002.

Gray, Ellen, 'The gay joke is becoming a staple of network TV', *Philadelphia Daily News*, 1 September 1999.

Green, Seth, 'In Step With . . .', interview by James Brady, *Parade*, 17 December 2000.

Green, Michelle Erica, 'Darla and Topolsky Are More Than Bad Girls', *Fandom Inc.*, September 2000.

Greenman, Jennifer, 'Witch Love Spells Death', *News Review*, 6 June 2002.

Gross, Ed, 'Triangle' review, *SFX*, issue 75, March 2001.

Hallett, Andy, 'Smells Like Green Spirit', interview by Tom Mayo, *SFX*, issue 81, August 2001.

Hanks, Robert, 'Deconstructing Buffy', *Independent*, 1 July 2002.

Hannigan, Alyson, 'Slay Belle', interview by Sue Schneider, *DreamWatch*, issue 43, March 1998.

Hannigan, Alyson, 'Net Prophet', interview by Paul Simpson, *DreamWatch*, issue 55, March 1999.

Hannigan, Alyson, 'Willow Blossom', interview by John Mosby, *DreamWatch*, issue 73, October 2000.

Hannigan, Alyson, 'Alyson's Wonderland', interview by Jeffrey Epstein, *Out*, August 2001.

Hannigan, Alyson, 'Witchy Willow', interview by David Miller, *TV Zone*, issue 143, October 2001.

Harrington, Richard, 'Unsung *Buffy*: Props for A Magical Musical Moment', *Washington Post*, 2 July 2002.

Harrington, Richard, 'Spike gives *Buffy* a darker, sexier tone', *Washington Post*, 11 August 2002.

Head, Anthony Stewart, 'Bewitched, Bothered & Bewildered', interview by Paul Simpson, *DreamWatch*, issue 54, February 1999.

Head, Anthony Stewart, 'Speaking Volumes', interview by David Richardson, *Xposé*, issue 39, October 1999.

Head, Anthony Stewart, 'Heads Or Tails', interview by Paul Simpson and Ruth Thomas, *DreamWatch*, issue 69, May 2000.

Head, Anthony Stewart, 'My Kind of Day', *Radio Times*, 30 September 2000.

Head, Anthony Stewart, 'Ripping Yarns', interview by Paul Simpson and Ruth Thomas, *SFX*, issue 80, July 2001.

'Hell is for Heroes', *Entertainment Weekly*, issue 505, 1 October 1999.

Hensley, Dennis, 'Sarah Michelle Gellar Vamps it Up', *Cosmopolitan*, June 1999.

Hibbs, Thomas S, 'Buffy's War: Good and Evil 101', *National Review*, 24 May 2002.

Highley, John, 'Beer Bad' to 'Pangs', *Xposé*, issue 42, January 2000.

Holder, Nancy (with Jeff Mariotte and Maryelizabeth Hart), *Buffy the Vampire Slayer: The Watcher's Guide Volume 2*, Pocket Books, 2000.

Huff, Richard. 'WB Net Returns to Gender-Build on Initial Appeal Among Young Women', *New York Daily News*, 14 September 1999.

Hughes, David, 'Slay Ride', *DreamWatch*, issue 42, February 1998.

Innes, John, '"Buffy" attackers escape jail term', *Scotsman*, 29 March 2002.

Johnson, Kevin V, 'Fans Sink Teeth into Bootlegged "Buffy"', *USA Today*, May 1999.

Johnson, RW, 'The Myth of the 20th Century', *New Society*, 9 December 1982.

Keveney, Bill, 'When it's quality vs. ratings, casualties abound', *Charlotte Observer*, 31 August 2000.

Kincaid, Lisa, 'Three's Company', *Xposé*, issue 67, May 2002.

King, Stephen, *Danse Macabre*, Futura Books, 1981.

Kramer, Clare, 'Glory Days', interview by Nick Joy, *Starlog*, issue 24, March 2002.

Kramer, Clare, 'Profile', interview by Paul Simpson, *SFX*, issue 90, April 2002.

Kurtz, Frank, 'Whedon Talks *Buffy* Resurrection', *New York Daily News*, 17 July 2001.

Lagos, Marisa, 'Dad Wanted Attias to Have "Normal Life"', *Santa Barbara Daily Nexus*, 29 May 2002.

Laight, Rupert, 'Demon Lover', *Starburst*, issue 284, March 2002.

Lambert, Brian, 'The WB network contemplates life after *Buffy*', *St Paul Pioneer Press*, 17 July 2001.

Lane, Andy, *The Babylon File*, Virgin Publishing, 1997.

Lewis, Randy, 'Musical *Buffy* finally lands in stores', *Los Angeles Times*, 23 September 2002.

Littleton, Cynthia, 'UPN sked has WB feel; Fox goes Conservative', *Hollywood Reporter*, 17 May 2001.

Lowry, Brian, 'Actresses Turning Down Roles of Teens' Mothers', *Los Angeles Times*, 29 April 1999.

Lowry, Brian, 'WB Covers A Trend Too Well', *Los Angeles Times*, 29 June 2000.

MacDonald, Ian, *Revolution in the Head* – Second Edition, Fourth Estate Ltd, 1997.

MacKenzie, Kate, 'Last Days of *Buffy* a Kind of Living Death', *Australian*, 18 July 2002.

Madden, Michelle, 'Total Faith', *Mean*, July 2001.

Mansfield, Sonia, 'Women on Top', *San Francisco Examiner*, 27 December 2001.

Mansfield, Sonia, 'Endgames', *San Francisco Examiner*, 27 May 2002.

Marsters, James, 'Sharp Spike', interview by Cynthia Boris, *Cult Times* Special 9, Spring 1999.

Marsters, James, and Caulfield, Emma, 'Vamping It Up', *Alloy*, Summer 2000.

Marsters, James, 'It's Only Rock & Roll, But I Spike It!', interview (with Four Star Mary) by Tom Mayo, *SFX*, issue 81, August 2001.

Marsters, James, 'Loves Bites', interview by Abbie Bernstein, *DreamWatch*, issue 89, February 2002.

Marsters, James, 'Love in Vein', interview by Ian Spelling, *Starlog*, issue 24, March 2002.

Marsters, James, 'Demon Lover', interview by Rupert Laight, *Starburst*, issue 284, April 2002.

Mason, Charlie, '*Buffy* Lowers its Bawdy Count', *TV Guide*, 10 July 2002.

Matthews, Richard, 'Boldly staying in with *Buffy* and *Friends*', *Daily Telegraph*, 4 July 2002.

Mauger, Anne-Marie, 'Staking their Claims', *Sky Customer Magazine*, January 2001.

May, Dominic and Spilsbury, Tom, 'Return to Sunnydale High for *Buffy* Season 7', *TV Zone*, issue 153, July 2002.

Mayo, Tom, *SFX Presents Buffy the Vampire Slayer The Unofficial Episode Guide to the First Four Seasons*, Future Publishing, 2000.

McDaniel, Mike, '*Buffy* Lauded for Gay Character', *Houston Chronicle*, 18 May 2000.

McDaniel, Mike, '*Buffy* will get back to basics for fall season says network chief', *Houston Chronicle*, 15 July 2002.

McFarland, Melanie, 'Musical *Buffy* could be a grave mistake for vampire slayer', *Seattle Times*, 6 November 2001.

McIntee, David, *Delta Quadrant: The Unofficial Guide to Voyager*, Virgin Publishing, 2000.

McIntyre, Gina, 'Slay Anything', *Hollywood Reporter*, 21 May 2001.

McLean, Gareth, 'Last Nights' TV: A real death in Buffyland', *Guardian*, 21 April 2001.

Meltzer, Dana, 'Raising the Stakes', *Guardian*, 5 January 2002.

Metcalf, Mark, 'Buffy's Master', interview by Mark Wyman, *Starburst*, issue 245, January 1999.

Miller, Craig, 'Xander the Survivor', *Spectrum*, issue 17, March 1999.

Miller, Craig, '*Buffy the Vampire Slayer* Fourth Season Episode Guide', *Spectrum*, issue 25, January 2001.

Moore, Ronald D, 'Moore the Merrier', interview by Jim Swallow, *SFX*, issue 74, February 2001.

Mosby, John, 'UK-TV', *DreamWatch*, issue 71, August 2000.

Mosby, John, 'Last Writes', *Impact*, issue 127, July 2002.

Murray, Steve, 'Cracking the closet door: More visibility for gay characters on TV', *Miami Herald*, 9 July 2002.

Naughton, John, 'Buffy up on *Buffy*', *Radio Times*, 29 June 2002.

Newman, Kim, *Nightmare Movies: A Critical History of the Horror Movie From 1968*, Bloomsbury Publishing, 1988.

Norman, Matthew, 'Biological Warfare and the Buffy Paradigm', *Guardian*, 10 July 2002.

'No Sex Please, it's *Buffy*', *DreamWatch*, issue 89, February 2002.

Noxon, Marti, 'Soul Survivor', *DreamWatch*, issue 63, November 1999.

Noxon, Marti, '"Nasty" Noxon', interview by Andy Mangels, *DreamWatch*, issue 90, March 2002.

Noxon, Marti, 'Slay it with feeling', interview by Steve Eramo, *TV Zone*, issue 154, August 2002.

Ogle, Connie, 'Something's fangtastically wrong in Emmyland', *Miami Herald*, 23 July 2002.

O'Hare, Kate, 'Silent Buffy', *Ultimate TV*, 13 December 1999.

O'Hare, Kate, 'WB's Core Series *Buffy* and *Angel* Cross Time and Space', *TV Weekly*, 12 November 2000.

O'Hare, Kate, 'While *Buffy* Rages, *Angel* Still Flies', *St Paul Pioneer Press*, 15 April 2001.

O'Hare, Kate, '*Buffy* reaches end of run on the WB', *St Paul Pioneer Press*, 20 May 2001.

O'Hare, Kate, 'Fist of fury – TV's high-flying on-screen battles', *St Paul Pioneer Press*, 14 April 2002.

Owen, Rob, '*Pow! Bash! Bam!* WB, UPN trade barbs over *Buffy*', *Post-Gazette*, 17 July 2001.

Peary, Danny, *Guide For the Film Fanatic*, Simon & Schuster, 1986.

Petrozzello, Donna, '*Buffy* Exec Feels Slayed by "Insult"', *Daily News*, 19 March 2001.

Pierce, Scott D, 'Buffy Sings!' *Deseret News*, 3 November 2001.

Pirie, David, *The Vampire Cinema*, Galley Press, 1977.

Plath, Sylvia, *Collected Poems*, Faber & Faber, 1981.

Poniewozik, James, 'How the *Buffy* coup could change television', *Time*, 23 April 2001.

'Potty About Paganism', *Alternative Metro*, 24 August 2000.

Pruitt, Jeff and Crawford, Sohpia: 'The Hitman and Her', *Science Fiction World*, issue 3, August 2000.

'Queen of the Damned', *FHM*, issue 114, July 1999.

Ramlow, Todd R, ' "I Killed Tara": Desire and Death on *Buffy*', *Pop Matters*, 4 June 2002.

Richardson, David, 'Snyder Remarks', *Xposé*, issue 37, August 1999.

Rigby, Jonathan, *English Gothic: A Century of Horror Cinema*, Reynolds and Hearn, 2002.

Robins, J Max, '*Buffy* Goes Too Far for the British', *TV Guide*, 17 March 2001.

Robson, Ian, 'Action Replay: Buffy's Show'll Slay You' ('The Freshman' review), *Sunday Sun*, 9 January 2000.

Roeper, Richard, 'Buffy Crackdown Won't Strike Heart of Problem', *Chicago Sun-Times*, 27 May 1999.

'Role Offers New Blend', *Evening Chronicle*, 12 February 2001.

Rose, Lloyd, 'Outcast Buffy Embodies Teen Angst', *Washington Post*, October 1998.

Roush, Matt, 'The Roush Review', *TV Guide*, 3 April 1999.

Roush, Matt, 'The Roush Review – Buffy Rocks: Better Late Than Never', *TV Guide*, 10 July 1999.

Roush, Matt, 'Shows of the Year '99', *TV Guide*, 25 December 1999.

Roush, Matt, 'The Roush Review', *TV Guide*, 1 April 2000.

Roush, Matt, 'The Roush Review: End Games', *TV Guide*, 16 June 2001.

Roush, Matt, 'Spaced Out – *Roswell* Beams to UPN with *Buffy*', *TV Guide*, 7 July 2001.

Roush, Matt, 'Great Performances: Emma Caulfield', *TV Guide*, 27 October 2001.

Roush, Matt, '*Buffy* Reborn: Slayer is full of life – and song', *TV Guide*, 24 November 2001.

Rubinstein, Julian, 'Politically Correct', *US Magazine*, October 1999.

Rutenberg, Jim, '*Buffy* Moving to UPN, Tries to be WB Slayer', *New York Times*, 21 April 2000.

Rutenberg, Jim, 'Media Talk: Hold the Tears in Vampire Slayer's Death', *New York Times*, 29 May 2001.

Sachs, Robin, 'The Eyes Have It', interview by Paul Simpson and Ruth Thomas, *DreamWatch*, issue 68, April 2000.

Sangster, Jim and Bailey, David, *Friends Like Us: The Unofficial Guide to Friends* [revised edition], Virgin Publishing, 2000.

Sansing, Dina, 'Secrets of Sarah', *Seventeen*, August 2001.

'Sarah gets a spanking: *Buffy* star forced to eat humble-pie after "Quit" gaff', *Daily News*, 30 January 2001.

'Sarah Michelle Gellar: American Beauty', *FHM*, issue 128, September 2000.

Schneider, Michael, '*Roswell* Joins *Buffy* for UPN Fall Lineup', *Variety*, 16 May 2001.

Sellers, John, 'Slay You!' *Maxim*, March 2002.

Sepinwall, Alan, 'Delaying Episode Could Make *Buffy* Target of Witchhunt', *Network Star-Ledger*, May 1999.

Sepinwall, Alan, '*Buffy* Network Switch Could Slay TV Industry Practices', *St Paul Pioneer Press*, 29 April 2001.

Silverman, Steven S, ' "Buffy" on Big Move: Nervous', *People*, 17 July 2001.

Simpson, Paul, 'Red Shirt Robia', *DreamWatch*, issue 59, Summer 1999.

Simpson, Paul and Thomas, Ruth, 'Interview With The Vampire', *DreamWatch*, issue 62, October 1999.

Simpson, Richard, '*Buffy* bites the dust', *Evening Standard*, 25
    May 2001.
'Single Women: If The She Fits, Air It', *St Paul Pioneer Press*, 6
    January 2000.
'SMG going out with a bang', *Cult Times*, issue 82, July 2002.
Spines, Christine, 'Getting Buffed!' *Glamour*, October 2000.
Spragg, Paul, 'Welcome to the Hellmouth', *Cult Times* Special 9,
    Spring 1999.
Springer, Matt, 'Crusin' Sunnydale', *Buffy the Vampire Slayer*,
    issue 3, Spring 1999.
Springer, Matt, 'The Evil That Geeks Do', *Entertainment Weekly*,
    20 May 2002.
Stanley, John, *Revenge of the Creature Feature Movie Guide*,
    Creatures Press, 1988.
Stanley, TL, 'Buffy the Rules Slayer', *Los Angeles Times*, 20 May
    2001.
Stanley, TL, 'Is it the end of the road for *Buffy-Angel* connec-
    tion?' *Los Angeles Times*, 21 May 2001.
Steel, Bill, 'Beautiful Buffy's Back, Big Boy' ('Anne' review),
    Journal, 31 March 2000.
Streisand, Betsy, 'Young, hip and no-longer-watching-Fox', *US
    News & World Report*, 15 Nov 1999.
Strong, Danny, 'Big Man on Campus', interview by Matt
    Springer, *Buffy the Vampire Slayer*, Fall Special 1999.
Summers, Montague, *The Vampire, His Kith and Kin*, Kegan
    Paul, Trench, Truber & Co., 1928.
Sutherland, Kristine, 'Source of Denial', interview by Paul
    Simpson, *DreamWatch*, issue 58, July 1999.
'The Boo Crew', *Entertainment Weekly*, issue 505, 1 October
    1999.
'Today's Trout' ('Earshot'/'Bad Girls' preview), *St Paul Pioneer
    Press*, 27 April 1999.
'The Top Fifty SF TV Shows of All Time!' *SFX*, issue 50, April
    1999.
Topping, Keith, '*Buffy the Vampire Slayer* Season One', *Dream-
    Watch*, issue 55, March 1999.
Topping, Keith, '*Buffy the Vampire Slayer* Season Two', *Dream-
    Watch*, issues 57, 58, May, July 1999.
Topping, Keith, '*Buffy the Vampire Slayer* Season Three', *Dream-
    Watch*, issues 60, 61, August, September 1999.
Topping, Keith, 'The Way We Were', *DreamWatch*, issue 58, July
    1999.

Topping, Keith, *Hollywood Vampire: A Revised and Updated Unofficial and Unauthorised Guide to Angel*, Virgin Books, 2001.

Topping, Keith, *High Times: An Unofficial and Unauthorised Guide to Roswell*, Virgin Books, 2001.

Topping, Keith, 'Body Rock', *Intergalactic Enquirer*, March 2001.

Topping, Keith, 'Teenage Kicks', *Intergalactic Enquirer*, April 2001.

Topping, Keith, '*Sed Quis Custodiet Ipsos Custodes?*' *Intergalactic Enquirer*, May 2001.

Topping, Keith, 'Changing Channels', *Intergalactic Enquirer*, August 2001.

Topping, Keith, *Inside Bartlet's White House: An Unofficial and Unauthorised Guide to The West Wing*, Virgin Books, 2002.

Topping, Keith, *Beyond the Gate: An Unofficial Guide to Stargate SG-1*, Telos Publishing, 2002.

Topping, Keith, 'Has *Buffy* Jumped the Shark?' *Shivers*, issue 97, May 2002.

Topping, Keith, 'TV Reviews', *Shivers*, issues 94–98, 2002.

Trachtenberg, Michelle, 'Summer's Dawn' interview by Ian Spelling, *Starburst*, issue 272, April 2001.

Trachtenberg, Michelle, 'Dawn Tomorrow', interview by David Miller, *TV Zone*, issue 143, October 2001.

Trachtenberg, Michelle, 'Fast Times at Sunnydale High', interview by Nick Joy, *Starburst*, issue 289, August 2002.

Tucker, Ken, 'High Stakes Poker', *Entertainment Weekly*, issue 505, 1 October 1999.

Udovitch, Mim, 'What Makes *Buffy* Slay?' *Rolling Stone* issue 840, 11 May 2000.

van Beek, Anton, 'Bite Me!' *Total DVD*, issue 21, January 2001.

Wagner, Chuck, 'Punk Shocks', *SFX*, issue 49, March 1999.

Whedon, Joss, interview by AJ Jacobs, *Entertainment Weekly*, 25 April 1997.

Whedon, Joss, 'How I Got To Do What I Do', interview by Wolf Schneider, *teen movieline*, issue 1, March 2000.

Whedon, Joss, 'Whedon, Writing and Arithmetic', interview by Joe Mauceri, *Shivers*, issue 77, May 2000.

Whedon, Joss, 'Blood Lust', interview by Rob Francis, *DreamWatch*, issues 71, 72, August, September 2000.

Whedon, Joss, 'Prophecy Boy', interview by Matt Springer with Mike Stokes, *Buffy the Vampire Slayer*, issue 20, May 2001.

Whedon, Joss, interview by Gina McIntyre, *Hollywood Reporter*, 21 May 2001.

Whedon, Joss, 'Buffy R.I.P?', interview by John Mosby, *Dream-Watch*, issue 84, September 2001.

Whedon, Joss, interview by Tasha Robinson, The Onion AV Club, 5 September 2001.

Whedon, Joss, 'The Wonderful World of Whedon', interview by Ian Spelling, *Cult Times*, issue 79, April 2002.

Williams, Zoe, 'The lady and the vamp – a buff's guide to *Buffy*,' *Guardian*, 17 November 2001.

Wilson, Steve, 'Web Sucks TV's Blood – *Buffy* Fans Bite Back', *Village Voice*, May 1999.

Wright, Matthew, 'Endings and New Beginnings', *Science Fiction World*, issue 2, July 2000.

Wurtzel, Elizabeth, *Bitch*, Quartet Books, 1998.

Wyman, Mark, 'The *Buffy* Guide Season Two', *Xposé*, issue 29, December 1999.

Wyman, Mark, 'Anno I', *Cult Times* Special 9, Spring 1999.

Wyman, Mark, '*Buffy* Joins The Banned – A Fable For The Internet Age', *Shivers*, issue 68, August 1999.

Wyman, Mark, 'Crush' to 'The Body', *TV Zone*, issue 140, July 2001.

Wyman, Mark, 'Entropy' to 'Grave', *TV Zone*, issue 152, July 2002.

Errata from *Slayer*
(Third Edition, 2002)

The last edition of *Slayer* was 488 pages, and approximately 170,000 words, long. Inevitably in such a massive work, the odd error cropped up (this is a long-winded way of saying that this author is only human). Listed below are various corrections and additions to the text.

Page 45, **7**, 'Angel' – **References:** *Spider-Man* ('with power, comes responsibility').

Page 63, **12**, 'Prophecy Girl' – **References:** *The Master's 'Where are your jibes now?' is a question Hamlet asks Ophelia.* Except it isn't. It's a question Hamlet, rhetorically, asks Yorick's skull.

Page 72, **13**, 'Some Assembly Required' – **References:** *The Effects of Gamma Ray Radiation on Man in the Moon Marigolds* is a possible influence on the plot (the school science fair, the embittered mother and the name of Willow's project).

Page 77, **15**, 'School Hard' – **Notes:** Much of the continuity in **15**, 'School Hard', concerning Spike's origins is contradicted (or, at least, expanded upon) in **85**, 'Fool for Love'. In particular, Giles states he can find no historical reference to a vampire named Spike implying that, until recently, Spike was still using the name William. However, in 'Fool for Love' we discover that he took the name Spike almost immediately upon becoming a vampire, taking exception when Angel continues to call him by his human name.

Page 85, **18**, 'Halloween' – **References:** *Star Trek* (Cordy's description of Angel as 'a Care Bear with fangs' is similar to how Spock's pet Sehlat was described.

Page 133, **32**, 'Go Fish' – **References:** *The title is from Rose Torche's 1994 lesbian movie.* 'Go Fish' is also the name of a popular card game in the US which was probably the initial source of Torche's title. It's the game, incidentally, that Dawn and Xander are playing in **112**, 'Doublemeat Palace'.

Page 154, **38**, 'Beauty and the Beasts' – **References:** Pete's 'you shouldn't make me angry' is a probable allusion to *The Incredible Hulk*.

Page 201, **50**, 'Doppelgängland' – **Notes:** *This is a genuinely groundbreaking piece of work in any context – all the way to the suddenly explained 'oh f—' reprise from* **43**, *'The Wish'*. However, the scene of Evil-Willow dying in 'The Wish' does *not* feature her mouthing 'Oh f—'. This, presumably, means that during the production of 'Doppelgängland' Joss Whedon inserted a head-shot of Alyson Hannigan's line into the previously filmed 'The Wish' sequence. Though it would be wonderful to be able to say that this had been a classic example of the series' foresight and attention to detail, sadly, it's not true.

Page 272, **65**, 'Something Blue' – **References:** *The daily soap Passions ('Timmy's down the bloody well')*. Many fans believe this to be a reference to the *Lassie* movies – in which Timmy *was* frequently down a well, or something similar. Since *Passions* does include a character called Timmy, the matter remains unresolved.

Page 279, **66**, 'Hush' – **Did You Know:** Among the extras at Maggie Walsh's dream-lecture in the opening scene is future *Angel* star Andy Hallett. Many of the exterior sequences were filmed on one of the backlots at Universal Studios.

Page 325, **78**, 'Restless' – **References:** Xander's line, 'It's a gay romp', may be an allusion to *The Producers*.

Page 328: *James Marsters (Spike, 79–94, 96–100)* should read James Marsters (Spike, 79–93, 95–100).

Page 329: *Adam Busch (Warren Mears)*. Several sources (some, quasi-official) give the spelling of Warren's surname as Meers, which is the one I've used in this edition.

Page 359, **86**, 'Shadow' – **References:** *Xander mentions 'Bipperty, Bopperty, Boo' (from Bedknobs and Broomsticks)*. It's actually from *Cinderella*.

Page 366, **88**, 'Into the Woods' – **References:** The title may refer to Stephen Sondheim and James Lapine's stage musical of the same name; a darkly amusing take on fairy tales, in which various characters get what they want but ultimately find that there's no such thing as 'happily ever after'.

Page 381, **91**, 'Blood Ties' – **References:** Dawn's present to Buffy – a photo surrounded by shells – may be an oblique allusion to *Dark City*, a movie about reality and false memories, in which one character remembers a place called Shell Beach which never really existed.

Page 446, 'Paleo' – **References:** The pterodactyl in the 1860s is an allusion to a famous photo (allegedly) of Civil War soldiers and a dinosaur which has appeared in the *Fortean Times*.

Logic, Let Me Introduce You To This Window: Early in the novel it is stated that if a dinosaur fossil is broken or incomplete a full manifestation cannot take place. So, why doesn't Angel simply break the fossilised Tyrannosaurus egg?

Page 454, 'The Outsiders': *The great taboo 's' world ('sex') was finally spoken (by of all people Joyce) in* **29**, 'Passion'. As one reader points out, this is factually inaccurate. The first use of the word 'sex' in *Buffy* occurs as early as **3**, 'The Witch' (the line is even quoted on page 34). Albeit, it's used in a very different context.

The previous edition also listed French episode titles to **90**, 'Checkpoint', German titles to **78**, 'Restless' and UK Transmission Dates on BBC2 to **78**, 'Restless'. While all of the season five episodes have now been broadcast in Germany and on the BBC, the final four remain to air in France at the time of writing.

Ep.	German Title	French Title	UK Transmission Dates (BBC2)
79	*Gegen Dracula*		23 August 2001
80	*Lieb Schwesterlein Mein*		30 August 2001
81	*Der Doppelte Xander*		6 September 2001
82	*Initiative lässt grüßen*		13 September 2001
83	*Sein und Schein*		27 September 2001
84	*Familienbande*		4 October 2001
85	*Eine Lektion für's Leben*		11 October 2001
86	*Schatten*		25 October 2001
87	*Alles Böse Kommt von Oben*		1 November 2001

Grrr! Arrrgh!

A return to a lighter, funnier *Buffy* is promised for season seven following a year many saw as being too grim for too long. While Joss Whedon is looking forward to taking the show back to its wittier roots, he also believes *Buffy* accomplished what it set out to do last year: make a more solitary heroine face the inner demons that accompany maturity. 'Every year has its criticism,' Joss told *USA Today*. 'I do think we hit a few of the same notes too many times. But I'm proud of many of the things we did.' It seems Les Moonves agrees with him. 'Joss thinks it got a little too dark and off-track last season,' the UPN executive told Mike Duffy. 'Next year will be lighter.'

Speaking at an Academy of Television Arts and Sciences symposium in June 2002, Joss noted that when he first saw the footage of Tony Head's scene at the climax **121**, 'Two to Go' he instantly realised how much season six had missed Giles's presence. 'I'm going to England to shoot some second-unit with Tony and Alyson,' Joss told *Sci-Fi Wire* at the same time. 'Our first production values ever. Usually it's "We're in Venice. Hand me that goblet."' Asked about his general approach to next season, Joss added, 'it's something I've been gearing towards since the beginning. The climax will be the biggest thing we've ever done. I am looking for closure next year because we're making a more positive statement. This year was just about surviving.' Filming took place near Tony Head's home, Bath, in late June. Afterwards, Joss motored to London and, so legend has it, spent three hours buying comics in Forbidden Planet. Now *there's* a man who's got his priorities in life sorted.

'Season six was fantastic, but it had a darker tone,' Joss told an online interview. 'Some of the episodes depressed the hell out of me. Next year we're going back to our original mission statement, to the positive view of female empowerment. This year was about adult life and relationships – and making really bad decisions. Next year will still be scary, different and strange. People will stop abandoning Dawn. Willow won't be a junkie anymore. Buffy won't be dead. The theme for this year was: "Oh, grow up." In season seven it'll be *Buffy Year One*.'

One of the most popular fan rumours circulating during the summer was that Mark Metcalf, who played The Master in *Buffy*'s first season, is scheduled to appear next year. *Entertainment Weekly* ran a news item indicating that Buffy will be quitting the Doublemeat Palace to work at the rebuilt Sunnydale High as a guidance counsellor. 'Sarah's very upset about not getting to wear the [Doublemeat] hat anymore,' Joss told *TV Zone*. Joss has also been quoted as saying that 'everyone's worst nightmare will wreak havoc in Sunnydale'. Spike, it seems, will remain a vampire, albeit one with a soul. Jane Espenson reportedly indicated that the 'perfect moment of happiness' problem was something specific to the Angel's curse, and will not be a problem for Spike. Meanwhile, Joss told *scifi.com* that he hopes to bring back the surviving duo of the *troika*, Jonathan and Andrew, 'because they made us laugh'. Much has also been made of Whedon's assertion that Amber Benson may be returning even if the character of Tara won't be. Speculation is rife that Benson, who has written Buffy-related comics, may sign on to write for the show. 'I don't know, and even if I did, I couldn't tell you,' Amber told *Birmingham News*. 'On *Buffy*, one minute you're dead, the next you're giving birth to some horrible creature.' Also, popular former guest stars like Clare Kramer (Glory), Adam Busch (Warren) and, if a schedule can be arranged, Eliza Dushku (Faith), could return. Although with Seth Green's successful movie career, we're unlikely to see Oz back in the near future. The impression so far given is that several of Buffy's greatest enemies of the past might be back for some kind of Who's the Hardest? competition early in the season. Kim and Kelley Deal of rock band The Breeders are also alleged to be making a cameo. The pair were contacted after Joss heard

their version of the '*Buffy* Theme', which has become a
mainstay of The Breeders' live set. 'Last year was about the
dark side of power and confusion,' Joss told the *Orlando
Sentinel*. 'This year is about the joy of power. It's about
Buffy becoming more proactive in her fight against evil.'

Tony Head, meanwhile, will definitely return. 'We
worked out a deal,' Tony told the *New York Daily News*.
'[I'll be in] a minimum of ten episodes. Thank God I work
for somebody who isn't remotely Hollywood,' he noted.
'Usually, they say, "You do what we want you to do, or
you're not coming back at all." [Joss] is such a cool guy.'

'We are [the same] in the sense of living, the difference
between being a young adult and being a child at the same
time,' Sarah Michelle Gellar said concerning her alter ego
when she appeared on *The View* in July 2002. 'As we both
grow into adulthood I have a big responsibility but I'm still
a young adult. Buffy is basically a single mom with a
full-time job. So I think there are comparisons.' Alyson
Hannigan believes that Willow's greatest challenge in the
coming year will be 'winning the fans love back. They
probably hate me now,' she told a convention audience. 'I
just hope they forgive my evilness in the last few episodes.'
Hannigan added that Willow's addiction to magic will
remain an issue for the character. 'Once you go that far,
you deal with it for the rest of your life. She's got to have
time to recover.' James Marsters told *Sci-Fi Wire* that he
doesn't know if Spike will turn out to be good or evil. 'I
could be unleashed as the big villain, or I could be goody
two-shoes,' he said. But Spike's attempted rape of Buffy in
119, 'Seeing Red', *will* cause a rift between him and Dawn.
'It will not be easy,' Michelle Trachtenberg notes. 'I think
he's the one that Dawn has connected to the most, because
he's never treated her like a child. She'll handle the
situation in an adult way, but she won't let him get away
with it.' Dawn will also face teen dating issues. 'I've heard
a couple of rumors that Dawn will have guys coming in
and out. I think this is the year that Dawn matures.'

The opening episode of season seven will premiere on 24
September 2002. It's called 'Lessons', written by Joss

Whedon and will concern Dawn's first day at the newly reopened Sunnydale High. The episode will introduce two new recurring characters in Dawn's classmates: Kit Holbern (a sensitive goth girl who sees visions of dead people) and Carlos Trejos (an apparent loser with interesting levels of heroism). Her Willow and Xander, seemingly. We'll also be introduced to Principal Robin Wood, a compassionate and likeable African-American who is aware of Buffy's chequered past and enlists her to work for the school's Outreach programme. The episode introduces the season's big-bad, a creature who can assume numerous different forms. Following this, the episode 'Beneath You,' appears to refer to Buffy's opinion of Spike in **85**, 'Fool for Love' and will deal with the ramifications of Spike's return to Sunnydale, and to his new with-soul status. Buffy reluctantly allows Spike to help her fight a worm-demon who, it turns out, was made the way he is by Anya's wish granting. Jane Espenson's 'Same Time, Same Place', sees Willow's return from England and focuses on the activities of a demon called Gnarl. 'Help', introduces a girl named Cassie, whom Buffy counsels at school. Cassie knows that she's going to die, but not why or how. The episode features the first indications that Spike had been changed forever by his acquisition of a soul. In 'Selfless', written by newcomer Drew Goddard, Anya grants a woman's wish, but the vengeance leaves Anya guilt-ridden. She asks that the spell be undone, knowing the price of such reversal is the life of a vengeance-demon. Is she willing to make the ultimate sacrifice? The episode features numerous flashbacks, including a missing scene from **107**, 'Once More, With Feeling', and sees the return of Olaf (see **89**, 'Triangle') and Halfrek. 'Him' features the introduction of a Cordelia-like character in Dawn's class called Lori and a football player, Skyler, who has done something similar to Xander in **28**, 'Bewitched, Bothered and Bewildered'. Spike and Xander end up as a team as all of the women are spellbound.

It is quite possible that next season will be *Buffy*'s last. Indeed, Nick Brendon more or less announced this during

an Australian convention in May. Emma Caulfield recently
noted that she will definitely be leaving at the end of season
seven as she only signed a three-year contract. UPN
Entertainment president Dawn Ostroff has confirmed,
however, that some *Buffy* cast members have contract-
options that extend beyond the end of season seven even if
Sarah Michelle Gellar isn't one of them. 'Obviously, we
would love to have Sarah back,' Ostroff told the *Daily
News*. 'That is, by far, the best situation for us. But short
of that, we are just starting to explore what that means.'
Rumours have been flying around all summer of a
Buffyless series (or perhaps a Dawn spin-off) for the
2003–4 season. 'Yes, that has been given [some] thought,'
Joss told *E! Online*. 'Every variation of everything has been
given thought. What's going to happen is so unknown to
me it's kind of exciting.' Interestingly, Joss told *Sci-Fi
Wire*: 'Dawn is now the age Buffy was when the show
began. And what's nice about that is it gives us the
opportunity to tell more high-school stories which were the
centerpiece of the show, and which we only got to do for
two and a half years.'

Meanwhile, Joss's new series for Fox, *Firefly*, is according to Marti Noxon 'a science-fiction western. The show
takes place in the wake of a universal civil war in which the
government wanted to unite all of the planets. The
government won, so the guys on our ship, who fought for
independence, are cruising the periphery of the universe.
They aren't heroes; they do salvage work, some of which
isn't legal. It's not like most sci-fi shows where everything's
in black and white. The government isn't all bad, but they
do some bad stuff.' The show will concern human interac-
tions and problems experienced by its ensemble cast. Joss
had apparently been mulling the concept over for a couple
of years, but reading up on the American civil war finally
crystallised an idea. 'I wanted to make something that's
about a guy who fought for the South, lost and doesn't like
anybody anymore,' he said. 'This show isn't about the
people who made history. I wanted to do a show about
people who are not "super", just working class; the people

history steps on.' The show will be produced by Mutant Enemy and 20th Century Fox. In a clear sign of its belief in Joss, Fox has taken the unusual step of committing to airing at least thirteen episodes, starting in autumn 2002. 'It's wicked Joss-like. It's not like any show set in space that I've ever seen,' said Gail Berman, a collaborator who was pivotal in bringing *Buffy* to our screens and is now president of Fox Entertainment. The pilot episode 'The Train Job' is written by Joss and Tim Minear and introduces viewers to the regular cast led by Nathan Fillions as Captain Mal Reynolds, while subsequent episodes will be by Minear, Jane Espenson, Drew Greenberg and former *Dark Angel* writer Jose Molina.

So, *Buffy*, *Angel* and *Firefly* are all active and ongoing. The long-talked-about *Buffy* animated series has recently been green-lighted by the Fox Kids network. And Tony Head's cherished *Ripper* project simply awaits everyone involved having the time to complete it. I seem to say this every year as summer ends and everyone gets ready for another season, but these are exciting times for *Buffy the Vampire Slayer* and its creator, along with his talented young cast and crew as they continue to make (in every sense of the word) television history.